Why St. Peter Could Not Become a Catholic Priest Today

by
Edgar Davie

TABLE OF CONTENTS

Securing Papal Power
Anti-Popes and Cardinals
Cardinal-Nephews
Opposition
A Failed Papacy
Keep the Faith, Change the Church

WHY Priests? A Failed Tradition

Thirty five years ago this author, a committed Catholic layman, experienced what some religious teachers term being "reborn". Although 46, this event became a formative experience. Catholics understand we are reborn at baptism but this event became a special experience. As faithful Catholics our family of wife and seven children, all of whom graduated from excellent parochial schools, religiously followed Church teaching. At that time our faith and beliefs became more important.

This faith experience ultimately led to an interest in the Bible and its eternal truths. However, only short passages are read during weekly Mass, and being an average Catholic I had not read through it. Beginning to investigate the Bible it became apparent that others viewed scripture and Christian history far differently than do Catholics. Recalling my youth I remembered anti-Catholic preaching broadcast via radio in my small East Tennessee home town. As I grew it became apparent some of my friends were personally concerned for me should I remain Catholic. This too brought back youthful memories of criticism from non-Catholic friends who held a far different view of Christian history, believing that Catholicism altered Apostolic teaching and was no longer the original Church left to us by Jesus. This possibility was very disturbing and led me on a determined search for the truth.

After a study of differing beliefs between Catholics and others these differences became apparent. Especially concerning were differing views on our sacraments, the supremacy of scripture, and their rejection of Christian traditions not explained in the New Testament. In order to discover the truth a plan was conceived – examine history. I reckoned, at the death of the last Apostle who replaced them and what did they teach on these subjects? Thus, I began a study into the origins and formation of scripture, ancient church canons, infallible papal declarations and Christian history as it developed over the centuries, leading to our different beliefs of today. I did not stop there; what about the origins and development of other religions, particularly Protestantism, Judaism, and Islam? It seemed simple; merely discover Christianity's earliest beginnings and beliefs as taught by those who first followed the Apostles.

After ten years of investigation I wrote a book: *Before the Bible: beliefs and practice of the first Christians*. Relying on recorded Church history I was able to answer all accusations posed by non-Catholics and happily concluded that, historically speaking, the Catholic Church is the visible, organized Church left to us by Jesus, and that today's Church is the modern remnant of that original Church. Moreover, this Church had conquered the pagan world exclusively through preaching long before the New Testament existed, which is relied on by others as the only source of faith known to exist; I also discovered that tradition and history not contained in scripture is an important part of Christianity. Finally, feeling vindicated in my beliefs I continued to read Christian history, tradition, and scripture. Now content with my beliefs I began a lifelong pursuit in search of the historical Jesus and His Apostles. This pursuit eventually lead to new concerns.

Having been an abused child revelations of priestly sex abuse were greatly disturbing to me. In my first book I vigorously defended the vow of celibacy which is presented as a personal choice freely made by our priests, even believing some Apostles renounced marriage, becoming chaste in an attempt to imitate Jesus' lifestyle. I realized some priests were married when called by Jesus, but passed it off as unimportant because it seemed apparent celibacy became universal as a free choice by priests sometime after Constantine in 325 AD - the point in history where my book had stopped. Only intending to discover original Christian beliefs before the New Testament was known to exist, c. 30-400 AD, I had stopped, not wishing to examine the history of unsavory churchmen who later failed to live Christian lives as did the Apostles. Unfortunately, that's when the story of ascetic celibacy begins.

It is more than disturbing. It is traumatic when one discovers they are misled by those whom they rely upon for guidance and the teaching of truths, on which our Faith was founded. Slowly, I concluded this was the case on at least one important teaching, mandatory celibacy for our priests; a teaching which has now led to our current world-wide scandal surrounding sexually dysfunctional clerics of all ranks. Despite the disappointment of being misled by our Church hierarchy, along with our priests, I remain Catholic, a member of the Universal Catholic Church as it was left to us by Jesus, a Church with priests who were married fathers in the beginning, and where women leaders were included in the Church of Christ.

There is deep unrest and disaffection within the Catholic Church today. Worldwide from Asia, Africa, and Europe to North and South America demographics reveal the Church is failing in much the same way it was in 1139 AD, when mandatory celibacy was finally and successfully forced upon the priesthood. Only the truth can set us free from this past. For these reasons this author writes in service to Jesus of Nazareth, a Jew. He did not leave us with mandatory celibacy. Therefore, this book is merely one more expression of world-wide unrest, and often total disaffection.

Finally, this book will seem rather strident and confrontational to some who view it as an affront to Church authority and Hierarchical leadership. It is intended to be so. Sadly, for this reason the spiritual blessings God has bestowed upon our Church will not be our primary focus.

Book Notes

Vatican: In this book the term "Vatican" will be used throughout to indicate the ruling authority of the Roman Catholic Church. The Vatican itself is a sovereign nation, it is not the Church, but today governs both theological and temporal affairs of Catholicism as a Theocratic nation state. This ruling authority, as presently constituted, arose only after Christianity was legalized by Emperor Constantine in the fourth century. The term Vatican came to be used only after the fall of the Papal States which ruled the Italian peninsula from 756–1860 AD.

Pope: The term "Pope" literally means "papa", derived from Latin during a time when others were also titled pope. This title entered Catholicism c.399 AD as a designation for the Bishop of Rome. Pope Siricius was the first to assume this title as Bishop of Rome after his election by the citizens of Rome. Among first Christians, all bishops, including the Bishop of Rome, were elected only by parishioners of their diocese. The term pope will be used in this book for all successors of St. Peter after his death in 67 AD.

Scripture citations: Citations are from the Catholic edition, *The Jerusalem Bible*. Occasionally, for clarity a very few citations are from the *New International Version* (NIV). This book attempts to present the historical development of Christianity, therefore Biblical quotations are intended only to reveal historical understandings of the authors at that time in Christian history.

Footnotes: The author has elected to leave most footnote citations from the World Wide Web for the convenience of readers since many documents are not easily obtained without difficulty and expense. In addition to providing website links, footnotes in this book can be read on the author's website,

www.illicitcelibacy.com/SPfootnotes

Vatican sites and some Catholic apologetic sites also publish information on the web and anyone wishing to research these footnotes may visit a public library and use their free availability to the web. There, these web footnotes may also be read immediately on the computer screen. Book citations are listed by author and title only.

INTRODUCTION: ABOUT THIS BOOK

The Catholic Church is the oldest Christian church. Founded by Jesus of Nazareth in 30 AD it today remains the largest Christian belief system, however, today more than one billion followers are aware their church and its leaders are under assault worldwide, resulting from scandals surrounding celibate priests, bishops and the papacy. Not since the Protestant Reformation has Vatican leadership faced such controversy, directed primarily at the Pope. Repeated Vatican controversy has eclipsed its spiritual writings and its ability to discuss theology is slipping away. Since 2002 the public revelation of abusive clerics, and now the revelation that women have been disenfranchised from their first century achievements as followers of Christ, the Catholic Church faces internal reform. The leadership of popes who exercise power over faithful Catholics is becoming irrelevant. Today, Catholic scholars believe the source of this public irrelevance began in the second century after the first generation of Christian leaders, all of whom were Jews, had died. Replaced by a new generation of non-Jewish Christian leaders during a time of persecution, changes appeared. Only today have the consequences of these early changes begun to denigrate the Catholic hierarchy and its power over faithful Catholics.

This book will focus on papal changes introduced into ancient Christianity following the death of Jesus and His Apostles, changes that occurred during a time when Catholicism was the only Christian belief system; these changes are today alleged by growing numbers of Catholic historians to have originated with second century beliefs and practice not taught by Jesus and His apostle. Manifested in the fourth century, and contrary to original Christian belief, these doctrines are now viewed as the source of today's international scandals surrounding abusive Catholic priests, and misogynistic doctrines prohibiting women from important Church positions they held during the time of Christ and His Apostles. For this reason one must examine these modern scandals, scandals now explained by these ancient changes, changes that today threatened the church.

In 2002 members of the America Catholic community were confronted with troubling reports of sexual abuse committed by our celibate Catholic priests, primarily against young boys but now recognized to be prevalent among women and young girls. Initially these depressing reports left faithful Catholics angry and appalled, angry with the secular media and appalled with the prospect of dysfunctional priests. Catholics have long known segments of secular media to be antagonistic toward Catholic moral precepts that are opposed to modern society's secular moral-egalitarianism. Celibate Catholic Priests have been revered as men "set apart" since before the 19th century when increasing numbers of European Catholics immigrated to America, but today priests are under assault. It was the celibate priesthood on whom the foundation of Catholicism and our Catholic society relied for leadership. Catholic priests such as Father Flannigan who created Boys' Town as a home and school for homeless, abandoned and neglected young boys. Priests such as those portrayed by Bing Crosby in the movie 'Bells of St. Mary' elevated our celibate priesthood in the eyes of Americans. Surely, Catholics believed, our priests were men set apart from average humans, men who renounce desires of the flesh in order to "Act in the place of Jesus" as servants of Christ. Surely, we believed, these highly publicized allegations were mere anomalies, published only to denigrate Catholicism. Unfortunately however it soon became evident this sad story was not limited to the American Church.

More disturbing were reports of clerical cover-up, assisted by senior clergy in order to avoid embarrassment or scandal within the Church. Abusive priests were quietly moved to unsuspecting parishes where there abuse continued.

It is acknowledged by historians today that sexual abuse by clerics of all faiths is not a modern phenomenon, but it is also known the Catholic Church, the only Christian denomination that denies clerical marriage, is the only church under assault worldwide for sexual abuse of its members. Most disturbing today is the discovery that priestly sex abuse has been commonplace for centuries, a truth eloquently expressed by a 71 year old nun as she revealed sexual and financial abuse in the Santa Rosa, California,

Diocese: "Sexual misconduct of clerics has been an abscess on the Body of Christ for centuries." Comments by those such as this good nun came as a shock to faithful Catholics, but this view was not surprising to knowledgeable Catholic historians of the 21scentury. Throughout the 20th century Catholic scholars came to believe historical church records can trace priestly sex abuse back to the earliest days of mandatory celibacy. Today, numerous Catholic historians regard three Papal Doctrines as the source of these modern scandals, doctrines that were not contained in original Christianity.

The origin and history of these Papal Doctrines are now believed to have been inspired during the second and third century when foreign beliefs first began to influenced many Christians; these events will be the focus of this book. Today these Papal Doctrines pose a threat to the Papacy itself; seen by a majority of Catholic scholars as heterodox these doctrines have become part of our present scandal.

THREE PAPAL DOCTRINES THAT TRANSFORMED THE CATHOLIC CHURCH

Initially more troubling for Catholic historians and theologians as they reexamine the law of celibacy, based solely upon papal doctrines, new problems concerning other infallible Doctrines arose, problems that cast doubt on the Papacy itself, doctrines that today have become a part of expanding scandals. These doctrines are: Mandatory celibacy for all clerics; denial of women's ordination to positions they originally held in the early Church, and finally, the mortal condemnation under all circumstances for women who practice birth control. Therefore this book will challenge the existence of a divinely endowed Papal Monarch, a Monarch that did not exist in first Christianity. Today this Papal Monarch is understood by many to be the source of heterodox doctrines that now defame the Church. Today, St. Peter would not be admitted into the Catholic priesthood.

Centuries ago independent Catholic historians, theologians and scripture scholars began to question infallible papal authority, defining popes as the sole human divinely graced by God with the authority to infallibly teach Christian faith and morals. This question is not new to many Catholic historians. Such questions have been raised since the early centuries and are now a serious problem in the 21th century. In response to these questions Pope John XXIII assembled Vatican Council II in 1962, the first Ecumenical Council since Vatican Council I of 1870. Nearly a century after Vatican Council I, and realizing Catholics often ignored Church teaching, Pope John XXIII announced it was time to "throw open the Church windows" and reexamine ancient teachings often ignored by faithful Catholics. With this announcement Pope John XXIII became a beloved leader. Concerned Catholic historian had already begun a reexamination of mandatory celibacy, women's' ordination and birth control. But tragically these desired reforms did not occur; Pope John XXIII died and Pope Paul VI a Vatican conservative, ultimately disappointed those seeking change with Vatican Council II.

Following the failure of Vatican Council II discontented Catholics remained largely silent from 1965 until the 2002 sex scandal; today renewed efforts to challenge these ancient doctrines are introducing serious problems for the Vatican hierarchy. This discontent was well expressed by the *National Catholic Reporter*.

"Rather than wring our hands over what the church has become under back-to-back popes who have acted in an arrogant and authoritarian manner, we should celebrate what Vatican II has already done for us. It has given us a new view of ourselves. It's made us more free, more human and more at the service of a world that Jesus loved. It has given us a new view of the church. It's our church. It's not the popes' church, or the bishops' church, or a priest's church. It has given us a view of our place in it. We can think, we can speak, we can act as followers of Jesus in a world that needs us."

Following that template it will be asserted in this book three papal doctrines originated with non-Christian beliefs and traditions after the death of Jesus and His Apostles, a time of chaos in early Christianity. No objection in this book will question new traditions of Catholic belief and practice that arose after the first Christians in support of our first Catholic beliefs.

Written by an author more experienced in technical literature than in scholarly literature, this book is presented as a condensed historical report of incidents during early centuries that brought about change. Therefore, since *tradition* and *history* are synonyms this book will revolve primarily around historical epochs of Christian beliefs, practices and traditions that affected Christianity; their effect on today's scandals is the subject of this book.

A wise old Monsignor whom I greatly respected once told me, "Edgar, your intellect informs your conscience and your conscious makes decisions, so nourish your intellect, search for truth and defend the Faith."

—Edgar Davie

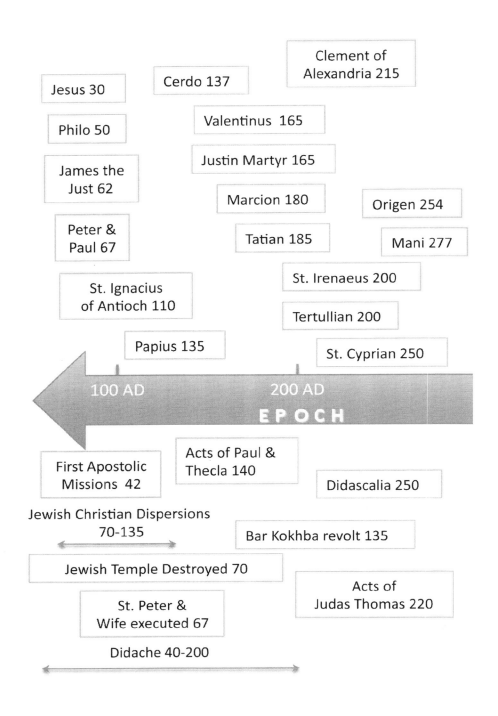

Constantine 337

Julius the
Apostate 362

St. Ambrose 379

St. John
Chrysostom 407

Pope Damasus 385

St. Gregory 389

Augustine 420

Pope Siricius 399

St. Jerome 420

300 AD   400 AD   500 AD

OF   CHANGE

Elvira Council 306

Dark Ages
Fall of Rome
476

Council of Nicaea 325

New Testament 400

Siricius Mandatory
Celibacy 385

Apostolic Constitution 375

CHAPTER ONE

INTRODUCTION:

Judaism, from which Christianity arose in c.30 AD is the oldest monotheistic religion, and its history of conflict with oppressors is widely known. From Moses, who led the Jewish exodus out of enslavement in Egypt, through the Babylon Exile c.550 BC, Judaism overcame important threats to their existence. However, few modern Christians are aware of the consequences and oppression following Alexander the Great's conquest of Palestine. Events during this time would affect Judaism and later Christians, both men and women. An understanding of changes that occurred during that time is particularly beneficial for modern Catholics, and for this reason our understanding of this event will be the first focus of this book.

ON THE ORIGIN OF FOREIGN BELIEF

"Asceticism. Rigorous abstention from any form of self-indulgence which is based on the belief that renunciation of the desires of the flesh and self-mortification can bring man to a high spiritual state... Judaism did not believe that the freedom of man's soul could be won only by the subjugation of the flesh, a belief which was central in religions based upon anthropological dualism."[1]

—Jewish Virtual Library

Early Christianity engaged Hellenistic culture generally, and more specifically Greek philosophy, from the end of the first century on.[2]
—The influence of Greek language, Philosophy and Culture on Jews and
—Early Christians.

1

HELLENISTIC BELIEF AND ITS LATER EFFECT ON CHRISTIAN-JEWS

Few Christians are familiar with the decades of religious and social trauma inflicted on ancient Judaism, a religious and social trauma that would later affect Christian beliefs and teachings. Although beginning with Alexander the Great's conquest of ancient Palestine three centuries before Christ, it is only in modern times that the lingering consequences of Greek asceticism, imposed during that time, have begun to become apparent for present day Catholics. Asceticism, as conceived before Christ by the ancient Greek philosopher, Plato, is a dualistic belief that posits a conflict between the body and soul. The belief defines the body as being weak and subject to sin, thus requiring a lifestyle of abstinence from worldly pleasures with the aim of pursuing religious and spiritual goals, and ultimately salvation. This ascetic belief was first conceived c.348 BC during a period when ascetic philosophy permeated the Greek world of politics, art and religion. While not discussed in Christian churches today, this historical epoch was destined to later affect Christianity four centuries later and because of this, its teaching and influence should be understood by modern Christians. This epoch in Jewish history, which came before Christ imprinted an instinctive and visceral rejection by all Jews regarding all things pagan, was where asceticism was given birth; and it would be the Jewish descendants of this oppressive time who would later become the first Christians. During His life, Jesus instructed His Apostles as they spread the Gospel: "Do not turn your steps to pagan territory...go rather to the lost sheep of the house of Israel." Matthew 10: 5

Before Christ, Judaism was the only monotheistic religion. Secure in their isolated Mediterranean world, the Jews remained immune to encroachment of foreign beliefs since the time of Abraham. Three hundred years before Christ, and relatively secure in their isolated world, it is understandable why Judaism felt threatened by an invasion of foreign forces. With the prospect of subjugation by Alexander the Great and a potentially devastating war seeming imminent; it is instructive for modern Christians to understand this pre-Christian Jewish world from which Jesus of Nazareth and Christianity would later arise; a world divided between Orthodox Judaism and Greek-Hellenistic pagans.

A historical examination of the origin of today's Papal Doctrines that were later imposed on Christianity in the second century after Christ, and the affect they had on Christianity after the death of Jesus and His Apostles, is a story of importance for today's Catholics.

PAGAN OCCUPATION

"In the aftermath of the conquests of Alexander the Great, Greek culture spread widely and came into much closer contact with the civilizations of the Near East and Egypt. The most significant impact of Greek religion was the importation of foreign deities and the development of new philosophical systems."[3]

—Hellenistic Religion

Having existed in their homeland for a millennium, the Jews would confront for the first time a threat never before experienced. Terrified by an impending war with Alexander c.331 BC, they believed it would be more favorable to negotiate than to fight, especially after being given assurances that while their nation would be occupied; they would be permitted to continue their ancient religion and holding sacrosanct the great Jewish Temple and their Jewish Law, the Torah. But ominously, along with this conquest came Alexander's pacification policy termed "like-mindedness." This policy was imposed by Alexander in order to introduce Greek culture and learning into all subjugated nations. This was a brilliant plan designed to encourage assimilation of religions and religious beliefs among all subjugated peoples. The policy was primarily intended to bring all conquered ethnic cultures into unity and harmony with Greece, while at the same time ostensibly permitting Jewish religious autonomy.

"Some years before, when the Greeks, who had conquered the entire known world first met the Jews, they were astonished. They had never before encountered people such as this. The Jews were different from anyone else they had ever encountered. They were the only monotheists in the world, and they subscribed to a worldview totally different from anyone else's - namely, that everything that exists had been created and is sustained by one infinite, invisible and caring God." [4]

Even with Alexander's assurances, those practicing Judaism and its tribal culture were appalled, but nevertheless submitted to this blending, which included their introduction to the pantheon of pagan gods and practices: the Canaanite god Baal, the Egyptian god Amon and the Persian god Ahura Mazda, who became identified with Zeus; the goddess Astarte, Egypt's Isis, and Horus and Artemis of Ephesus. For the more intellectually inclined, Plato and Stoicism became popular. For the consumption of those pagans beneath the intellectuals there were a myriad of gods, myths, cults and fables that controlled the common man. However, as onerous as this attempted indoctrination was, the Jews remained faithful to their one God *Yahweh* and *shunned* the plethora of pagan practices that slowly came to envelop them as increasing numbers of Hellenists penetrated their homeland.

As time passed, there arose throughout Palestine knowledge and rejection of all gods and goddesses introduced by their pagan overlords. The eastern Mediterranean became a religious melting pot with new religions seemingly springing from the ground, and apart from the Jews it became a religiously egalitarian world which enveloped them. They continued to shun pagan influences while remaining a controlled culture for two centuries, until the arrival of Greco-Syrian ruler, Antiochus IV Epiphanies, who in 173 BC began a Jewish persecution that inevitably lead to Jewish rebellion, and a virulent Jewish animus toward paganism that has not abated to this day.

It began when "Antiochus IV, heeding the advice of Hellenized Jews, believed the majority of the Jewish nation was ready to accept Greek culture. Antiochus decided to turn the temple at Jerusalem into a Greek temple of Zeus or Dionysus. The strong resistance of the people led to the first known instance of religious persecution in history: worship of God was forbidden and the Jews were forced to worship other gods."[5]

Under Antiochus' occupation the Jewish world would be turned upside down with a forcible assault by pagan beliefs not hitherto experienced. This change was shockingly assisted by the defection of the Jewish High Priest, Jason, who embraced the

4

Hellenistic lifestyle, and became a thoroughly Hellenized Jew who went so far as to abandon his Jewish name, Jesus. Embracing his newfound love of Greek culture he supported a Hellenist movement within Judaism itself. Jason's change brought visceral opposition from the captive Jews, but ultimately he would transform Jerusalem into a Greek city; following his example many Jews apostatized. Young priests took up the Greek language, dress, and engaged in athletic sporting contests. Since these athletic events were performed in the nude, many young priests desperately attempted to hide their mark of circumcision with surgical procedures.

Much of this sad epoch in Jewish history is revealed in Old Testament books of 1 and 2 Maccabees (Catholic Bible) where, writing of High Priest Jason and this forced Hellenization we read of the Jewish revolt: "Godless wretch that he was and no true high priest, Jason set no bounds to his impiety; indeed, the Hellenizing process reached such a pitch that the priests ceased to show any interest in the services of the altar; scorning the Temple and neglecting the sacrifices" 2 Maccabees 4:12-14.

High Priest Jason made every effort to Hellenize the average Jew, even to the point of sending money for sacrifices to Hercules in the city of Tyre, a fatal mistake. Seeking power, Jason greatly miscalculated Antiochus' true intentions when he attempt to seize control in 167 BC, an event we also find recorded in the Old Testament. "Raging like a wild animal, he [Antiochus] set out from Egypt and took Jerusalem by storm. He ordered his soldiers to cut down without mercy those whom they met and to slay those who took refuge in their houses and bringing about a massacre of women and children. In the space of three days eighty thousand were lost, forty thousand meeting a violent death and the same number being sold into slavery." 2 Maccabees 5:11–14

"Not long after this the king sent an Athenian senator to force the Jews to abandon the customs of their ancestors and live no longer by the laws of God; also to profane the temple in Jerusalem and dedicate it to Olympian Zeus. They also brought into the temple things that were forbidden, so that the altar was covered with abominable offerings [swine] prohibited by the laws. A man could not keep the Sabbath or celebrate the traditional feasts,

nor even admit that he was a Jew. A decree was issued order-
ing the neighboring Greek cities to act in the same way against
the Jews: 'oblige them to partake of the sacrifices, and put to
death those who would not consent to adopt the customs of the
Greeks.' It was obvious, therefore that disaster impended. Thus,
two women who were arrested for having circumcised their children were publicly paraded about the city with their babies hang-
ing at their breasts, and then thrown down from the top of the
city wall. Others who had assembled in nearby caves to observe
the Sabbath in secret were betrayed to Philip and all burned to
death." 2 Maccabees 6: 1-11

This time in Jewish history was so important that it is recorded in the *Septuagint* Bible. The Old Testament Septuagint version
used by the Catholic Church is presented here because it describes
an important historical event in Judaism's survival and its later
effect on Christianity. Married Jewish priests were vilified by the
plethora of pagan priests who denigrated Jewish priests for rejecting Plato's ascetic philosophy of celibacy and the temptations of
women, declaring that the Jewish priesthood had descended to
the baseness of carnal sex and, therefore, were unable to medi-
ate between man and the divine. Even more devastating, the great
Jewish Temple around which the lives of all Jews revolved, the place
where precious sacrifices were offered to God during Holy gatherings such as Passover, was debased. One can only imagine the
calamity visited on average Jewish families, not merely in Jerusalem
but across the Empire. Since the Babylon captivity c500 BC, Jewish
population centers had sprung up across the Empire, described as
the *Diaspora.* Within this dispersion Jewish enclaves existed from
Egypt to Rome and Persia, and the brutal impact of Antiochus'
acts affected the entire Jewish world. The lingering effect of this
ancient pagan assault on Judaism became formative in Jewish history, forever instilling an animus toward all things pagan and bringing about an unforgettable Jewish revolt that would instill a total
rejection of Hellenistic paganism by those Jews who later became
the first Christians. Not only was this epoch an assault on Jewish
people, it was an unforgivable assault on their God that would be
handed down from generation to generation and linger for centuries, later dramatically affecting the early Christians.

THE MESSIANIC HOPE

"Yahweh your God will raise up for you a prophet like myself, from among yourselves, from your brothers, to him you must listen. This is what yourselves asked of Yahweh your God at Horeb on the day of the Assembly."

—Deuteronomy 18:15-16

This Jewish epoch of occupation and persecution introduced changes within Judaism that lasted until after they were forced from Palestine in the second century AD. Not only did this religious trauma bring about divisions within Judaism, it arrived with Hellenistic-pagan influences that also reinforced the ancient Jewish desire for their promised Messiah. During this Jewish occupation, pleas to God for the promised Messiah to rescue them abounded. When would He finally arrive?

Remarkably, after more than a century of pagan occupation Orthodox Jews, the Maccabees' (Hasmoneans), successfully revolted during the years c.164 BC, in one of the most remarkable events in Jewish history. During this revolt the Jews were finally able to regain their freedom, and upon escaping Antiochus' dominance, the Jewish Hasmonean Dynasty ruled until 37 BC, even after Rome annexed Palestine in 63 BC. This successful Hasmonean overthrow of Palestine's pagan rulers would be followed by a century of relative peace, and in honor of the overthrow of paganism Judaism established *Hanukkah,* the *Festival of Lights.*

Following centuries of occupation many Jews believe their new Roman occupiers, while more benign, actually portended the impending arrival of their long-expected Messiah, and during this relative time of peace, hopes escalated with fertile expectations that the Messiah's time was close. Never before in Jewish history had conditions been more favorable for His arrival. But after nearly two centuries of Hellenistic indoctrination, damage remained; Hellenism had not vanished and with this lingering and damaging legacy of Alexander's introduction of pagan thought, it continued to influence some Jews and later some Christians, Plato's ascetic philosophy remained in the minds of many.

THE ASCETIC INTRUSION INTO CHRISTIANITY

"The Hellenization of the Jews in the pre-Hasmonean period was not universally resisted. Generally, the Jews accepted foreign rule when they were only required to pay tribute, and otherwise allowed to govern themselves internally. Nevertheless, Jews were divided between those favoring Hellenization and those opposing it, and were divided. . . conflict broke out."[6]

—Hasmonean Dynasty.

Pre-Christian Judaism heavily influenced later Jewish-Christians and the successful Jewish overthrow of Hellenistic rulers remains among the most important religious wars in history. It halted Judaism's slide into the ascetic pagan Hellenism instigated by the apostate High Priest, Jason. This war would leave Judaism divided, a division that later affected Christians. This acceptance of Plato's ascetic philosophy by some and its resistance by Orthodox Judaism would one day confront Jesus and His Apostles as He began to teach. While these confrontations are recorded in the New Testament, they are rarely recognized in context by average Catholics. Because of this, it is helpful for modern Catholics to identify those contending Hellenist and Jewish factions that influenced the Christian movement.

In *Antiquities of the Jews,* first century Jewish historian, Flavius Josephus, 37-99 AD, describes the contending Jewish movements of his time. Most of Jesus' Apostles are believed to have been Pharisees, a powerful political party in the ruling theocratic Sanhedrin. This powerful group was a social/religious movement and a school of thought among Jews during the Second Temple period, which began under the Hasmonean dynasty 140–37 BC in the wake of the Maccabean Revolt. Well known in the New Testament, the Pharisees were a powerful group who confronted all pagan thought. However, Jesus' teachings threatened their autonomous teaching authority, causing them to frequently confront Jesus over the few Orthodox Jewish Laws He "Completed." Then there were the Pharisees' political adversaries, the Sadducees, they were the other powerful party among the Temple's ruling class in the great Jewish Sanhedrin who, while rejecting asceticism, were more secular in that they rejected the concept of resurrection after death. Still, Hellenistic beliefs remained in the mind of some. Outside of the Sanhedrin, two notable Jewish theological movements accepted ascetic celibacy. They were the Essenes and the Cabala, two little known but important and influential groups not mentioned specifically in the New Testament. It would be these two and lesser known movements that would exert the most damaging influence on second century Christianity after Jesus' death.

THE ESSENES

"In fact, the apocalyptic literature belonging to the second and first pre-Christian centuries contained the chief elements of the Cabala; and as, according to Josephus, such writings were in the possession of the Essenes, and were jealously guarded by them against disclosure, for which they claimed a hoary antiquity."[7]

—Jewish Encyclopedia, Cabala

Only in recent times have average Christians come to understand the importance of the Essenes. In 1946, the discovery of ancient Jewish beliefs and practices, both orthodox and heterodox were uncovered among the famous Dead Sea Scrolls. This ancient Jewish literature reveals new understandings of pre-Christian times and permits an examination of Judaism before the time of Jesus, providing clues to the practice of celibacy among Jewish Essenes and their ascetic Hellenistic influences. While some Essenes were married, a fundamentalist sect of Essenes separated and withdrew to Qumran about 15 miles from Jerusalem c.160 BC and abandoned Orthodox Judaism following the Hasmonean revolt against Antiochus IV. While sometimes amicable, these groups were at the core of the inter-Jewish conflict.

Catholic historian Will Durant and wife Ariel authored *The Story of Civilization*. In Part III, *Caesar and Christ*, writing of the Roman civilization and Christianity from their beginnings to AD 325 wrote of the ascetic Essenes, "They derived their doctrine and practice from the stream of ascetic theory and regimen circulating through the world of the last century before Christ; possibly they were influenced by Brahmanic, Buddhist, Pharisee, Pythagorean and Cynic ideas that came to the crossroads of trade at Jerusalem." What Durant describes here is the result of Hellenistic "like-mindedness" established by Alexander, not from Orthodox Judaism. Many historians note the growth of celibate practices that spread rapidly in the first century BC, no explanation is offered for the phenomena other than Hellenism, which followed Alexander's conquest of the western world.

Shortly after the successful Hasmonean revolt, the Essenes rejected the newly installed Hasmonean Kings who saw themselves as a Royal Priesthood, a ruling class differing from the traditional non-royal High Priesthood. The Essenes believed this high priesthood to be apostate because it remained only within the Hasmonean Dynasty – a change from historical Judaism. It is not a leap of logic to believe Jesus and his cousin, John the Baptist saw the Jewish Priesthood of their day in much the same light, while at the same time rejecting the Essenes' Hellenistic dualism (soul versus body). On the one hand, Essenes were a highly literate and scholarly group who believed themselves to be devout Jews; while on the other hand they read and investigated widely into many belief systems. Although they were not a political movement, their influence became important.

Possessing a large library of eclectic material, the Essenes included ancient religious literature from sources other than Judaism among their Dead Sea Scrolls. Found among this Essene literature were writings from the *Septuagint*, the Catholic version of the Old Testament that was rejected by Jewish Scribes as Hellenisticly inspired, thus indicating Essene familiarity with Egyptian beliefs where asceticism was widely practiced. In 90 AD a decision to reject the Esseneic Septuagint Bible was made authoratively by a synod of Jewish rabbis, as it remains today. Disputed books which the Catholic Church retain and Jews rejected are: Tobit, Judith, Wisdom of Solomon, Sirach, Baruch, First and Second Maccabees, and parts of Daniel and Ester which were written in Greek. Today Protestants accept only the Jewish Canon. Most scholars believe Essene celibacy was influenced by both *Neo*-Pythagoreans from Egypt as well as the *Mystery Religions*[8]. These beliefs were incorporated into the Essenes' unorthodox ascetical practices. In essence, the Essenes were devout Jews who came to accept asceticism and were no longer Orthodox Jews.

While they were a small cult, historically speaking, the effect of the Essenes' religious philosophy was huge throughout Palestine. Essenes considered themselves the elect and withdrew from society, as Christian monks would later do. Being possessed of secret knowledge (Gnosticism) and practicing ritual purity, association with the unclean world was forbidden. In his book, *Birth of Christianity*, John Dominic Crossan explains the following regarding Essen celibacy, their "emphasis on celibate asceticism is, however, much more their Hellenism than their Judaism speaking."[9] It must be noted that non-ascetic married Essenes lived throughout Palestine and shared the same rejection of the Jewish High Priest. In Jerusalem the Essenes were firmly established in New Testament times, so much so that a small city gate on the southwest wall of Jerusalem was called the "Gate of the Essenes."

JEWISH GNOSTICISM OF ALEXANDRIA EGYPT

"Jewish Gnosticism unquestionably antedates Christianity...Judaism had experienced close contact with Babylonian-Persian ideas for at least that length of time, and for nearly as long a period with Hellenistic ideas."[10]

—Jewish Encyclopedia, Cabala

"Alexandria was, in addition, one of the chief seats of that pagan and Christian speculation known as Gnosticisms."

—New Advent Catholic Encyclopedia. Alexandria.

Modern Christians unfamiliar with the ancient tenets that dominated all religious beliefs of the first century, when Christianity was considered merely a strange new sect, can become confused when attempting to understand their origin. Not taught during seminary formation, priests and theologians also have little understanding unless they devote extensive personal time to the study of ancient gods, myths and philosophies. However, during the twentieth century Catholic historians have begun to revisit the influence ancient pagan centers, such as Alexandria, Egypt, exerted on the ascetic movement after Christ's death. Alexander founded Alexandria c.331 BC as the capital of Egypt and it soon replaced Athens as the theological center of Hellenistic thought; a most egalitarian center where both pagan and Jewish scholars began to conflate their disparate beliefs. Later, when Christianity began accepting pagan converts, c.49 AD, this blending of Hellenistic philosophy and Christian thought became prominent in Alexandria, c.50AD. Having surpassed Athens as the center of Hellenistic philosophy, the ancient Library of Alexandria was the largest and most significant such structure in the ancient world. It functioned as a major center of Hellenistic scholarship from its construction in the third century BC until the Roman conquest of Egypt in 30 BC. Alexandria became the intellectual capital of the world, famous for its library which in the 3rd century BC was said to have contained 500,000 volumes.

Containing the writings of all Hellenistic philosophy, the religiously egalitarian Ptolemaic dynasty sought to include the Jewish Scriptures, and to that end employed Jewish Scribes to translate their Jewish Bible, the *Septuagint,* a Hellenisticly inspired Greek translation now rejected by Jews and Protestants. It is often identified with Hellenistic Judaism which predates Christianity.

Philo of Alexandria

"Philo came from an aristocratic family which had lived in Alexandria for generations...a family who were noble, honorable and wealthy... educated in the Hellenistic cultures of Alexandria, Rome, Greece and Ancient Egypt, and particularly in the traditions of Judaism and the study of Jewish traditional literature and in Greek philosophy."[11]

—Philo

While the importance of Philo of Alexandria is little known by modern Christians, it is critical to understand his influence, because his writings would later mislead many Christians. He was a peer of Jesus, although the two of them never met. This most influential Jewish teacher-philosopher's writings ultimately did

12

more to mislead second and third century Christians than did the Essenes.

A brilliant scholar, Philo used philosophical allegory to fuse and harmonize the Greek philosophy of Plato with Old Testaments prophets such as Moses in an effort to harmonize the two beliefs. His method followed the practices of both Jewish scholars and Stoic philosophy. In the third century AD we find his allegorical interpretations cited by several Church Fathers; but brilliant as he was, Philo was rejected within Judaism because his ascetic-dualistic contrast between God and the world appears in both Platonism and in Neo-Pythagorism, which are anathema to Judaism. History records that no Jewish Hellenistic movement more effectively influenced later Christian asceticism than did Philo's *Cabala* (Kabbalah) movement, which began in the second century before Christ and was later popularized in Alexandria, Egypt; as described by Adolf von Harnack in his *History of Dogma*, "The role of Philo in synthesizing Judaism with Hellenism paved the way for later Hellenistic Christians." The Jewish Encyclopedia provides information on this movement under "Gnosticism" and "Cabala," from which the quotations below are drawn.

Cabala's originators did not limit their beliefs to the Jewish Torah alone, they claimed secrets were imbedded throughout the prophetic Old Testament books and in ancient apocryphal writings; believing this hidden information to be "received doctrines" they obtained from the "Jewish Fathers." These received doctrines allegedly could be "traced back to the Prophets as well as Moses on the Mount of Sinai." In other words, Cabala discovered new and secret knowledge (*Gnosis*, from Gnosticism i.e., newly discovered hidden knowledge) hidden in the Old Testament; in the same manner Christian Gnostics of the second century would claim to find secret revelation in the New Testament. Such secret knowledge was condemned by Orthodox Jews; and Cabala was believed to be a deviant within Orthodox Judaism since the second century BC when Ben Sira warned against it in his sayings, "Thou shall have no business with secret things." (Ecclus. lii. 22)

The chief characteristic of Cabala's secret belief was that, unlike Scriptures, it declared that the Law given to Moses by God said, "These words shalt thou declare, and these shalt thy hide."

This teaching is typical of Gnostic apocrypha. Since its inception Cabala, as other Gnostic movements, intended their message for the *elect* only. Within Cabala both marriage and sex were forbidden because, as we will shortly discover, both the Cabalists and Essenes were splinter groups from the same Hellenist belief. Both insisted Satan ruled the earth and that the propagation of children would only further his reign.

Being a Hellenized Jewish philosopher, Philo was the first scholar to interpret biblical Scriptures allegorically, thus allowing a new and mystical interpretations of Moses' writings. We belabor Philo here because, influential as he was at the time of Christ, Philo led a group of likeminded followers called *Therapeutae* that later influenced Christianity, described by historians as "an esoteric circle of illuminati, of 'wise men of vast influence.'" Contrary to Judaism and later Christianity, a major belief of Jewish Therapeutae was their ascetic philosophy, i.e., to live a contemplative ascetic life and free themselves from the temporal bonds of soul and body, that is, absolute sexual abstinence. It is here that we first see the enigma of Hellenistic philosophy intruding into the Gospel of Christ. This belief was later rejected by Jesus who taught, "This is why a man must leave his father and mother and cling to his wife, and the two shall become one body." Matthew: 19-5 Philo preached marriage was a threat to one's soul.

The Cabalists vanished during a conflict with the Greek Hellenist in Alexandria, Alexander, in 115–118 AD. However, we will later discover a variant of their theological belief reappearing among Christian philosophers of the second century, a syncretized religious system based on secret knowledge, not faith. For this reason, it is difficult for modern Christians to accept that such a mystical belief of a supposedly brilliant Jewish scholar would be accepted by rational Christians; this is a difficulty we will later address.

The Judaizers - Followers of Jesus

"Nazarenes: A Sect of primitive Christianity; it appears to have embraced all those Christians who had been born Jews and who neither would nor could give up their Jewish mode of life."[12]

—Jewish Encyclopedia

"'It is believed by many scholars that this false messianic movement, also called the 'Judaizers,' was the birth of the Ebonite group'"

—Dangers of the False Messianic Movement

Rarely known by average Christians, two sects, the Nazarenes and Ebonites were devout Jews who followed Jesus and the Apostles, only to later be condemned as heretics by fourth century Christians for their refusal to abandon Jewish Law.

The New Testament is replete with information describing faithful Jews, who for centuries awaited the arrival of their prophesied Messiah to be sent by God, who would be the expected savior and liberator of the Jewish nation. But as we know from reading the New Testament such religious groups are not specifically identified, they were merely part of several Jewish sects active during the time of Jesus, such as the Zealots who committed suicide *en masse* in their fortress at Masada rather than surrender to Roman forces following the destruction of the Jewish Temple in 70 AD, or the Sacarii, a group known as "dagger men" who assassinated Roman sympathizers. We read nothing of the Ebonites in the New Testament and the Nazarenes are mentioned only once in passing. The Ebonites were faithful Jews who followed their Messiah. While unknown by most Christians, these two groups, along with the majority of Essenes who were married, rejected the asceticism of their brothers at Qumran and followed Jesus. These groups were at the core of the Jesus movement. The Ebonites[13] and Nazarenes[14] were important, and it is helpful to understand them since their Jewish beliefs were identical with those of the Apostles prior to Jesus' arrival. These two Jewish sects were known as the *Judaizers*, and while followers of Jesus, they continued to be Law abiding Jews. According to the

15

fourth century Church historian Epiphanius, the Nazarenes were originally Jewish converts of the Apostles, who fled Jerusalem following Jesus' prophecy of the coming fall of Jerusalem in 70 AD. They settled in Pella where Jesus' young cousin, Simeon, became bishop. The Nazarenes were similar to the Ebonites in that they considered themselves Jews who maintained an adherence to the Law of Moses. They only used the *Gospel of the Hebrews* written in Aramaic, the Jewish language of that time. The Gospel of Matthew is today believed to be a later expanded Greek version of the lost original. The Nazarenes followed only this Gospel. However, unlike half of the Ebonites they accepted the Virgin Birth. Lost in the fog of history, many scholars believe both the Nazarenes and Ebonites were originally one movement that later separated over differing views of Judaism.

An important reason for understanding these two groups is their acceptance of Jesus as the Messiah while remaining Law abiding Jews, much to the distress of later Christians who in the third century rejected them. Disappearing from history, they were later accused of heresy for failing to accept Hellenistic philosophies, which by then influenced new generations of Christians. The second epitaph above is an example of the heretical charges that exist today.

The following are beliefs adhered to by both groups that, while causing great angst for some later Christians, were acceptable to other first century Jewish-Christians: "They accept Messiah in such a way that they do not cease to observe the old Law of circumcision and the Sabbath, nor did they celebrate the common meal [Mass]"; "they believe the Messiah was the Son of God born of the Virgin Mary." And importantly for our study, they rejected all ascetic pagan philosophies and closely followed the first Biblical command in Genesis 1:28, "Be fruitful and multiply." Holding such beliefs, Church historian Epiphanius wrote in 395AD, "At present they strictly forbid virginity and continence as is true of other sects likewise." In essence, for many later Christians, even though they followed the Messiah, Nazarenes and Ebonites were heretics.

Whatever ones' view of these ancient Jews may be, understanding them is of paramount importance for Christians. Their

Jewish-Christian rejection of Plato's ascetic philosophy was identical with that of Jewish-Christians in the first century during the life of Jesus and His Apostles. Had Jesus come preaching asceticism requiring any Jew to abandon marriage, and thus propagation of the family, He would have been summarily rejected.

LEGACY OF THE ASCETIC PHILOSOPHY FOR SECOND CENTURY CHRISTIANS

As we look back over Jewish history, it is apparent throughout the Bible that confrontation between ancient Jews and their pagan adversaries appeared throughout the Old Testament i.e., Daniel in the Lion's Den and the Babylon Captivity 550 years before Christ; these confrontations were always successfully overcome, often by converting the pagans. However, following two centuries of occupation under Alexander and Antiochus IV's conquest, the existence of pagan philosophies would not be exorcized from Judaism until after the destruction of Jerusalem and the Great Temple by the Romans c.70 AD, 40 years after Christ, a time when Jews and Jewish-Christians began to separate. Only after the Romans slaughtered 80,000 Jews and expelled Judaism from Palestine, would the Jews be free of this pagan philosophy, as it remains today. Only in 1948 were Jews permitted to return to Judea; but tragically, pagan converts to Christianity in the second century AD would reintroduce the ascetic philosophy of celibacy and superiority of virginity. For modern Christians to grasp this threat posed by Plato's Hellenistic philosophy one must understand its vast departure from the original Jewish belief upon which Christ instituted His church. Initially, Jews and early Christians accepted only revelations from God as opposed to esoteric philosophies of man, but at the time of Christ this ascetic philosophy dominated all religious belief-systems, all that is, except the Jews and Christian-Jews who followed their Messiah, Jesus of Nazareth.

CHAPTER TWO

FIRST CENTURY JUDAISM

NOTE: The purpose of this chapter will be to historically describe Jewish cultural, theological and societal foundations upon which Christ formed Jewish-Christianity during the first century, along with the reality that asceticism was rejected by Jewish-Christians, as it was by the first Jew, Abraham.

"Enjoy your life with the woman you love, through all the fleeting days of your life God has given you under the sun; for it is the lot assigned to you in life."

—Ecclesiastes 9:9

It's helpful to understand the Jewish world into which Jesus was born and from whence He called His disciples. In order to understand the nature of Jesus of Nazareth and His Jewish-Christian followers we need to examine the common world view they shared. A full understanding of their tribal culture is often difficult for modern Christians to get their minds around because it was so vastly different from modern societal norms, and is largely unknown today. An analogy that may help shed light on first century Judaism and its world view is to examine the Muslim world of today, a culture which continues to be organized around tribal norms handed down through succeeding generations for more than three thousand years.

Muslims of today are descendent of Ishmael, the son of the first Jew, Abraham, and his concubine Hagar. Hagar was presented to Abraham by his wife, Sarah, because she was incapable of childbearing at her advanced age. From this union of Hagar and Abraham came Ishmael, who would later become the father of the Muslim faith. Arrangements such as this were normal within tribal societies because propagation of the family and the tribe were crucial to their continued existence in an isolated adversarial world. Later, with Sarah's miraculous birth of Isaac and the expulsion of Hagar and Ishmael, we find the beginnings of two tribal cultures who would oppose each other, even to this today. However, while history has been unkind to the Jews, the Muslims have carried their tribal culture into the twenty-first century. Muslims and Jews of today have differing views of God's will for them, but their societal norms of culture, family, and worship remain very similar. Aside from their differing theologies, an observation of Muslim culture today provides some insight into the tribal culture of Jews during the time of Jesus. As we know, Islam has no celibates.

For readers interested in an in-depth historical exposition of first century Judaism, a book that should be consulted is *Daily Life in Palestine at the Time of Christ* by the French Catholic scholar and historian Henri Daniel-Rops, from which some of this section is drawn[1]

THE FAMILY

"Yahweh God said, 'It is not good that man should live alone. I will make for him a helpmate.'"

—Genesis 2:18

"In Israel the family was the essential basis of society, the cornerstone of the entire building...its members really did feel of the same flesh and blood; and to have the same flesh and blood meant having the same soul. Legislation [Torah] had taken this principle as its base and had developed from it: the Law and also the multiple commands in order to uphold the permanence, the purity and the authority of the family."

—Daniel-Rops

As one contemplates the origins of Judaism the ineffable wisdom of Jewish laws become apparent. Judaism began in an isolated pastoral area of the world with the assemblage of twelve nomadic tribes, each self-governed but with a common allegiance to their Law, and to their one God. This was unique and original in human history. Jewish laws and societal norms arose from the practicalities of governing isolated tribal groups, each consisting initially of perhaps 50–300 individuals in the early days. As the Jews later settled into towns and villages, the family remained more than a social entity. Each family was also an individual religious community with religious feasts over which the family's father presided and in which family members took part. Passover, first celebrated within the family, was a family religious feast in addition to later becoming a major holiday Exodus 12:3, 13:8. This religious family theocracy would later remain with Jewish Christians as we see fathers converting to Jesus and bringing the entire family with them Acts 16:34.

"Nothing could break the tie of blood and it was of first importance for a man to make sure of the perpetuation of the family, that is, to marry. A text upon which Rabbis commented in these strong words was: 'a bachelor is not truly a Man at all'. And celibacy was thought of as an anomaly... a disgrace, a sin."

—Daniel-Rops

Polygamy was common in early Judaism and while it continued to be practiced during Jesus' time, it had become less the norm than the exception. Earlier, especially among Jewish kings such as David and Solomon, who provided themselves with harems as a sign of their authority and power, polygamy was near universal. Upon marriage a new and independent entity took its place in the tribal community. This new entity could look only to itself and its extended blood relatives for support, and for this reason the enlargement of this new family entity through the addition of children was imperative. It was God's command that they should propagate. Jesus' family members were tradesmen/carpenters, consisting of five brothers and at least two sisters. They were responsible for their family's growth, stability and well-being, with only their relatives to turn to in cases of emergency. In their attempt to increase the family through children few ordinary men could afford two or three wives, however, if the first wife was barren a man was obliged to take a second wife or a concubine with no repudiation of the wife of his youth, "Does a man cast off the wife of his youth? Says your God." Isaiah 54:6 Some rabbis, however, permitted men only four wives, a practice later adopted by Muhammad for Islam.

Historically, Judaism's rejection of ascetic pagan beliefs was fundamental to their tribal laws and culture; it was this tribal culture that Jews depended on to increase the family unit with children and the tribe for growth, prosperity and security. It is important to note that we find this same societal organization today among Muslims, who also descend from Abraham. Nothing was more important than increasing the family; King Solomon had 700 wives. Considered by Jews to be the first Biblical command, Genesis 1:28 states, "Be fruitful, multiply and fill the earth." To that end God said, "It is not good for man to live alone, I will make for him a helpmate." Genesis 2:18. A notable change for Christianity that would later occur is found in Exodus 28:1 when God commanded Moses, "From among the sons of Israel summon your brother Aaron and his sons to be priests in my service." Apparently, God in the Old Testament wanted only married priests, but, as Catholics we are now told God of the New Testament desires only celibate priests.

Forever, Jews have been required to marry by age 20 and men were permitted multiple wives and/or concubines. A rabbinical tractate, Kiddushin 29-6 states: "The holy one - may He be blessed - curses the man who at 20 was not married." Abraham sired Ishmael with his concubine Hagar, and Isaac was born of his wife Sarah. Childbirth to increase the family was so important that men whose married brother died without progeny were required to impregnate the widow; children of the deceased brother's wife were believed to extend his brother's family lineage. And contrary to Catholicism today, rabbis permitted contraception in circumstances when childbirth threatened the mother's health; vinegar soaked sponges were used as an IUD.

21

The consummate rejection of all pagan philosophy and Jewish devotion to the Torah was revealed in a rabbinical antidote. A rabbinical student asked, "Since I now understand all of Torah may I study Greek philosophy?" Replying with a citation from Joshua 1:8 the rabbi answered, "'The Torah shall not depart from your mouth, you shall meditate on the Torah day and night.' Therefore, search out the hour that is neither day nor night and devote it to the study of philosophy." During previous centuries it had become a matter of survival for Jews to reject pagan philosophies.

Parents arranged marriages for their children, male and female. According to the Law, girls were not to marry before twelve and a half, and it was highly unusual for children to choose their spouse. A rabbinical tradition existed stating that God had arranged the marriage forty days before the boy's birth and another rabbi advised the father to marry off his son "while he still had his hands upon his neck" Such measures were important because marriage would increase the family. This was a primary consideration in all tribal cultures such as Jews and early Christians. Celibacy had no place.

Perhaps the Old Testament explained Jewish animas toward paganism best, "Make no pact with the inhabitants of the land [pagans]...or else you may choose wives for your sons from among their daughters, and these, prostituting themselves before their own gods, may induce your sons to do the same." Exodus 34:14-16

OBLIGATORY MARRIAGE

Addressing the Jewish laws of His day, Jesus was asked a question by adversarial Pharisees having to do with the obligation of a man to marry the childless wife of his deceased brother in order to provide offspring. These descendants would then be considered children of his deceased brother; thus propagating his brother's family and lineage Matthew 22:23-31. This law, as described in the Talmud was in effect at the time of Jesus and based on a passage in the Old Testament Book of Genesis. In that case, a man refused to faithfully follow the Law and as a result, lost his life. "But Onan, knowing the child would not be his, wasted his seed on the ground every time he slept with his brother's wife, to avoid providing a child for his brother. What he did was offensive to

Yahweh [God] so he brought about his own death." Genesis 38:9 This practice of marrying the deceased brother's childless widow is continued to this day within Islam. Nothing was more important to the Jews of Jesus' day than the propagation of children and the family lineage. The thought of celibacy or virginity was *anathema*.

During the early years after Jesus' death all of His followers were Jews from within this Judaism. It is these first Jewish-Christians and the Jewish world view which they possessed that we ask the reader to recall as we describe the development of Jewish-Christianity. With this background, let us further examine those apostles whom Jesus chose.

THE TWELVE

As we examine the origins of Christianity an important point to notice about the twelve Apostles is they were called individually and personally by Jesus, as described in the New Testament. Jesus knew these men to be married. During his lifetime Jesus was called Rabbi, yet He departed from the practice of other rabbis by personally selecting His Apostles. Other rabbis actively proselytized followers.

Among the initial twelve Apostles selected by Jesus were Peter, Andrew, James (brother of John), John, Philip, Thomas, Bartholomew, Matthew (Levi), Simon the Zealot, Thaddeus and Judas. In addition to the twelve, Jesus called at least seventy Disciples, "After this he appointed seventy two others and sent them out ahead of him in pairs...." with authority to "...cure those who are sick and to announce 'The Kingdom of God is near you'" Lk 10: 1-20. We must acknowledge that all these men were what might be termed ordinary Jewish men. They were men from a tribal culture, and followed Jewish Law as handed down to them in the Torah, "God created him, male and female he created them. God blessed them, saying to them, be fruitful, multiply," Genesis 1:27-28. The Jews considered this to be the very first command given by God to humankind. Failure to marry and reproduce was believed to be a sin.

Indicating their continuing support of Jewish traditions that were formed during Temple worship throughout their lives, an incident occurred shortly after the death of Jesus and the fallen

Apostle Judas Iscariot that required the selection of a new Apostle to replace him. "We must choose someone who has been with us for the whole time that Jesus was traveling around with us...and he can act as a witness to the resurrection." Acts 1:21-22 Two men were nominated and after praying for God's guidance, "They then drew lots for them, and as the lot fell to Matthias, he was listed one of the Apostles." Acts 1:26 Of this incident Bernard Ruffin relates an interesting story in his book, *The Twelve*. Commenting on the common Jewish practice of casting lots, he says, "All offices and duties of the Temple were settled by lot." During that time before the Temple's destruction, names of candidates for Temple-religious office were written on small stones, placed in a container, and shaken. The first name to fly out was elected. It was in this same Jewish manner that Matthias was selected to become an Apostle.

What do we know, scripturally, of these first men? Biographically very little, except they were married middle class Jews of moderate education. In order to understand the lack of biographical information revealed in scripture we need only listen to their preaching, "For it is not ourselves that we are preaching, but, Christ Jesus as Lord, and ourselves as your servants for Jesus sake." 2 Corinthians 4:5 While much is known of these men from extra-Biblical literature of the first century it is scriptural silence on their personal lives that will later be exploited by celibacy apologists as they seek to create a far different historical picture of these men than existed in the first century. Coming from a tribal culture similar in many ways to Muslims of today, celibate males were as rare as hen's teeth within Judaism. Marriage and children were not only the norm, they were expected. One need only read the Old Testament to discover the joy in a tribal culture associated with the "first born" or the lamentations of barren wives. Both Peter's wife and mother-in-law are mentioned in scripture Matthew 8:14; 1 Corinthians 9:5, but later different explanations of first century priestly marriage will arise in order to foster a far different picture. For this reason let us examine some of these men.

Jesus' Family

Surprisingly, we know more about some of Jesus' relatives than might be expected. After Jesus' death the Apostles elected St. James, the brother of Jesus to the position of leadership for the Christian-Jewish community. St. James served until 62 AD, thirty two years after Jesus' death. This is surprising to modern Christians who believe St. Peter was the leader of the first Jewish-Christian community, when in fact that honor went to St. James.

The Bishop of Jerusalem who followed James in 62 AD was Jesus' first cousin, Simon (also Simeon). Simon was the son of Clopas, who was brother of St. Joseph, Jesus' father Luke.24:18. Simon remained bishop until his crucifixion under Emperor Trajan, c.106 AD. As we can see from this historical record, it was married men and relatives of Jesus who led the Jerusalem Church as bishops until the end of the first century. Jude (Judas) was another married brother of Jesus who traveled as an evangelistic missionary along with his wife. St. Jude wrote the New Testament "*Letter of Jude.*" Besides those brothers, ancient historian Julius Africanus of Emmaus described additional relatives of Jesus late in the first century who, "From the villages of Nazareth and Kokhaba they traveled around the rest of the land and interpreted the genealogy they had [from the family traditions]..." We will have occasion to discuss St. James again.

Few Christians realize Jesus had brothers, cousins, uncles, and aunts etc. as active participants in spreading the Gospels. Most are listed in the Bible as being present at the crucifixion.

Aside from anger directed toward Jewish-Christians by Jewish leaders because they refused to take up arms in Jewish revolts, Jews of the Christian sect lived side by side with their Jewish neighbors in Jerusalem until after the Temple's destruction in 70 AD. It was only after 90 AD that they were excluded from local Synagogues. While Jewish Temple authorities, for political reasons, were able to execute St. Andrew and St. James over a 40 year period before the destruction of the Temple, Christian-Jews remained Jews, as well as Christians who lived amicably with other Jews until 135 AD. They were all married and the prospect of mandatory celibacy in this tribal culture remained unimagined.

Historian Ruffin identifies the occupation of nine Apostles; six were fishermen, two were civil servants and one a carpenter, all were married.

Catholics wishing to understand first century Apostolic preaching should read the New Testament Epistle of James.

CHAPTER THREE

THE JEWISH JESUS

*"Peter stood up with the eleven and addressed them in a loud voice...
Men of Israel, listen what I am going to say: Jesus the Nazarene was a
man commended to you by God"*

—Acts 2:22

*"Pilate wrote out a note and fixed it to the cross; 'Jesus the Nazarene,
King of the Jews'."*

—John 19:19

In 167 BC the successful Jewish revolt brought freedom from Greek-pagan overlords and provided a century of stability and freedom, allowing Judaism uninterrupted religious autonomy until agreeing to be annexed by Rome in 37 BC, with assurance the Temple and the Torah would remain sacrosanct. Unfortunately, while pagan philosophies were no longer forced upon them, a residue of the pantheon of Greek-pagan gods and Plato's ascetic philosophy left a lingering effect on many Jews. It was into this conflicted Jewish world that Jesus of Nazareth was born, and we will see these lingering effects reappeared among new Christians in the second century AD.

As the scripture citations above detail, Jesus of Nazareth was born a Jew. He lived as a Jew, and He died a Jew. Before there was a pagan convert to Christianity, before there was a Christian in Rome, there were only Jewish-Christians who followed their Jewish Messiah and the Torah; it would be twenty years after Jesus' death before pagan men were permitted to become Christians without first converting to Judaism and undergoing circumcision.

To understand these first Jewish-Christian followers of Jesus, one must historically understand the Jewish societal foundation, culture and beliefs of Jews of that time. Secure in their monotheistic beliefs after two centuries, Jews were free to assert their beliefs and challenge Plato's ascetic philosophy. Jewish animus toward pagans remained and is a major focus of this book; however, in the second century the Jewish nature of Jesus would be more mythologized than divinized by pagans. Even today, 2000 years after Jesus, modern Christians often have difficulty separating Jesus' divinity from His human and Jewish nature, prompting second century non-Jews to imagine Jesus was not human at all, but a god who appeared in fleshly human form. To that end, the Catholic Church infallibly declares that Christ possessed both a human and divine nature, with a duality of wills, stating: *"Each of the two natures in Christ possesses its own natural will and its own natural mode of operation."*[1] With this infallible definition that both Jesus' human and divine nature operates independently, it becomes more difficult for the Church to insist He remained forever chaste as a Jewish man. How these two natures "operate" individually is unknown, as is His historical relationship with Disciple Mary Magdalene. But we can be assured that during Christ's life, Jesus of Nazareth's human nature as an itinerate Jewish rabbi/teacher with numerous followers, both men and women, was immediately recognizable as a charismatic Jewish prophet.

Typical of Jewish families, Jesus was the youngest of two sisters and five brothers: St. James, who later became the leader of Christianity, Joses (Joseph), Simon and Judas. All of whom worked with His artisan father to support the family. Little is known of Jesus' childhood other than the Biblical accounts of the flight into Egypt with his father Joseph and mother Mary in order to escape King Herod's "slaughter of the innocents." However, apocryphal writings of the second century such as *The Infancy Gospel of Thomas* describe Jesus as a sometimes bratty youth, but still the miracle worker when He[2] is reported to have raised a childhood friend from the dead following a fatal accident. Writings such as this were not included in the New Testaments, but were extremely popular well into the middle ages. Early literature such as this continually mystified the humanity of Jesus and lingers today. In real life, however, Jesus was viewed by his Sanhedrin challengers as simply a Jewish man, similar in many ways to the seventeen pseudo-Messiahs who appeared during the first century before and after His death. To his adversaries, Jesus remained throughout His life merely a trouble maker. We will later see voluminous second century apocryphal literature that has no place in Orthodox Christianity, fostering apocryphal beliefs of Jesus.

Jesus at Qumran

"Jesus' behavior reflects the Qumran-Essenes. He kept the Sabbath, but on a different day from traditional one, just like the Qumran Essenes. They followed a solar calendar, which meant the Sabbath fell on Sunday instead of a Saturday."
—*The Secret Initiation of Jesus at Qumran*, Robert Feathers

Today, information from the Dead Sea Scrolls is believed by some historians to demonstrate Jesus spent considerable time with the ascetic Jewish sect of Essenes[3] at their monastic compound at Qumran several miles from Jerusalem, as did Flavius Josephus and Jesus' cousin St. John the Baptist. The Catholic Church attempts to squash the idea of Jesus associating with the Essenes. Although names of individuals in the Essene community at Qumran are not listed, author Robert Feathers in his book, *The Secret Initiation of Jesus at Qumran,* presents a plausible case that Jesus did spend time there, perhaps after the death of His earthly father Joseph. Jesus' time with the Essenes would have occurred shortly after the Biblical story of Mary and Joseph losing Jesus in the Temple when He was about 13, Luke 2: 41. Father Joseph is believed to have died shortly thereafter and it is known the Essenes accepted young boys brought to them by parents who could no longer provide for them. Essene scrolls dwell voluminously on the coming of a royal messiah in the line of David, and a later connection between the Jesus movement and the non-celibate Qumran community is also known. If Jesus was truly the Son of God, as we believe, it is also acceptable that He would have mingled with, and fully understood all segments of Judaism,

29

especially with a sect that lived in His community. Some Christians have difficulty recognizing the depth of other Jewish movements, both modern and ancient.

Having renounced what they believed to be apostate transgressions of the Jewish Temple authorities during the first century BC, the Essenes withdrew to Qumran where they congregated in communal life dedicated to an ascetic search for what they believed to be true Judaism, voluntary poverty, daily immersion and abstinence from worldly pleasures, as recorded in their scrolls. While it is likely Jesus spent time with the Essenes at Qumran, He left before His ministry began. It is known that following His departure to begin His ministry, Jesus rejected asceticism which forbids alcohol, consumption of meat and marriage. Jesus preached a different message.

When speaking of pagans Jesus instructs His followers, "Do not give dogs what is holy; and do not throw your pearls in front of pigs, or they may trample them and then turn on you and tear you apart." Matthew 7:6. In Matthew 11:19 and Luke 7:34 Jesus confronts the Pharisees on the subject of asceticism when He states: "For John the Baptist comes, not eating bread, nor drinking wine, and you call him possessed, yet the Son of Man comes eating and drinking and you say 'look, a glutton and a drunkard.' " And, on the subject of marriage Jesus teaches: "Have you not yet heard that the creator from the beginning made them male and female, and that is why a man *must* leave father and mother and cling to his wife, and the two shall become one body. They are no longer two therefore but one body." Here Jesus is referring to Adam and Eve who became "One body" Matthew 19:5 (We will cite this passage several times). From teachings such as this we are assured Jesus did not preach ascetic celibacy. Additionally, there is no evidence in the New Testament what-so-ever that Jesus, through the "operation" of His human nature and free will did or did not marry. The suggestion that Jesus may have married first appeared in an ambiguous statement by St Ignatius of Antioch in his letter to St. Polycarp c.108AD. It would be c.160 AD before St. Justin Martyr suggested it would not have been "appropriate" for the Son of God to have married.

JESUS' TEACHING ON MARRIAGE

It was while quoting God in the Old Testament that Jesus taught, "Have you not read that the creator from the beginning made them male and female, and that He said:" this is why a man must leave his father and mother, and cling to his wife, and the two shall become one body." Matthew 19:4f, Genesis 2:24, Genesis 1:27.

Jewish-Christians, secure in their monotheistic beliefs after two centuries of occupation were free of pagan persecution, but Jewish-Christian animus toward pagans remained. Scribal law declared it a sin to eat at table with "unclean" pagans. Marriage was forbidden, and social intercourse didn't exist.

No statement in scripture more cogently expresses Jesus' instructions to his Jewish followers regarding their Jewish faith than what is found in the Gospel of Matthew when He instructs His apostles, "Do not imagine that I have come to abolish the Law or the Prophets. I have not come to abolish, but to complete them. I tell you solemnly, till heaven and earth disappear, not one dot, not one little stroke, shall disappear from the Law until its purpose is achieved" Matthew 5:17-19. Throughout His lifetime, as with all Jews, Jesus shunned pagans when preaching His Gospel; He instructed the disciples, "Do not turn your steps toward pagan territory...go rather to the lost sheep of the house of Israel." Matthew 10:5. Only after the resurrection did Jesus instruct His apostles to "Make disciples of all nations." Matthew 28:19. Still, after Jesus' death and the lingering concerns of previous pagan influences, it would be 20 years before Gentiles were permitted to become Christian without first undergoing circumcision and converting to Judaism.

What follows here are the two most important changes in Jewish law that were "completed" by Jesus, changes often taken out of cortex by ascetic apologists. (First) Jesus rejected the divorce of a legitimate marriage for any reason other than fornication, thus changing Mosaic Law permitting divorce under any circumstance Matthew 19:9. With these changes Jesus permitted all Christians, even today, to choose the unmarried state of their own free will. (Secondly) following His denial of divorce Jesus was asked by disciples, "Is it not advisable to marry?" In reply to this

31

question Jesus spoke of celibacy, comparing celibacy to becoming a eunuch. He stated, "It is not everyone who can accept what I have said [about celibacy], but only those to whom it has been granted. There are eunuchs born that way from their mother's womb, there are eunuchs made so by men and there are eunuchs who have made themselves that way for the sake of the kingdom of heaven...let anyone accept this *who will* [or "can"]. Matthew 19:11f. Nowhere does Jesus suggest that perpetual virginity is superior to marriage or that abandoning intercourse with one's spouse is necessary under any circumstances.

Surprising to many Catholics is the acknowledgement by celibacy apologists that neither Jesus nor His apostles required celibate priests, bishops, deacons or nuns. Perhaps the most authoritative acknowledgement by Vatican celibacy apologists that all Christians were permitted to freely choose marriage or celibacy appears in the book, *The Apostolic Origin of Priestly Celibacy,* by the Jesuit, Christian Cochini, S.J. who writes:

"The early centuries of the Church had no law on celibacy as it is understood in modern times, i.e., a law stating as a primary condition for admission to the Orders [priesthood] the obligation of rejecting marriage." [4]

This acknowledgement today by Catholic theologians contradicts what miss-informed Catholics have forever been taught, i.e., the laity continues to be taught Jesus' permission of celibacy was in reality a request of celibacy for His disciples who wished to become priests. As we examine the twelve apostles called by Jesus, they are known to be law abiding Jews and therefore married when called, for this reason the Apostles accepted Christ's gift of free-will choice of Sacramental Matrimony. These two changes, the prohibition of divorce and permission to accept or freely reject marriage are recorded by the Apostles, and therefore are Doctrines of Christ. As we proceed we will discover these doctrines of Christ have been nullified, and the devastating consequences of this nullification.

CHAPTER FOUR

JESUS' DEATH

"Having arisen in the morning on the first day of the week, He appeared to Mary of Magdala from whom He had cast out seven devils. She went and told those who had been His companions."

—Mark 16:19

The magnitude driving this Jewish movement as they continued to follow their risen Messiah is understandable as we read Jewish historian Josephus Flavius c 94 AD.[1] As a young man, Josephus spent time with the Essenes in Qumran as some historians today believe Jesus did. Josephus was both a Jewish Priest and general during the Roman-Jewish war of 70 AD. Captured, he was later allowed to write the history of Judaism late in the first century. Josephus said of Jesus, "About this time there lived Jesus, a wise man, *if indeed one ought to call him a man.* For he was one who wrought surprising feats and was a teacher of such people who accept the truth gladly. He won over many Jews and many Greeks. *He was the Messiah.* When Pilate, upon hearing him accused by the men of the highest standing among us, had condemned him to be crucified; those who had come in the first place to love him did not give up their affection for him. *On the third day he appeared to them restored to life. For the prophets of God had prophesied these and countless other marvelous things about him* and the *tribe* of the Christians, so called after him, has still to this day not disappeared." Josephus was born 37 AD and reared in Judea; he grew up with Christians and knew them well.

From this account, we first note the italicized texts are suggested by some detractors to be insertions into Josephus' writings by later Christians. This allegation is improvable, but inconsequential to our point here that an eminent Jewish historian and peer, Flavius Josephus, identifies Jewish-Christians as a Jewish Tribe firmly ensconced within Judaism at the end of the first century. We also must note the term "men of highest standing among us" refers strictly to the priestly and aristocratic Jewish leadership and not to average Jews, among whom Jewish-Christians were included. Jesus was executed under Roman Procurator Pontius Pilate at the instigation of Jewish Temple political-theological authorities – not by "The Jews," of whom Christian-Jews were a part. We will later examine anti-Semitism among Christians but it did not exist in the first century. At that time, animosity between Christian-Jews and Jewish authorities was strictly political and theological *within* Judaism.

Today, many Christians imagine the Apostles as having begun spreading the Gospel in other lands immediately after Jesus' Crucifixion; however, this is not how things developed. During those first 12 years after Jesus' death and long before the New Testament was written, the Apostles, Jews that they were, remained at home in Judea and began gathering together the "sayings of Jesus." These sayings would become the earliest beginnings of the New Testament during these first shrouded years, a time viewed by scholars as an "historical dark period" because few events outside of those recorded in the Bible are extant. The Bible, however, informs us of the death of St. Stephen who became the first Jewish-Christian martyr, and the conversion of St. Paul, who assisted in Stephen's death before converting during his encounter with Jesus in a "vision" on the road to Damascus at around c.32-33 AD. During those first 12 years, the Christian sect of Judaism remained in their Jewish homeland where the Apostles regularly met in Jerusalem or in Peter's home in Capernaum; all the while gaining Jewish converts from neighbors and friends, much to the distress of Temple authorities. Some commentators refer to these meeting places as a Christian Synagogue.

In 42 AD, fully 12 years after Jesus' crucifixion, Peter and Apostle James (St. John's brother) were arrested by Temple authorities who were concerned about the Christian's success. The Apostle James was executed but Peter miraculously escaped from jail and fled successfully to Rome. This brief incident began the first meaningful migration of Christian-Jewish leaders from Jerusalem into the pagan world, and was to be the starting point for Christian evangelization across the empire. By then, however, Christianity had already grown by word of mouth. When Peter first arrived at Rome in 42 AD he found Christians there who heard his speech twelve years earlier in Jerusalem, along with many others present that day from around the Empire, Africa, Asia, Europe, and Persia.

Roman historian and senator, Tacitus, c.100 AD, explains Christian growth from an adversarial third-party point of view when he wrote, "Christus, the founder of the name, had undergone the death penalty in the reign of Tiberius by sentence of procurator Pontius Pilot and the pernicious superstition was checked for the moment, only to break out once more, not merely in Judea, the home of the disease, but in the capital itself, where all things horrible or shameful in the world collect and find vogue." (Tiberius, Annals 15.44) This fleeing and persecuted sect of Jews was neither Hellenist nor celibate. Initially, Christianity's spread was by word of mouth and preaching. After 42 AD preaching alone remained the norm for more than two centuries. There was no New Testament.

JESUS' BROTHER ST. JAMES THE JUST BECOMES CHRISTIAN LEADER

"Eusebius of Caesarea (260-340 CE), Archbishop under Constantine, tells us in his "Ecclesiastical History" that James was "The lord's brother, who had been elected by the Apostles to the Episcopal throne at Jerusalem,"'

—Ecclesiastical History" 2.23

"The Gospel of Thomas sayings relate that the disciples asked Jesus, "We are aware that you will depart from us. Who will be our leader?" Jesus said to him, "No matter where you come [from] it is to James the Just that you shall go, for whose sake heaven and earth have come to exist."

—Epiphanius' Panarion 29.4

35

During the life of Christ it was Philo of Alexandria, a little known Jewish-Hellenistic scholar whose philosophical allegory, failed to fuse and harmonize the ascetic Greek philosophy of Plato with Old Testament prophets. Philo's ascetic influence on later Christians has been omitted from modern discussions concerning the Church's support of the ascetic philosophy; therefore Philo is omitted from early Christian studies of celibacy. In a similar manner St. James falls into the same category of intentionally omitted Christians who led the formation of Christianity after Jesus' death. No two figures in Christian history have been more covertly censored by future scholars in an effort to present a nuanced Christian history that continues to support Hellenistic asceticism.

As noted in the two Epigraphs above, it is universally agreed St. James the Just, Jesus' brother, became the leader of Christianity after Jesus' crucifixion, not St. Peter. This comes as a shock to modern Catholics. We are taught St. Peter was the chief apostle and pope. James, not Peter, followed his brother Jesus as leader of the movement we now call "Christianity." St. Peter, however, remains "First among equals" among the apostles.

As leader of Jewish-Christianity, James was strict. He carefully monitored apostolic teaching with an eye towards protecting Jewish laws left unchanged (completed) by Jesus. From ancient writings attributed to the second pope, Clement, but composed by a later unknown writer we find these historical instructions. "The Church at Jerusalem having been governed by James for a week of years, the Apostles return from their travels, and at James's request state what they have accomplished. A record was compiled by Clement of discourses involving the spostle Peter, together with an account of the circumstances..."[2] It is acknowledged that James carefully monitored apostolic teachings during a time when Hellenists were becoming enamored with Jesus as the Son of God, and were attempting to find similarities between Plato's philosophy and Jesus, similar to those proposed by Philo of Alexandria.

James in his own way was highly puritanical; he had taken the same rigorous Nazarite religious vow described in the Old Testament, as did Samson who lost his hair and his eyes for the love of Delilah. The term Nazarite refers to Jews who consecrated their lives to God by abstaining from wine or cutting the hair on one's head. Abstinence from wine was not categorized as ascetic; rather it was considered a *fast* because all Jews married. James was a married man whose wife accompanied him as they traveled and evangelized for 32 years after Jesus' death 1 Corinthians 9:5. We read this description of "the Lord's brother" by historian Eusebius, c 280 AD, "James the just, a Jew whose beard was never touched by a razor. He obeyed the Law and was respected by all citizens." He wrote the "Book of James" in our New Testament scripture. Some say it was the first New Testament book c.47 AD.

James, as Christian-Jewish leader after Jesus' death was extremely successful in persuading fellow Jews that Jesus was their long awaited Messiah. Comfortable among all Jewish sects, he moved into Jerusalem's married Essene quarters, all of whom became Christians. For this reason, and his success converting Jewish neighbors, a plot by Temple authorities was conceived in much the same manner as the one against Jesus. James' assassination occurred in a similar manner during a change of Roman Governors, when Roman authority was temporarily absent. We have from Jewish historian Flavius Josephus the following account of James death (an almost current account).

"*[The Roman Governor]* Festus was now dead, and [his successor] Albinus was still on the road. So [the High Priest] Ananus assembled the Sanhedrin of Judges, and brought before them the brother of that Jesus who was called Christ, whose name was James, and some of his companions. And when he [Ananus] had formed an accusation against them as breakers of the [Jewish] Law, delivered them to be stoned. Those of the city who were considered the most fair-minded and who were strict observers of the law were offended at this. They therefore sent to King Agrippa urging him, for Ananus had not been correct in the first step [convening the Sanhedrin], to order him to desist from any further such actions...King Agrippa, because of Ananus' actions, deposed him..." (Antiquities 20.9.1)

This death was no more than the same power politics that constantly surrounded the Temple and its power brokers who continued to see the Christian sect of Judaism as an ongoing threat to their authority, control, and wealth since the death of

Jesus. An indication of James' support among ordinary Jews as well as Christians is evidenced by this description of James by historian Hegesippus c. 150 AD, a time before the concept of a monarchial pope was conceived. "Control of the Church passed to the apostles together with the Lord's brother James, whom everyone called the Righteous, for there were many James', but this one was holy from his birth; he drank no intoxicating liquor and ate no animal food; no razor came near his head; he did not smear himself with oil, and did not bathe. He alone was permitted to enter the holy place [Temple], for his garments were not of wool but of linen. He used to enter the sanctuary alone and was often found on his knees, beseeching forgiveness for the people, so that his knees grew like a camel's from his continually bending them in worship of God and beseeching forgiveness for the [Jewish] people. Because of his unsurpassed righteousness he was called 'the Righteous' and...'Bulwark of the people. '" Truly, James was a Jew's Jew as well as Christianity's leader.

This anecdotal evidence is presented merely to demonstrate the continuing Jewishness of Christianity in Judea. The first Christians possessed a Jewish-Christian nature that remained through the first century until shortly before the holocaust of 135 AD; a disaster which forever divided Jews from Jewish-Christians. By then, Christians were moving quickly into the pagan world while retaining their Jewish-Christian nature with no thought of embracing asceticism.

Only when we investigate third century Christianity will we discover why Philo and St. James are marginalized in Christian history. Today Christian historians acknowledge that St. James, Jesus' older brother, was leader of the Christian movement until his death in 62 AD and following his death no Christian legitimately replaced him, ever. A point to be discussed later will be that, following James' death all Apostles and later bishops will be considered equals. Dr. James D. Tabor in his commentary, *The Jewish Roman World of Jesus*, writes, "I use Ebonite/Nazarene as an historical designation to refer to those original, First century and largely Palestinian followers of Jesus, gathered around Yaaqov (St. James) in Jerusalem, who were zealous for the Torah, but saw themselves as part of the New Covenant Way inaugurated by their 'True Teacher' Jesus. James is a key and neglected figure in this whole picture. As the blood brother of Jesus, authority and rights of guidance were passed on to him."[3]

Gentiles admitted to Christianity

"I rule then, that instead of making things more difficult for pagans who turn to God, we send them a letter telling them merely to abstain from anything polluted by idols, from fornication, from meat from strangled animals and from blood."

—St. James. Acts 15: 19-20

During the first century AD entrance of pagan proselytes into Judaism was rigorous and demanding. Judaism with its many laws and practices was unique in history as they diligently guarded against the introduction of foreign thought, considering themselves elite. For generations after Alexander, Jewish animus toward paganism was handed down through succeeding generations. Scribal law declared it a sin to eat with gentiles because they did not observe Jewish ritual purity laws. Proselytes were also to understand they were not and never could be on a par with them. A passage in the Jewish Mishna, a commentary on Jewish Law, states that proselytes should pray in the synagogue thusly, "O God of *your* fathers." (M. Bikkurim, 1.4)

Few Christians today appreciate the sanctity with which Jews held their Jewish Law; always, converts were expected to follow the Torah and its laws. Yes, St. James as leader of Christianity, as all Nazarites, was married and as with all Jewish-Christians in the beginning, he scrupulously followed Jewish Law. Children were circumcised on the eighth day, rules of purification were observed and the Sabbath was kept as a day of rest. Until 49 AD, two decades after Jesus, all converts in Judea were required to obey all Jewish Law, bringing about a problem among Christian-Jews. When word came to St. James in Jerusalem that St. Paul was preaching pagan converts need not be circumcised or observe Jewish Law, problems arose. Upon hearing of this James reacted strongly, precipitating the first near schism in Jewish-Christianity with his insistence that all converts must follow Jewish Law. This development became serious enough for St. James that he assembled a council for Apostles in Jerusalem during 48-49 AD. Acts Chapter 15.

Again, Christian-Jews were forced to deal with the pagan problem. Initially the council was in turmoil because certain Pharisees who had converted to Christianity insisted all converts must be circumcised according to Jewish Law. This was a huge issue since Paul in his travels had by then been accustomed to accepting Gentiles without subjecting them to Jewish Law, a law foreign to pagans. Writing of this counselor event eight years later, c.57, to his followers in Galatia, Paul described the situation, "It was not till fourteen years had passed that I went up to Jerusalem again. I went with Barnabus and took Titus with me. I went there as the result of a revelation, and privately I laid before the leading men the Good News I proclaimed among the pagans; I did so for fear the course I was adopting or had already adopted would not be allowed. And what happened? Even though Titus who had come along with me is a Greek, he was not obliged to be circumcised. The question came up because some [Judaizers] have furtively crept in to spy on the liberty we enjoy in Christ Jesus, and want to reduce us all to slavery [of the Law]. I was so determined to safeguard for you the true meaning of the Good News that I refused even out of deference to yield to these people for one moment." Galatians 2:1-5

Prior to this council, pagans admitted into Christianity in Judea had dutifully followed the whole of Jewish Law as had St. Stephen 20 years earlier. Later, as might be expected, history reveals many Jews who did not accept this councilor decision and remained adamantly opposed to any religious association with gentiles who did not fully convert and accept Jewish law. Historians term these Jewish converts who continued to reject all pagans, *Judaizers.* In passing we must ask the reader to acknowledge the differences between the terms Jewish Authorities, Judaizers, Jews, and Jewish-Christians. All were Jews living together, but with different theological/political agendas; they were all Jewish.

Finally, after a lengthy debate it was through Peter's intervention and his description of how the Holy Spirit was bestowed by God upon pagan converts who did not follow Jewish Law, "In fact God, who can read everyone's heart, showed His approval by giving them the Holy Spirit just as He does to us. God made no distinction between them and us since He purifies their hearts by faith." Acts15:7-9. This silenced the Elders who then allowed Paul and Barnabas to speak of their similar success through the Holy Spirit.

Happily, with this St. James also agreed and ended the discussion with his authoritative decision, *"I rule then"* that pagan converts must be instructed to "abstain from idols, from fornication, from meat of strangled animals and from blood." Until this council, twenty years after Jesus' death, the question of pagan converts had not been settled and some theological differences would continue between Paul and James over salvation by faith or by "works of Jewish Law." It was only with this council that pagan converts were welcomed with open arms by Christian-Jews. Prior to that time, absolutely no thought of mandatory *ascetic* celibacy existed within Orthodox Judaism or Christianity because it did not exist in Jewish Law.

This permission for pagan conversion was approved at a time when all Christian-Jews believed Jesus would return during their lifetime, but when Jesus failed to return this conversion permission would prove to be a great problem in the second century.

It should be noted the death of St. James under High Priest Ananus in 62 AD resulted from intra-Jewish Temple politics and James' great success converting Jews, not pagans. Christianity's belief that Jesus was the final, ultimate, and complete sacrifice posed a threat to both the Temple and its income, which came from animal sacrifice, whether two turtledoves or a bull. Jesus' sacrificial death also posed a great threat to the High Priesthood itself. This episode, the admission of gentiles defines the concern Jewish-Christians such as St. James had early on regarding pagan influences among non-Jewish converts, resulting from aberrant beliefs the Apostles knew to reside among pagans.

While Jewish-Christians in Jerusalem were concerned with gentile conversions it was already too late to stop the influx. As early as 33 AD, before the Apostles began to convert pagans, it had already begun by word of mouth shortly after the death of the first Christian martyr, Stephen Acts 6:1-8. "Those who escaped the persecution because of Stephen's death traveled as far as Phoenicia and Cyprus and Antioch but they proclaimed the message to Jews only. Some however...went to Antioch where they preached to the Greeks...and a great number were converted to the Lord." Acts 11:19-21. At that early date pagan converts were still expected to observe Jewish Law. We recall that when St. Peter first arrived in Rome in 42 AD he was met by Jews who heard him preach that first day in Jerusalem. Merely seven years after that first trip to Rome when this Council of Jerusalem was held, Christianity had become well entrenched in Rome as part of a large Jewish colony that had existed for more than a century, and by that time also included pagan converts. There a similar confrontation surrounding Jewish Law between Christians and Jews occurred c.52 AD, "All the Jews were making constant disturbances at the instigation of Chrestus [Christ], and he [Emperor] expelled them [all] from Rome."[4] Later we find some converted Jews who were forced from Rome will reappear as Christian leaders. It is important to realize that in 42 AD when Peter first visited Rome, the Apostles confined conversion to those who were prepared to become Jews. This history is presented merely to reinforce the Jewish nature of original Christianity; ascetic celibacy of any kind was not taught by Jesus and it was not up for discussion during the Apostolic council that admitted pagans, because *mandatory* celibacy was rejected by Jewish-Christians.

NOTE: To complete the relationship of Paul and the Ebonites and Nazarenes, the term *Judaizers* appears twice in the text above, they were the "some who do not belong to the brotherhood" according to Paul. Apparently Paul and the Judaizers never saw eye to eye ... they use the Gospel of Matthew only, and repudiate the Apostle Paul, maintaining that he was an apostate from the Law." With such comments one understands later divisions between Jews and Christian-Jews.

ANTI-SEMITISM

Twice above we have noted Jewish-Christians lived together in harmony with other Jews in their Palestinian homeland among life-long friends and neighbors, many of whom became Christian-Jews. However, beginning in the second century when Jewish Christians became strangers in a pagan world, new converts to

Christianity knew practically nothing of His Jewish nature, but with the later arrival of "Patristic Fathers" we will find the first traces of anti-Semitism. Attempting to separate Jesus from Judaism, "the Jews" became a convenient scapegoat. It would become "the Jews" who killed the Son of God. This scandalous epitaph has followed Judaism since that time, bringing disgrace on all Christians. Nothing could be further from the truth. Two scriptural examples explain the error of this slander.

In the book of Mark we find: "He went into the Temple and began driving out those who were selling and buying; He upset the tables of the money changers...And He taught them...you have turned it into a robbers den. This came to the ears of the chief priests and the scribes, and they tried to find some way of doing away with Him." Mark 11:15-18. The consummation of this plan to "do away with" Jesus came quickly; within days Jesus was arrested and convicted of breaking Jewish Law as described by Mark: "The first thing in the morning, the chief priests together with the elders and scribes, in short the whole Sanhedrin, had their plan ready." Mark 15:1. Understanding the potentially volatile nature of circumstances such as this, it was Pilate's custom to favor the Jews by releasing one prisoner at festival time, the choice in this instance being either Jesus or a notorious killer, Barabbas. "When the crowd went up and began to ask Pilate for the customary favor Pilate answered them, 'Do you want me to release for you the king of the Jews?' For he realized it was out of jealousy that the chief priests had handed Him over. The chief priests, however, had incited the crowd to demand that he should release Barabbas for them instead. Then Pilate spoke again. 'But in that case, what am I to do with the man you call the King of the Jews?' They shouted back, 'Crucify him.' Why? Pilate asked them 'What harm has he done?' But they shouted all the louder. 'Crucify him.' So Pilate, in order to placate the crowd released Barabbas for them and, having ordered Jesus to be scourged, handed Him over to be crucified." Mark 15:8-15.

This simple story is transparently surrounded by spurious political/theological conflict successfully executed by Jesus' adversaries. Temple authorities wished to "do away with Him." During a festival gathering of pilgrim Jews from across the Empire attending the Passover festival, it became a simple matter for the chief priests to incite turmoil "out of Jealously" among the pilgrim "crowd," few of whom were familiar with Jesus other than from temple propaganda misleading the uninformed. In the second century it then became easy to interpolate this story for uninformed converts. Only by abandoning canonical Scripture can the origin of this event be challenged.

The spurious nature of anti-Semitism's first entrance into Christianity is clearly exposed by Jewish historian Flavius Josephus. Describing the assassination of Jesus' brother James with a similarly premeditated plan, he describes the true nature of Jewish support for the Jesus movement in his description of James' death, and the resulting backlash from average Jews: "And when he [Ananus] had formed an accusation against them [James and his followers] as breakers of the [Jewish] Law, delivered them to be stoned. Those of the city who were considered the most fairminded and who were strict observers of the law were offended at this." Two thousand years later we find Jews still wrongly vilified based on second century Apocrypha introduced by the Patristics whom we will later describe.

Jews First

"You worship what you do not know; we [Jews] worship what we do know; for salvation comes from the Jews."
—Jesus to the Samaritans, John 4:22

Few Christians realize this newly formed sect, the Jewish-Christians, did not initially seek gentile-pagan converts. Conversion of non-Jews was not their goal in the beginning. The Apostle's primary mission was to announce to Jews around the world their Messiah had finally arrived, and the Kingdom of God was at hand; always, the term "Kingdom of God" was preached by Jesus as the *presence* of God's rule on earth, not merely the ascension into Heaven. It was to be lived out on earth. Moreover, their Messiah would return again, and soon! During His life, Jesus strictly confined the Gospel to Jews alone as he instructed His Apostles, "Do not turn your steps toward pagan territory, and do not enter

44

any Samaritan town; go rather to the lost sheep of the House of Israel. And as you go, proclaim the *Kingdom of God* is close at hand." Matthew 10:5-7 This passage describes a Jewish movement within Judaism at the time of Christ as they followed their Jewish Messiah; no passage in the Bible better describes original Christian-Jews before gentiles appeared; the first mission of the Apostles to these widely dispersed Jews was "believe, and be prepared, for the Messiah will soon return."

Later, Paul would be primarily known for converting gentiles, however, the mission of all Apostles was to the "Jews first." Paul consistently preached "The Good News is the power of God's salvation – to Jews first, but Greeks as well." During Paul's journeys his first charge was to first visit Synagogues in order to make the vital announcement of the Messiah's arrival and only after this first announcement did he seek pagan converts. These instructions are given in scripture, "...the brothers immediately sent Paul and Silas away to Boroea, where they visited the Jewish synagogue as soon as they arrived." Acts 17:10 Before the first century many Jews had dispersed around the world for half a millennium following the Babylonian exile of 500 years earlier. Therefore, the Apostolic mission was to inform those Jews in the *Diaspora* who had lost contact with Jerusalem and consequently continued to awaited their Messiah; from Babylon to Gaul, from Africa to England, even Jewish slaves in the Roman mines of Spain and Sardinia were to be preached to.

Apostolic missions of Jewish-Christians were so focused on informing all Jews of the arrival of their messiah that they made special efforts to reach the ten lost tribes of Israel. These tribes once composed the northern kingdom of Israel before vanishing from history during the Assyrian conquest of 722 BC. They had been carried off into captivity, never to be found again. The original Apostles preached in all these areas before their martyrdom; this was done because, as Paul said in Romans 2:9, "Pain and suffering will come to all who do evil, Jews first, but Greeks as well." In the beginning, these missionary travels by Jewish-Christians remained first and foremost committed to saving their Jewish brethren across the far flung Empire.

But, as Paul continued his mission to the pagan Gentiles he would continually be confronted with the problem of exorcising the life-long ascetic beliefs that the pagans often had difficulty shedding, primarily ascetic celibacy. Supporting Catholic teaching on the efficacy of celibacy and virginity over the married state, we are told today that Paul himself accepted ascetic celibacy. Let us examine Paul's teaching.

At that same time Jewish-Christian missionaries traveled the Roman world; house-churches were established with ordained *Presidents* 1Timothy 3:2 who then ordained other clerics and deacons from their own community, both urban and rural.

CHAPTER FIVE

ST. PAUL ON CELIBACY

"St Paul not only continued his pre-conversion celibacy as a Christian but recommended it for those who would be dedicated to serving God."[1]

—Catholic Answers

"I would like everyone to be like me, but some have one gift [celibacy] and some have another."

—St. Paul. 1 Corinthians 7:6

In the epigraphs above St. Paul taught, "I should like everyone to be like me but some have one gift [Celibacy], some have another." 1 Corinthians 7:6 Celibacy apologists today insist Paul was speaking here of the gift of celibacy versus marriage, and that he remained forever celibate. Scholars have recently come forward to challenge the belief of Paul's life-long celibacy. According to Daniel-Rops, Paul apparently began to experience a change around 54-55 AD. Rops says of Paul: "St. Paul may have shown partiality for celibacy at first but it is certain that among the earliest Christians several apostles, St. Paul among them, as well as leaders of the Church were married." Daniel-Rops apparently bases his conclusion partly on Paul's statement in 1 Corinthians 9:4, "My answer to those who wish to interrogate me is this: Have we not every right to eat and drink? And the right to take a believing wife with us, like all the other Apostles and the brothers of the Lord and Cephas [St. Peter]?"

In order to address the Vatican position on Paul's words in Corinthians concerning marriage vs. celibacy, let us first place Paul's statement in context. Chapter seven in First Corinthians begins thusly: "Now for the answer about which you wrote," 7v.1, here Paul is prepared to answer a question posed by the Overseer of Corinth - one of the most pagan cities of the Empire. The majority of this letter is concerned with sinful lapses of Church members that occurred since his last visit and of specific concern was the reappearance of pagan influences such as eating food sacrificed to pagan gods, and of celibacy.

Regarding these titles of early Christian leadership we should note the terms, *Overseers* and *Elder* were interchangeable, as Paul described when addressing the "Elders" of Ephesus: "Be on your guard for yourselves and all the flock of which the Holy Spirit has made you 'Overseers,' to feed the Church of God." Acts 20:28-29 The Church Hierarchy of today did not exist in the Deposit of Faith; St. Peter himself tells us: "To the Elders among you, I appeal to you as fellow Elders...Be *shepherds* of God's flock that is under your care...not lording it over those entrusted to you, but being examples to the flock." 1 Peter 5:1-3 In the second century these titles will become "Bishops".

Here, in his letter to the Corinthians, we find St. Paul fulfilling his duty as a "shepherd". In chapter six Paul's first sentence identifies the source of contention among the Corinthians when he says, "How dare one of your members take up a complaint in the law court of the unjust [pagans] instead of before the saints." 6v.1. So, we know therefore that pagan influence was at work. Corinth was similar to other large cities with pagans and celibate pagan priests who were held in high esteem for their celibacy (as the Church teaches today). There is little doubt here that the Overseer posed a question concerning the efficacy of celibacy, a question which had been raised by Hellenist influences from outside his Church. Additionally, the bishop's question was not merely about priestly celibacy but about celibacy for all Christians.

Now let us continue with Paul's answer to the question. "Yes, it is a good thing for a man not to touch a woman; but, since sex is always a danger let each [every] man have his own wife and each [every] woman her own husband." 7v.2 In this passage Paul does not differentiate between priests, who did not yet exist, and laymen. Paul's answer is clearly an endorsement of marriage, but we know Paul was unmarried at that time because he indicates in 7v.9 that widows would do well to remain unmarried *"like me, but if they cannot control their sexual urges, they should get married."* and in 7v.25 he says of his celibacy. "About remaining celibate I have no directions from the Lord...but if you are married do not look for freedom" This one statement, "no directions from the Lord," and "if you are married do not seek your freedom." forever removes Church allegations the Apostles felt a compunction to abandon their wives and imitate Jesus. It is only two chapters later 9v.3 when Paul makes the statement that he should be allowed to take a wife along on his missionary travels as did St. Peter. What was he thinking of if not marriage?

These passages in First Corinthians were written in the spring of 55 AD but only one year later in 1 Timothy 4:1 he says, "hypocrites will say marriage is forbidden." Daniel-Rops saw a change over time in Paul's position on celibacy when Paul said in 1 Corinthians 7:6: "This [celibacy] is only a suggestion not a rule," clearly invalidating all mandatory celibacy. Paul then immediately says 7v.9, "If they cannot control their sexual urges, they should get married, since it is better to be married than to be tortured." Finally, in his letter to the Ephesians three years later in c.58 AD we have this beautiful statement on marriage, "Husbands should love their wives as Christ loved the Church and sacrificed Himself for her to make her holy... in the same way husbands are to love their own wives as they are to love their own bodies, for a man to love his wife is to love his own body...and that is the way Christ treats the Church because it is His body. For this reason a man *must* leave his father and mother and be joined to his wife, and the two shall become one body. This mystery has many implications; but I am saying it [marriage] applies to Christ and the Church." Ephesians 5:21-32.

This striking comparison of Jesus and the Church, the Body of Christ, to a married couple becoming one body sounds strange indeed for one who would chose to remain celibate. This text is the most ringing endorsement of marriage in the entire New

Testament, especially his use of the word "must." Did Paul ultimately marry in order to avoid torture?

Contrary to Jesus' teaching supporting marriage, later apocryphal books such as *Acts of Paul and Thecla* would insist all Christians should remain celibate or abandon marriage. Written c.160 AD by an unknown author, this book was one among many apocryphal 'Acts' supporting an unknown author's apocryphal assertions. It is clearly spurious but as with all apocrypha a grain of truth is often present. Based on Paul's teaching above to the Corinthians supporting all marriages we know the Thecla story is spurious, but the prospect of a marriage upon which the story was based cannot be ruled out.

Two centuries later, the great Hellenist celibacy proponent Bishop Origen c. 250 AD recognized the word "yokemate" in Philippians 4:3, written c. 58 AD, to mean *wife* when Paul wrote: "I plead with Euodia and I plead with you loyal *Sygyzus* [yokemate or companion] to be a true companion, and help these women since they have contended at my side in the cause of the gospel"

Disturbed that Paul may have married, and attempting to defend Paul's perpetual celibacy in order to support celibacy, Origin insisted Paul's was a marriage of propriety only, to Lydia, with whom Paul lived in Philippi Acts16:11-15. This was necessary, Origen assured, because it would have been unseemly for Paul to live as a single man with a single woman. But 20 years earlier St. Clement of Alexandria had also believed St. Paul had married and offered a slightly different reason for the relationship, "Even Paul did not hesitate in one letter to address his *consort*. The only reason why he did not take her about with him was that it would have been an inconvenience for his ministry." Clement of Alexandria: *Stromata*.[2] At the time of Paul, long before celibacy became a law it was becoming commonplace for pagan converts, who knew little of Jesus' Jewish nature, to insist the Apostles surely abandoned their wives in order to imitate Jesus, therefore denying Paul's marriage.

Today, the Jewish apologist Hyam Maccoby[3] repeats allegations by Jewish antagonists against Paul in his day. Early Jewish detractors claimed Paul was a Hellenized Jew from Tarsus, one of the most pagan cities of the Empire. They insisted Paul became enamored with the prospect of marrying the High Priest's daughter; and then, alleging Paul was rejected, he abandoned the Torah and became a follower of Christ. Only later, after years as a Christian, scholars then claimed Paul considered marriage. As with many such points of contention it is impossible to discern all the facts from available documents, but his perpetual celibacy is now seen by independent historians to be apocryphal.

Paul never met Jesus in the flesh, only in a vision. How much of Jesus' teaching he received is unknown. It was three years after his conversion in c. 33–34 AD that he traveled to Jerusalem for a two-week visit with St. James, Jesus' brother, and St. Peter. He went again in c.44–45 AD and again to the Council meeting of c.48–49 AD. Therefore, after 20 years of meetings and traveling with various Apostles, in addition to his trips to Jerusalem, he had ample time to learn of the human Jesus during His time on earth. Many scholars pose the question, "If Paul was the promoter of celibacy as alleged by celibacy apologists why did he not point to Jesus celibacy as the shining example of its correctness, not just for himself but for all Christians?" Never did Paul point to Jesus' celibacy as a lifestyle to be followed. There is absolutely no evidence anywhere, from any source, which indicates Jesus wished his Apostles to remain chaste during His life or after His resurrection.

Vatican apologists frown on private exegesis such as this when interpreting scripture in a manner contrary to their teaching, but this letter to the Corinthians was important for more than merely instructing the bishop. It reveals the spread of Christianity was accomplished through House-Churches such as this one in Corinth, and the qualifications of leaders selected by Paul and his disciples. These leaders should have been capable of identifying Hellenistic philosophies that might mislead pagan converts such as those at Corinth. Considering the numerous House Church leaders and bishops that Paul instructed and/or corrected over a period of near 30 years it is worth examining Paul's comments on Hellenistic philosophies that could cause problems for Christians.

ST. PAUL ON ASCETIC PAGAN PHILOSOPHIES

"In my speeches and sermons that I gave, there were none of the arguments that belong to philosophy;...And I did this so that your faith should not depend on human philosophy but on the power of God... we still have a wisdom to offer those who have reached maturity, not of a philosophy of our age as do the philosophers of our age, which are coming to their end. The hidden wisdom of God which we preach in our mysteries that God predestined to be our glory before the ages began."
—St Paul to the Church in First Corinthians. 1 Corinthians 2: 4-7

In the second century "The church fathers were also infected by this virus [asceticism], too enthusiastic about the potential of Greek philosophy as preparation for the gospel, despite a formal adherence, 'the Trinity plays almost no role whatever in the living-out of the Christian life." [4]
—The Influence of Greco-Roman Culture on Early Christianity

As it was with the problems that confronted the Overseer of Corinth, so too would others be confronted with problems concerning non-Christian philosophies. During this time when there was no New Testament, faith in Christ was taught orally, and St. Paul was prepared to instruct them. Paul was surely most qualified to expound on Judaism's pagan adversaries. His early years were spent in Tarsus, a commercial and intellectual center where all religions competed, Gnosticism, Mithraism, Stoicism, and Platonism. Paul's parents sent him to Jerusalem as a youth to study the Law under the renowned Pharisee and scholar of Jewish Law, Rabbi Gamilial the Elder. As one investigates the historical record of Christianity's spread into the Roman world, a continually recurring theme will be an interminable confrontations between Hellenistic philosophies and the Apostles who were taught from childhood to shun them.

The epigraph above describes the second and third century influence of Plato's ascetic philosophy imbued into later pagan scholars prior to their Christian conversion that would remain with them. Asceticism would ultimately come to dominate a majority of Church leaders in the second century who, as converts from paganism knew little of Jesus' Jewish nature upon which He founded Christianity. Not only did St. Paul understand the threat Hellenistic philosophies posed to the Gospel, he realized it must be challenged as non-Christian and a threat to the Church. Being aware of the threat we find he continually admonished his disciples to be aware. In his letter to the bishop of Corinth, written in the spring of 55 AD, we find many subjects discussed, such as Dissension among the faithful, sexual sins and general Christian principles. But a most important matter is dealt with in the very first chapter of Corinthians; the intrusion of pagan philosophy set the tone for the entire letter. Replete in Paul's writings are admonitions concerning the threat of pagan philosophy.

In the spring of 55 Paul writes in 1 Corinthians 1:19 "As scripture says: 'I will destroy the wisdom of the wise'; where is the wise person? Where is the teacher of the law? Where is the [pagan] philosopher of this age? Has not God made foolish the wisdom of the world?" As he moves into the discussion of marriage and celibacy Paul issues one of his most cogent anti-ascetic comments on the subject of Christian marriage. "Do not Barnabas and I not have every right to eat and drink? And the right to take a Christian wife around with us, like all the apostles and the brothers of the Lord [James the Just] and Cephas [St. Peter]? 1 Corinthians 9:5 (spring 55)

Apparently, during the year 55 AD Paul was to confront ascetic philosophy several times as he pointed out the errors of one's pagan background regarding the belief in the superiority of perpetual chastity. In the fall of 55 AD he wrote to his disciple Timothy, who was actively recruiting new Christian leaders, saying, "The Spirit clearly says that in later times some will abandon the faith and follow deceiving spirits and things taught by demons. Such teachings come through hypocritical liars [pagans], they forbid people to marry and order them to abstain from certain foods, which God created to be received with thanksgiving by those who believe and who know the truth." 1 Tim 4:1-3

In this instructional comment to Timothy, Paul again identifies the dangers of asceticism by condemning abstinence from certain foods, "which God created to be received with thanksgiving by those who believe" as well as denial of Christian marriage. Paul embellishes his teaching in this letter when he instructs Timothy to ignore Gnostic philosophies – "Have nothing to do with pointless philosophical discussions and *agnostic* beliefs of the *'knowledge'* [Gnosticism], which is not knowledge at all." 1 Tim 6:20 (fall 55)

Three years later, in 58AD, Paul feels it necessary to confront ascetic philosophies, again to Timothy: "Have nothing to do with pointless philosophical discussions; they will only lead further and further away from the true religion. Talk of this kind corrodes like gangrene, as in the case of Hymenaeus and Philetus, the men who have gone right away from the truth...some people's faith cannot stand up to them." 2 Timothy 2:16. Later that year, Paul again feels it necessary to instruct the bishop of Colossae of the dangers he faces in challenging pagan philosophers. "Make sure you are not trapped by some second-hand empty rational philosophy based on the principles of this world instead of on Christ." Colossians 2:8.

Paul's approach to Hellenistic philosophy at the time of Jesus mirrored the Jewish Mishnah, an authoritative collection of material embodying the *tradition* of Jewish Law; it was taught orally and later compiled into texts. Here we cite a rabbi of Jesus' day on the subject of pagan philosophy. One Rabbi wrote, "A student asked 'since I have learnt the whole of the Torah may I now study Greek philosophy?'" The reply came with a scripture quotation from the Old Testament (Joshua 1:8), "'This Book of Torah shall not depart from your mouth but you shall meditate on it day and night, now go and search out at which hour it is neither day nor night and devote it to the study of Greek philosophy." Mishnah, *Menachoth,* 99b

Time and again, as one follows the development of Christianity anecdotal comments such as Paul's will continually confront errors that repeatedly confuse the ever spreading House-Churches and their leaders.

House Church Leaders

"He should not have been married more than once."

—St. Paul

No epoch in Christianity better reveals its Jewish foundations than does the development of house-churches and their leaders such as the bishop of Corinth, until late in the second century. In the face of scripture presented here below it is truly remarkable that mandatory celibacy should ever have been imposed upon Christianity in light of the early church practice left to us by the example of Jesus, who selected only married Apostles. He would, however, select both married and single Disciples, both men and women, a practice continued by His Apostles.

After Jesus' death the Apostles remained committed Jews who continued to evangelize, spreading the Faith throughout the Empire often accompanied by their wives. On their missionary journeys the Apostles went first to larger cities with Jewish populations in order to inform them of their risen Messiah and, upon establishing churches, select others who would further spread the Faith to rural communities and villages. Judaism, from its beginning with Abraham was a patriarchal society ruled by men. This patriarchal tradition changed when the Apostles later approved both married and unmarried Disciples as House-Church leaders. However, in this patriarchal society most House-Church leaders remained primarily Jewish men who were husbands and fathers. The clearest teaching of this practice comes from St. Paul when he gives specific instructions to his disciple, Timothy, regarding the selection criteria for these men, bishops (Overseers) who were to be ordained in those different communities as they evangelized from area to area establishing new churches. Paul was clear in describing those who should be selected.

"The President Overseer must have an impeccable character. He must not have been married more than once and he must be temperate, discreet and courteous, hospitable and a good teacher, not a heavy drinker, nor hot tempered, but kind and peaceable. He must not be a lover of money. He must be a man who manages his own family and brings up his children to obey him and to be well behaved. How does a man who does not understand how to manage his family have responsibility over the church of God?" 1 Tim 3:1-7 Additionally, Deacons preparing for leadership were also to have the same sterling qualities "In the same way, Deacons must be respectable men whose word can be trusted... In the same way, the women [Deacons] must be respectable, not gossips but sober and quite reliable. V.8-13. This was Paul's constant message.

Three years later in correspondence to his disciple Titus he wrote, "The reason I left you behind in Crete was for you to get everything organized there and appoint Elders in every town, in the way I told you: That is, each of them must have an irreproachable character; he must not have been married more than once, and his children must be believers and not uncontrollable or liable to be charged with disorderly conduct. As God's representative he must be irreproachable: never an arrogant or hot tempered man, nor a heavy drinker or violent, nor out to make money; but a man who is hospitable and a friend of all that is good; sensible, moral, devout and self controlled." Titus 1:5-8 These standards for selecting ministers remained unchanged throughout the Universal Church during a time when the first generation of Apostles and their disciples selected the first generation of Church leaders, a time when married bishops remained our Tradition! Today, we Catholics are taught these Elders were expected to abandon conjugal relations with their wives, but today those same bishops would be denied ordination.

The Early Years and House Churches

"Christian missionaries made a deliberate point of gaining whatever households they could as lighthouses, so to speak, from which the Gospel could illuminate the surrounding darkness."
—*Evangelism in the Early Church*, Michael Green

"Now, about reaming celibate, I have no directions from the Lord, but give my own opinion..."
—St. Paul, *1 Corinthians 7:25*

Examining the historical absence of ascetic celibacy for House-Church leader, male or female, after Jesus' death in 30 AD, their importance must be brought into the discussion of Christianity's growth – Christians had no churches as we envision them today. An analogy for modern Christians might be the predicament in which Christians of China currently find themselves, often outlawed or under pagan threat. This expansion of Christianity by means of establishing Churches before the Sacramental Priesthood was instituted is little known to moderns but is informative; it introduces the first generation of Christian leaders during the life of the Apostles.

The first Christians were Orthodox Jews who throughout life worshiped in the Temple and offered what today we term the "Mass" in their homes. This practice would continue in Jerusalem until the Temple's destruction in 70 AD, forty years after Jesus. In the Bible St. Luke instructs us; "They went as a body to the Temple every day but met in their houses for the breaking of bread [Mass]" Acts 2:46. This statement describes Jewish-Christian growth during the first two centuries and it would be after 250 AD, more than 200 years after Jesus when this persecuted new sect of Judaism would emerge triumphantly from the shadows of history in all parts of the Empire. Persecutions of the third century would fail to crush this growing belief. Up until the end of the second century, history records that Christians gathered in the homes of Church leaders for "breaking of the bread," also known as the "Common Meal" described by St. Paul above in the book of Corinthians. But it would be quite different in the dispersed areas of the Empire, where local governments and local religions sought ways of persecuting this Jewish sect.

Evidence of Christian house churches is replete in scripture. The house of Jason in Thessalonica is mentioned Acts 17:5 when Paul explains why "a gang drug them off to the People's Assembly." The home of Crispus [a Jew]; Crispus, president of the Synagogue, is mentioned when his household became believers. Acts 18:8 The clearest example of House-Church leaders is found in 1 Corinthians 16:19 when St. Paul mentions husband/wife leaders Aquila, and his wife Prisca (Priscilla) who taught Apollos. We will have occasion later to cite Apollos, the author of the Book of Hebrews. Luke speaks of Apollos as an "eloquent man" who had a "thorough knowledge of the Old Testament and taught about Jesus" Acts 18:25-27. Priscilla, in addition to being the wife of Aquila and co-worker with Paul was a missionary House-Church teacher. Aquila and Prisca "took an interest in Apollos and explained the words of God more accurately", belying efforts by opponents who insist women had no place in teaching men.

As time passed House-Churches became more prominent. About 80 AD the third Pope, Clement of Rome, recalls the preaching of Peter in a house church: "The master of the house welcomed us, and led us into a certain apartment, arranged like a theatre and beautifully built. There we found a considerable crowd waiting for us, who had come during the night..."[5] As the *Word* spread across the Empire house churches were its fundamental building blocks and it would be both married men, along with married and unmarried women elevated to the level of teachers and deacons. In another instance, Paul specifically identifies a woman House-Church leader as an "Apostle." Paul identifies her as a female relative, "Junia" and her husband, Andronicus, "Salute Andronicus and Junia [vs. *Junias*] my kinsman and my fellow prisoners who are of note among the Apostles." Romans 16:7 It is accepted by scholars that later papal concerns with a female "Junia", identified as an Apostle inserts the male designation "Junias," a male name that did not exist in antiquity in order to replace the female Junia. We find the male designation, Junias, appeared only after Pope Boniface VIII's Decretal, *Periculoso*, in 1298 AD, requiring nuns be perpetually cloistered in order to limit the growing power and influence of scholarly nuns and scriptural copyist such as St. Gertrude the Great, who had previously rendered the female, *'Junia'*.

Second Century House Churches

About 50 years after Paul, a House-Church is mentioned by Pliny the Younger 111 AD, a Roman official and historian who encountered Christian-Jews during his assignment under Emperor Trajan, 98-117 AD, as Governor of Palestine, located at the center of Roman authority in Pontus. Under Trajan it was illegal to be Christian, although not rigidly enforced. Even so, under Trajan

Jesus' cousin Simon, Bishop of Pella, and St. Ignatius of Antioch were martyred. Simon was crucified and Ignatius was slaughtered by animals in Rome. Christians had proven to be a problem for the Roman government with their refusal to worship Roman deities, especially the Emperor. Therefore, Pliny was instructed to investigate the sect and take appropriate measures. This investigation arose as a result of complaints by leaders of established pagan religions in an area located on the southern coast of the Black Sea where Jewish-Christians fled after 70 AD. In many such areas, the new influx of Jewish-Christians economically damaged pagan temples and their financially lucrative sacrifices. As a result, Christians were reported to Roman authorities for failure to worship the Emperor as a god.

Pliny communicated back to Emperor Trajan the results of his investigation, of a Christian House-Church "[The accused Christians] were in the habit of meeting on a certain fixed day before it was light, when they sang in alternate verses a hymn to Christ, as to a god, and bound themselves by a solemn oath, not to do any wicked deeds, but never to commit any fraud, theft or adultery, never to falsify their word, nor deny a trust when they should be called upon to deliver it up; after which it was their custom to separate, and then reassemble to partake of food – but an ordinary and innocent kind [Mass in a house church]. Even this practice, however, they abandoned after the publication of my edict, by which, according to your orders, I had forbidden political associations. I judged it much more necessary to extract the real truth, with the assistance of torture from two female slaves who were styled deaconesses, but I could discover no more than depraved and excessive superstition."[6] The deaconesses were tortured to death and Pliny's letter well describes the faith and religious practice of this minority sect of Judaism, demonstrating an early awareness of their separate identity, while remaining Jews.

This letter from Pliny was written during the perilous years between the fall of the Temple in 70 AD and the final Jewish revolution of 135 AD when Jews and Christians remained inseparable in the minds of Roman authority. Pliny also gives a flavor of the Christian community as his letter continued, "The matter seemed well worth referring to you—especially considering the numbers endangered. Persons of all ranks and ages and of both sexes are, and will be, involved in the prosecution. For this contagious superstition is not confined to the cities only, but has spread through the villages and rural districts: it seems possible however to check and to cure it..." This letter reveals the remarkable growth of Christian House -Churches before their final separation from Judaism; they were composed of people of all ranks and ages. We also find Christianity had by then spread to the villages and rural districts outside Judea.

It is notable here that Pliny sought information not from men but from two women leaders, both of whom were slaves and Deacons. Before sacramental priests appear in the later centuries women leaders played a vital role in spreading the Gospel, and as leaders there is no doubt these women were in charge of the liturgy. Often house churches are reported to have been jointly pastored by married couples, here we find two women. Though they were slaves, these women leaders were also important personages in that Christian community. Egalitarianism toward gender, race or social status was a hallmark of early Christianity.

HOUSE CHURCHES AND THE COMMON MEAL (MASS)

"What is of Prime importance...in the Common Meal traditions is the 'full and normal' meal that, as a communal share-meal, symbolized the presence of sharing God in both the life and death of Jesus."[7]
—*Birth of Christianity,* John Dominic Crossan

"Initially, these communities were all Orthodox Jews as described by one historian, 'The silent majority of those who awaited the coming of the Kingdom were careworn and decent householders, long used to the punctilious rhythms of Jewish life. Secure in their moral horizons.'"[8]
—The Body and Society, Peter Brown

Thus far we have examined the growth of Christianity from Jesus' crucifixion in 30 AD until the early second century, a time of dislocation for many Christian groups after the death of the last Apostle and before the Bar Kokhba revolution of c.135 AD, a time when early Christianity had spread from Roman Judaea in the west throughout the Roman Empire and beyond, to East Africa and South Asia and as far as India, bringing Jewish-Christian House-Churches into contact with alien religions. At the end of the first century, house churches remained primarily Jewish-Christian churches even though often in alien environments. At the 111 AD date of the House-Church described above, just south of the Black Sea, some Christians continued to await the return of Jesus while others chose to retreat to caves and await the inevitable "end of days." By about 250 AD asceticism had influenced many Christian-Gentile converts when groups known as the Desert Fathers became hermits, ascetics and monks who retreated to the seclusion of the Egyptian desert to await the Messiah's return. As these monastic desert communities grew, these gatherings of hermits and monks became the model for later Christian monasticism. But, at the same time House-Churches with their congregations of married families and leaders containing both Gentiles and Jews continued to worship their Messiah with the same rituals as in the beginning.

Among both local churches and metropolitan bishops, the Christian worship service had not changed. It consisted of a Common-Meal (Last Supper tradition) similar to the Last Supper of Jesus and His Apostles as explained in the New Testament, "They went to the temple every day but met in their houses for the breaking of the bread [Eucharist]; they shared their bread gladly and generously; they praised God and were looked up to by everyone." Acts 2:46 As membership increased, both the well-off and the poor attended this communal worship service with the more prosperous providing food for the poor. As in all Church services, proper decorum was expected by all. An excellent description of "proper" decorum in these meetings is presented by St. Paul in his letter to the Corinthians 1Corinthians 11:17-27 when he felt the need to chastise some.

St Paul teaches, "Now that I am on the subject of instruction I cannot say that you have done well in holding meetings that do you more harm than good. In the first place, I hear that when you come together as a community there are separate factions among you...The point is, when you hold these meetings, it is not the Lord's Supper you are eating if when it comes time to eat, every-one is in such a hurry to start his own supper that one person goes hungry while another is getting drunk; surely you have homes for eating and drinking in? Surely you have enough respect for the community of God not to make poor people embarrassed...I can not congratulate you on this." Clearly the Mass then did not con-sist merely of a small wafer of bread.

"For this is what I received from the Lord, and in turn passed it on to you: That on the same night He was betrayed, the Lord Jesus took some bread, and thanked God for it and broke it, and He said 'This is my body which is for you; do this as a *memorial* of me. In the same way He took a cup after supper and said 'This cup is the new covenant in my blood. Whenever you drink it do this as a *memorial* to me. Until the Lord comes therefore anyone who eats this *bread* and drinks this *cup* unworthily will be behav-ing unworthily toward the *body and blood of Christ*...Everyone is to recollect himself before eating and   drinking this cup; because a person who eats and drinks without recognizing the Body is eat-ing and drinking his condemnation."

Such chastisement from Paul was unusual but necessary in large communities such as Corinth, where these converts needed direction. Fortunately, Paul's teaching here, even though severe, establishes the fundamental Christian worship service that today, while vastly different, presents the same truths. Written 20 years after Jesus' crucifixion this early account assures us of the Eucharist's "Real Presence," at a time before the concept that only Sacramental Priests may consecrate (bless) the Eucharist.

CHAPTER SIX

WAR, CHAOS AND DISPERSION

"The rise of Christianity has occupied such a prominent place in the study of the history of religions that it has dwarfed an interrelated and perhaps more important question: the manner in which Judaism and Christianity separated from each other and came to conceive of each other as "the other". How did it come to be that Christians saw the Jews and Judaism as alien and different?"

—Council of Christians and Jews

Aside from the death of Christ, Rome's destruction of the great marble clad Jewish Temple, nearly blinding when gazed upon under a blazing sun, was the single most important historical event in first century AD history. It forever ended Jewish Temple sacrifice and began the separation of Jews from Christians. The magnificence of this building was equaled nowhere on earth at the time, not even in Rome. The Jews considered it the *dwelling place* of God. The vast wealth acquired by Rome from its plunder of the Temple was used to construct the great Coliseum of Rome.

By 62 AD and the assassination of St. James, the Jewish-Christian sect had expanded across the Empire far beyond its Jewish-Christian leadership in Jerusalem. Judaism itself was threatened by strained relationships with Rome, which would eventually result in violent conflict in 73 AD that devastated the Jewish nation. The defeat of this Jewish revolt also affected the Jewish Diaspora across the Empire. Many of the Jewish rebels were scattered or sold into slavery. Josephus claims that 1,100,000 people were killed during the siege of Palestine.

In 135 AD, another Jewish uprising led by the last pseudo-Jewish *Messiah,* Simon Bar Kokhba, had failed. Bar Kokhba despised

Christians after they refused to join his revolt. Bar Kokhba rallied the Jews who continued to seek a Messiah to his side – all except the Christians. A balanced report on this revolt by a Jewish historian describes the situation. "Bar Kokhba led a revolt against Rome in 135 C.E. One segment of the population however, refused to join the revolt and wage war under the banner of Bar Kokhba – the Jews who believed Jesus was the Messiah. Bar Kokhba killed a number of them, seeing them as enemies, heretics and traitors to the national cause."[1]

The Apostles, along with most Christians who had actually heard them preach or studied under them were gone. With this event, Christianity and Judaism began to separate as a holocaust by Roman legions ensued and the Christian community fled Jerusalem to the neighboring city of Pella, where Simeon, Jesus' cousin had earlier relocated as Bishop following the Temple's destruction. This Roman invasion precipitated the slaughter of 580,000 Jewish citizens and Jerusalem was razed to the ground. It would only be after the United Nations resolution in 1948 that the Jewish Nation would be allowed to return.

Since the death of Jesus, Jewish authorities continued to duel theologically with their Jewish-Christian rivals for the minds and hearts of Jews. The Jewish revolt under Bar Kokhba set in motion a series of anti-Semitic events over the next century that would forever separate the two faiths.

Oppressed and decimated, the Jewish people continued to grieve over the loss of their Temple and the end of Jewish Temple Sacrifice; the situation would only worsen. Banished from Jerusalem, the Jewish leadership relocated to Jamnia, close to the Mediterranean c.90-100 AD where they founded a school of Jewish Law and defined the official Jewish Old Testament Canon. They rejected the Egyptian translation, the Septuagint, because it contained rejected Hellenisticly inspired books used by Christians and Essenes. Among other theological items undertaken at Jamnia was the composition of a *blessing* against both Christians and the Essenes, "And for the slanderers [Essenes, Christians] let there be no hope and may all the evil in an instant be destroyed and all Thy enemies be cut down swiftly...blessed are You Lord who breaks down enemies and humbles sinners."[2] Much anti-Christian polemics of a vicious personal nature against Jesus, Mary and Paul were written during this time that would later be compiled into the Babylonian Talmud c.500 AD.

In a time span of less than 50 years, Christianity had dispersed from Palestine to Persia, Africa, Egypt, Asia Minor, England, Spain, Gaul and India. By the end of the first century Christianity had re-located throughout the Empire as converted missionaries preached the Faith. Within the Empire a common language, Roman roads and peace made this dispersion possible. Across this vast migration many accepted this new religion of Christ but confrontation sometimes occurred with pagan priests.

Circumstances in Rome, to where the center of Christianity had gravitated following the expulsion from Jerusalem, were different. The Jews were successful in re-acquiring their previously lost legal status as an *ancient religion*. In other words, Rome was now prepared to tolerate them legally and this Jewish legality brought protection for Jews under Roman law. At the same time, Christians wished to distance themselves from the Bar Kokhba revolt in the eyes of Rome, but as a new religion separate from Judaism. This separation proved to be illegal under Roman law and having separated from Judaism Christians lost their legal protection as Jews, bringing about new tensions between rabbis and bishops.

Jerusalem retained the prestige of being the city of Christ's death and resurrection but declined during the years of the Jewish–Roman wars (66-135AD). During this time Jerusalem's bishops became subordinates of Metropolitan bishops and the Holy Land soon lost its connection with Christianity; Separated from Judaism, the Christian movement became largely composed of Gentile-Pagan converts who had never met a rabbi and knew practically nothing of Christ's Jewish nature, allowing new and non-Jewish-Christian beliefs to intrude. This century would change Christianity as Gentile converts slowly accepted apocryphal teachings not contained in the Deposit of Faith, teachings that did not originate with Christ.

CHAPTER SEVEN

DEPOSIT OF FAITH

*"**The Deposit of Faith:** The Deposit of Faith is the body of doctrines handed down from Jesus to the Apostles, from the Apostles to their successors, and so forth to our times. The Deposit of Faith contains the complete body of doctrines that make up the Catholic Faith. Nothing new can be added that is not at least implicitly contained within the Deposit of Faith, and nothing can be taken away, for public revelation ceased with the death of the last apostle. The means by which the Deposit of Faith has been passed down to us is through the written word of God, as contained in the New Testament, and the unwritten word of God, handed down orally by the Apostles. The written word of God – the Holy Bible - exhorts us to hold fast to both the written and unwritten Traditions we have received – "therefore, brethren, hold fast to the traditions which you have received, whether by word or by epistle" (2 Thess. 2:14). Holding fast to both the written and unwritten Traditions is necessary to preserve the integrity of the Gospel."*[1]

—Catholic Answers

"There seems to be some kind of disconnect in the evolution of this system to safeguard the Deposit of the Faith for those who will be the future of the Church"[2]

—Catholic Women for Faith and Family

At the end of the first century the formative century of Christianity was complete. At the end of this period ancient Jewish animus' towards paganism and its attempts to crush Judaism remained visceral, both religiously and personally. Since the arrival of Jesus and the formation of Christianity during the life of Jesus and His Apostles, the entirety of the Christian belief-system was established, a time span known as *The Deposit of Faith.* This term has been mentioned earlier without definition; it is defined as the accepted foundation of all Christianity by all competing Christian religions. With that understanding the focus of this entire book will revolve around changes that occurred during the first three centuries, leading to *neo*-Christian Papal Doctrines that continue to affect Catholicism today. The two contrasting Catholic epigraphs above describe the Church's conflict today.

Since the time of Christ we have been taught the fullness and limitations of our doctrines are to be found only in this Deposit of Faith, which is defined as the source of all infallible Christian beliefs and teaching. Furthermore, we are told the totality of these beliefs is to be discovered *only* during the first years of Christianity before the death of the Apostles. Unfortunately the importance of this term, as consequential and simple as it is for all Catholic belief, is little understood and for this reason we must go there. The fundamental importance of this time period for Catholic belief is critical if we merely pause and consider the consequences of imposing some new doctrine not left to us by Jesus and the Apostles.

In later centuries uplifting new religious *traditions* of Christian worship and practice appear, that do not conflict with the Deposit of Faith and rightly remain with us today; but in Catholic teaching the Deposit of Faith is strictly limited to the *Holy Traditions* of Jesus that were left to Christianity during that first historical century, beginning when all Christians were Jews living in their Judean homeland. Again, this last point is central. Christianity began as a Jewish sect, composed totally of Orthodox Jews who followed Old Testament Jewish Law and the societal and theological norms not changed by Jesus. This will be the key to understanding the origins of *neo-Christian* "traditions" discussed in this book.

It was during those early years when gentile converts first appeared that Christianity was unchangeably founded. That's where the story begins. It was also during these years when many exciting events occurred, historical events which few Christians are aware of. Jesus of Nazareth was born in 9-6 BC during Quirihius' first mission to Palestine in 10-7 BC as military governor of the Roman Empire, with his seat of government in Syria. Jesus was executed in April of 30 AD under the reign of the Emperor Tiberius. Tiberius, in his palace on Capri did not know it, but a new force was being born that would one day inherit the empire. The last Apostle to die was St. John the Evangelist during the reign of Trajan, c.92-98 AD.

During this time-span Christianity was conceived, birthed, and grew into a belief system which had by the end of that time spread across the Roman Empire and far beyond. Initially as a Jewish sect, Christianity was challenged by Jewish Temple authorities who viewed it as an aberration arising from within. It would only be late in the first century when Christianity became theologically challenged by paganism and the religious dominance it held over the rest of the ancient world. This confrontation would linger long past the Deposit of Faith and it is the result of that confrontation with pagan beliefs which this book intends to address.

The importance to Christianity of Jesus' teachings during that time period was well described by Jesus himself when he instructed his Apostles, "Go therefore, make disciples of all nations... teach them to obey all the commands I have given you." Matthew 28:19-20. Jesus did not say "obey the commands of the Pope," and later, "He who hears you hears me, and he who rejects you rejects me, and he who rejects me rejects Him who sent me." Luke 10:16. With these statements Jesus commands his Apostles to teach *only* that which they received from Him. Later, St. Paul confirms Jesus' commandment when he wrote, "Stand firm then brothers, and keep the traditions that were taught to you, whether by word of mouth or by letter." Thessalonians 2:15. From these teachings it is accepted the Deposit of Faith contains both Scripture and Holy Tradition which is based on Jesus' teaching not included in scripture. For as St. John said, "There were many other things Jesus that did; if all were written down, the world itself, I suppose would not hold all the books that would have to be written." John 21:25. From such statements Christians are to only accept as Gospel the information Jesus and the Apostles left to us. The totality of Christian doctrine is contained within these first teachings. In defense of these sacrosanct teachings of Jesus, we shall later find another term in Church literature, "some new doctrine." This term will be used to protect the Deposit of Faith from some new doctrine not left by Jesus.

Other key historical events occurred during this time. The first Jewish-Christian martyr Deacon Stephen was stoned to death c.31-32 AD following Jewish accusations of blasphemy. St. Paul, an early opponent of Christianity who assisted in Stephen's death converted c.32-33 AD. Later, around 42 AD the Apostle James (brother of St. John) was beheaded in Jerusalem and Peter fled to Rome bringing a temporary exodus of Christian leaders from Jerusalem. Apostle James the Less, Jesus' cousin, was martyred by stoning in Jerusalem c.44 AD. Other than the four Gospels, Matthew, Mark, Luke and John, the first New Testament book to be completed was St. Paul's epistle to the Thessalonians in 49 AD. That same year an understanding was reached that allowed non-Jews to become Christians without having to observe Old Testament Jewish Law. Later, Apostle Philip was martyred at Greece c.54 AD while Jesus' brother James the Just was martyred in Jerusalem in 62 AD. The Apostle Barnabas was burned alive in Cyprus c. 64 AD. The Apostle St. Thomas was speared to death in southwest India c.60 AD. St. Peter, his wife Perpetua, and St. Paul were executed at Rome c. 67 AD, Paul was beheaded and Peter met his death by being crucified upside-down. That same year St. Mark was assassinated in Alexandria, Egypt.

Later in 70 AD the Jewish Temple in Jerusalem was destroyed causing the first mass exodus of Christians and forever ending Jewish Temple sacrifice, beginning the rapid spread of Christianity across the Empire. This occurred forty years after Jesus' death and it would be 135 AD, sixty-five years after the Temple's fall, one hundred and five years after Jesus' death, after the Deposit of Faith and the last Jewish rebellion against Rome when Christian and Jew began to separate during that last rebellion in which Christians refused to take part. However, by then Christianity was fully formed. The Deposit of Faith lingered until 98 AD but by then all Christian tradition from which the New Testament would come had already been preached. Later, after the Deposit of Faith new traditions will appear that support and embellished those first Holy Traditions.

During those intervening years the Apostles faithfully followed Jesus' teaching and continued to preach, teach and live the Gospel as He had instructed them. Catholicism has forever taught that during those years the entirety of Jesus teachings were revealed, practiced, preached, and written down in the New Testament. The Church therefore describes all of these first beliefs contained within the Deposit of Faith to be the alpha and omega of all Catholic belief. These beliefs and practices are to be understood by anyone who would comment on Orthodox Catholic belief.

Those years were an exciting historical time which unfortunately few Christians fully understand. During those early years the New Testament was begun. An ancient Christian writer who studied under St. John, Papias c.125 AD, described this beginning, "Matthew first gathered the oracles of the Lord." Apparently, Matthew first wrote an early Aramaic, or possibly Hebrew language version of his Gospel, because during the life of Jesus most Jews did not speak Hebrew, they spoke Aramaic – Jesus' cry *"Eli, Eli, lama sabachthani?"* Matthew 27:46 – is Aramaic. That first Aramaic version c.36 AD is lost. It is believed the current Gospel of Matthew is a later expanded Greek translation. Next, Mark traveled with Peter to Rome in 42 AD where he is reported to have penned the first version of his Gospel based on Peter's preaching there. Mark began his Gospel at the request of Roman citizens who cherished Peter's teaching and pled for a written copy after Peter left Rome at the conclusion of his first visit.

From the 30s and early 40s little secular history is available because the disciples initially remained in their Jewish homeland teaching and converting Jewish brothers and sisters. Our primary information for those years is confined almost totally to the New Testament texts that can be juxtaposed against then current secular history.

Initially, no thought was given to the systematic conversion of non-Jews such as the first martyr St. Stephen, a Greek who converted to Jewish-Christianity during the time when converts were expected to first become Jews and obey all Jewish Law. Few today realize that initially Christians were Jews who followed Jewish Law, including circumcision, food, cleanliness, sacrificial and Temple worship. It would be twelve years before the first missionary journeys began and only then because many Christians were forced to migrate into pagan dominated areas. Fortunately, from Paul's writings in the 50s we have voluminous information. With these writings we understand the beliefs and practices of the Christian communities that spread across the Empire during the Deposit of Faith, Galatia and Asia in Turkey, Macedonia and Achaia in Greece. From areas such as this we also learn of the beliefs and practices of this new Jewish sect in Philippi, Thessalonica, Ephesus and more. In addition to the New Testament, much extra-biblical historical information on our first traditions is available to us, and it is necessary to examine this historical time period if we are to understand neo-Christian Papal Doctrines – and their strangeness.

Currently, there are many religious persons of different theologies who hold the belief that God continued to provide new revelations (information) to humankind after Jesus. New information that, in addition to His revelation in the New Testament and the teaching of His Apostles, gives a more complete understanding of His will for us. A good example of those who believe in this new revelation after the Deposit of Faith are our Mormon friends. They believe their founder, Joseph Smith, discovered long lost writings equal in value to the Bible, from which they claim to be able to understand Jesus' original teachings more fully. Such a belief is totally contrary to dogmatically defined Catholic theology. While Catholicism believes the written Word and Tradition left to us at the death of the last Apostle may have become better understood over time, there will never be any more direct Revelations from God. This is a fundamental Catholic belief.

As we examine celibacy requirements for priests today an understanding of those first years will be the principle upon which our objections rest. Accordingly, it is essential for Catholics to fully understand the meaning of this term, *Deposit of Faith*. Perhaps it will be better understood if the term is expanded to Deposit of Faith and Morals, a term all Catholics are familiar with. Unfortunately, this term as critical as it is to Catholic Theology, is little known to average Catholics. This father of seven children, who are graduates from good Catholic schools, found none able to explain the Deposit of Faith or its importance to their fundamental beliefs. Such lack of understanding of our origins is systemic among Catholic Faithful.

THE ONE SOURCE OF CHRISTIAN INFALLIBILITY

To understand the importance to the Church of this term let us turn to Pope Benedict XVI. Several years ago during an interview with then Cardinal Joseph Ratzinger (Later Pope Benedict XVI), a question was asked on the possibility of new Revelations from God having been given to mankind after the death of Jesus. He was quite emphatic on this point as he answered, "No, Jesus was Revelation." His response is noteworthy because it is the first infallible principal of all Catholic theology, of which he was keenly aware.

In order for us to understand this underlying foundation of all Catholic dogma and doctrines upon which our teachings rest which is the primary focus of this polemic. No apparition of the Blessed Mother, private understanding of scripture or new traditions (including by this writer) may add to or take from our Deposit of Faith. This Catholic truth is *irreformable.*

During succeeding centuries we find what the Church later describes as the *development* of Doctrine and *fullness of understanding*. From this development the Church assures us it has come to a more comprehensible understanding of Jesus' revelation on such important matters as the Trinity, the number of Sacraments, infallibility, etc. By the same token, that which the Deposit of Faith does not contain is simply not there. There will never be an Eleventh Commandment nor mandatory celibacy found in the Deposit of Faith. In order to highlight the unchangeable nature of our first Revelations the Vatican has acknowledged that Jesus' statement to Peter, "I will give you the keys to the kingdom of heaven; whatever you bind on earth shall be considered bound in heaven" Mat. 16:19 pertains only to the 'binding' of Faith and Morals which are based on the teachings of Jesus. In order to define these first recognized infallible teachings let us turn to the authoritative on-line *Catholic Answers* which defines the Deposit of Faith as follows, "The source and fount of revealed truths, namely, Scripture and Tradition, which must be accepted by all true Christians on the Authority of God." We must note here the term "all Christians" includes the Pope.

Another statement on the Deposit of Faith was issued by Pope John Paul II in the Apostolic Constitution contained in the publication of our new Catholic Catechism issued following the second Vatican Council of 1965. His first sentence declares, "Guarding the Deposit of Faith is the mission which the Lord has entrusted to the Church and which she fulfills in every age."

Permit this writer to relay a personal analogy on the importance of the Deposit of Faith. Several years ago in an ecumenical meeting between my Church and a local Baptist Church, the Baptist minister spoke regarding fundamentals of Baptist belief. After his presentation he concluded humorously, "If it ain't Scripture, it ain't Baptist." A similar statement must be made of Catholic beliefs, "If it ain't in the Deposit of Faith, it ain't Catholic." While we will confine ourselves to Papal Doctrines here, one might let their mind wander to the many new beliefs now proposed by some who claim to be Catholic, yet are not to be found in the beginning, in the Deposit of Faith.

There is little need to further elaborate this point; it is as simple as it is basic. Addition to, or removal from the Deposit of Faith contradicts the teachings of Jesus. For this reason, any teaching that varies from those first teachings are to be considered apostate.

THE ENIGMA OF SCRIPTURE VS. TRADITION

"All Scripture is inspired by God and useful for teaching, for reproving, for correcting, for instructing in justice."

—2 Tim 3:16

"So then, brothers, stand firm and hold to the traditions we passed on to you, whether by word of mouth or by letter."

—2 Thessalonians 2:15

The source and authorship of "Scripture" and "Holy Traditions" contained in the Deposit of Faith is an enigma for Catholics,

73

including priests who do not invest years of personal investigation into ancient Christian and Jewish writings as described in the epigraphs above. Catholics understand that our faith in Christ is imbued into us through study of the Catechism and Infallible Church Doctrines as defined by the Church, both of which must be based on scripture and tradition contained in the Deposit of Faith. But, today questions by Catholics such as the previous epigraph above have arisen, *"There seems to be some kind of disconnect in the evolution of this system to safeguard the Deposit of Faith.* Such questions are not new; for centuries non-Catholic historians have alleged that post Deposit of Faith 'scripture' and 'traditions' have been erroneously relied on by popes when issuing Infallible Papal Doctrines, doctrines that altered Doctrines of Christ. All were based on Plato's ascetic philosophy that entered Christianity after the Deposit of Faith was closed.

New Testament Scripture and Tradition are two different subjects and since the origin of both are unknown by the laity an historical outline is helpful.

THE NEW TESTAMENT

There is consensus among Christians today that accepts the 27 New Testament books as canonical, but no consensus among Biblical scholars agrees as to when these books were written, estimates regarding the time-span range from First Thessalonians, 50-60 AD until Second Peter, 100-160AD. It was early in the fifth century, c. 400AD, before the New Testament was officially identified and separated from among a sea of non-Canonical Christian writings, writings that sprang up during the same period as the New Testament, causing great confusion regarding which books were of Apostolic origin. This occurred during a time before Christianity was established as the universally dominant religion.

For these reasons it cannot be said that Christianity was founded on New Testament writings that did not exist. Following the death of Christ the Church was initially aware of but three authorities: First, the Old Testament Hebrew Scriptures; second, the spoken word of Jesus; and third, the oral testimony and teaching of the Apostles. In the beginning no books were considered to have authority of themselves when Faith in Christ was spread orally by preaching alone; speaking of "spreading the Gospel" it was later explained by St. Paul when he taught in the Book of Romans 10:14-17, "They will not ask Jesus' help unless they believe in Him, and they will not hear of Him unless they get a preacher, and they will not have a preacher unless one is sent...so faith comes from what is preached, and what is preached comes from the word of Christ." We will later have occasion to note why St. Paul here mentions a "preacher" and not a "priest" being sent.

There remains a misunderstanding regarding the role, or lack thereof, of the New Testament. In nascent Christianity a meaningful antidote is helpful to explain the problem. (Arius) 256–336 AD, an ascetic Christian priest from Alexandria, Egypt was first to teach about the nature of God, and Jesus as a lesser god; Arius emphasized the Father's divinity over the Son, opposing the Trinity, making this a primary topic of the First Council of Nicaea convened by Roman Emperor Constantine in AD 325. Had Arius prevailed the Trinitarian concept would have been abandoned. This theological dispute lingered for a century.

In order to properly understand the historical role of New Testament controversy let us place ourselves in a Church in Caesarea (Palestine), c. 363 AD, 330 years after Jesus, in a Church where the Book of Hebrews was not approved by the bishop and therefore forbidden to be read in church. It is relevant to place ourselves in this church as the minister instructs the congregation to turn to the fourth chapter of the canonical book of Hebrews so that he could preach against a "false" priest such as Arius. Arius believed Jesus to be a lesser God. However, Hebrews also faced a problem when it taught, "...the word of God is something alive and active...No created thing [A lesser god] can hide from Him... since in Jesus, the Son of God, we have a High Priest who has gone through the highest heavens, we must never let go of the faith we have possessed [In Jesus]." Hebrews 4:12-14. Unfortunately, the Book of Hebrews was rejected in Palestine by this church at this time because it was not yet considered canonical. The book of Hebrews was nearly left out of the New Testament because it faced the same problem as did Arius; first, Arius rejected the Trinity, and secondly Hebrews merely described Christ as a "High Priest", therefore lowering Christ to the office of "priest".

Incidents such as this reveal why foreign teachings not contained in the Deposit of Faith were successful in misleading early Christian converts. Before 150 AD[3] the question had never been raised as to what books were sacred or how many there were. The early Christians were Jews and were taught by rabbis who had teaching authority, later it was Apostles such as St. Paul who had teaching authority during a time when Christians believed Christ would return during their lifetime; only during the second century after Christ did disputes arise regarding which books were permitted to be read in church, a dispute that lasted for centuries. Quite early-on in certain large Christian centers such as Rome, Antioch, Alexandria and Corinth, their bishops possessed some writings from the Apostles. These writings were considered authoritative but from city to city the lists of approved books would vary and none were necessarily the final word concerning theological disagreements among bishops.

These writings were laboriously copied by hand and spread to other communities, but communication and travel were slow and these writings were scarce. An entire city would do well merely to have in its possession a few books and those would be in the hands of their bishop. This was largely unimportant at the time since only about five percent of Christians were literate. The laity depended on hearing the Word preached to them during the worship service. By the beginning of the third century we find the four Gospels along with Paul's thirteen letters (Except Hebrews) were generally accepted. Yet, from one church to another and from east to west across the Empire we find that all the remaining books: Acts, Hebrews, James, 1&2 Peter, 2-3 John, Jude and Revelation, were to one degree or another not universally accepted.

With such early confusion over the importance of which "scriptural" writings should be accepted vs. authoritative preaching it is informative to read the opinion of an early bishop, St. Papias, the bishop of Hierapolis in Asia Minor, which was a crossroad of missionary travelers across the Empire. Papias was a friend of Bishop Polycarp of Smyrna and perhaps a "Hearer" of St. John, but assuredly a hearer of apostolic acquaintances. Papias wrote, "I do not delight in those who talk a great deal, but in those who teach the truth; nor in those who relate the commandments of others, but in those who relate the commandments given by the Lord to the faithful, and which are derived from truth itself. And then too, when anyone comes along who has been a follower of the presbyters, I would inquire about the presbyters' discourses: What was said by Andrew or by Peter, or by Philip or by Thomas or by James, or by John or by Matthew, or by any Disciples of the Lord...It did not seem to me that I could get much profit from the contents of books as from a living and abiding voice."[4] Unfortunately Papias well describes the diminished position of New Testament scripture in early Christianity.

Before departing this discussion regarding which books were accepted by different bishops across the Christian world as they individually labored to understand which were acceptable, and which could not be associated with the Apostles as late as the fourth century, it must be pointed out that all Christian bishops were autonomous and independent from authority of other bishops. Tragically, at this time of confusion among bishops in the early third century, the Christian movement consisted only of converts from paganism or descendants of previously converted pagans, and animas toward Jews existed. It was during this epoch of change in Christianity that apocryphal Gnostic literature was permitted to seduce the minds of many Church leaders.

APOCRYPHAL SCRIPTURE

"The author of Colossians 4:17 (St. Paul) tells his readers that they are also to read the letter sent to the Christians in the town of Laodicea. We don't have any authentic letters from Paul to Laodiceans, however...in the second century a couple of letters turned up, forged in Paul's name."
—*Scripture's Imposters*, Bart D. Ehrman. U.S. News and World Report Special Edition

"Apocrypha means 'hidden things' in Greek. The Apocryphical books of the Bible fall into two categories: texts which were included in

*some canonical version of the Bible at some point, and other texts of a
Biblical nature which have never been canonical."*[5]

—Internet Secret Text Archives.

The first epigraph above describes an instance of early
Christian Apocrypha based on what was alleged to be "newly discovered" secret knowledge of canonical Christian scripture. This
was similar to writings of the Jewish scholar Philo of Alexandria
whom we discussed as having discovered 'hidden things' contained in the Jewish Old Testament. Both epigraphs are based on
Jewish and Christian historical beliefs but were embellished with
false subjective information. Beginning late in the first century
AD a plethora of writings began to appear, alleging discovery of
new information from Jesus and the Apostles not contained in
the New Testament. It was not until the end of the fourth century
that all Christian literature was finally either accepted or rejected
by various Christian leaders, and by the end of the third century
great confusion existed.

Today, the number of apocryphal Christian writings are too
voluminous to list in a book such as this, but this is a subject that
all who wish to understand the validity of early Christian writings
should be familiar with. Who wrote it; to whom was it written,
when was it written and what was the source of their beliefs? As
we enter the second century, new apocryphal beliefs that seduced
many Christians will be discussed and explained, and for this reason it is helpful to at least be aware of these ancient writings which
can be found on the internet today. It is suggested for those interested in this subject that they examine EarlyChristianWritings.
com[6] This site includes writings of both early Christian scripture
and apocryphal writings, and is explained by unbiased scholarly
discussions and links to supporting historical information, permitting readers to juxtapose one against the other.

DIDACHE, THE JEWISH-CHRISTIAN CATECHISM

*"The Didache, in fact, is a very clear example of a text that is both
totally and profoundly Jewish and totally and profoundly Christian.*

—*Birth of Christianity,* John Dominic Crossan

It is of great importance to understand the Didache, an instructional manual originally composed by Jewish rabbis before Christ, for Gentile converts to Judaism. It was later expanded by Jewish-Christians with the addition of Jewish-Christians beliefs and practices, setting Christianity apart from Judaism. In essence this book may be considered the first Christian catechism, expanded by Christians before the New Testament existed. The first line reads, "Teaching of the Lord God to the Gentiles by the Twelve Apostles." Until the fourth century AD this document could be found across the Roman Empire where it was wrongly considered by some Church leaders to be a part of the New Testament; having been in use since shortly after 50 AD when the Council of Jerusalem first admitted Gentiles to Christianity without first converting to Judaism, it remained the most important Christian writing. For practicing Catholics these teachings will be familiar, but with the voluminous number of pseudo-Christian apocryphal writings this instructional Christian document is unfamiliar to modern Christians, so we will bring attention to only a few passages that were formative, describing subjects that may shed light on familiar Catholic beliefs and practices of today. The Didache is available on the internet with full text and scholarly comments.[7]

> "It [Didache] lets us see, probably the best we ever will, how early Christianity regulated its life.[8]
>
> —*The Didache*, Aaron Milavec

The opening statement of the Didache states: "The way of life is this" and proceeds to introduce subjects familiar to today's Catholics: *"Do not commit murder; do not commit adultery; do not seduce young boys; do not have illicit sex; do not steal; do not practice magic; you shall not murder a child, whether it be born or unborn."* This first section was contained in the original Jewish text, written during a time after the fall of their Greek occupiers, a time when pagans began to convert. In addition to the original Jewish Commandments against adultery and murder it was known that "Sins of the flesh" were rampant among ascetic pagan converts.

Concerning the Eucharist: *"But as touching the Eucharistic thanksgiving give ye thanks thus. First, as regards the cup: We give Thee thanks, O our Father, for the holy vine of Thy son David, which Thou madest known unto us through Thy Son Jesus; Thine is the glory for ever and ever. Then as regarding the broken bread: We give Thee thanks, O our Father, for the life and knowledge which Thou didst make known unto us through Thy Son Jesus; Thine is the glory for ever and ever."* In these early centuries before the Sacramental Priesthood we find each Christian was to individually say the Liturgy before consuming the Eucharistic meal.

After the Eucharist: *"After the Eucharist when you are filled, give thanks this way: We thank you, holy Father, for your holy name which you enshrined in our hearts, and for the knowledge and faith and immortality that you made known to us through Jesus your servant And after ye are satisfied thus give ye thanks... But permit the prophets to offer thanksgiving [Eucharistize] as much as they desire. Whosoever therefore shall come and teach you all these things that have been said before, receive him."* The terms *Apostle* and *Prophet* are synonymous in the Didache with the "Prophets" who had the right to freely formulate their Eucharistic prayers. Today the Vatican forbids deviations from Vatican approved liturgy.

Teachers: *"Whosoever therefore shall come and teach you all these things that have been said before, receive him... But concerning the apostles and prophets, so do ye according to the ordinance of the Gospel. Let every apostle, when he cometh to you, be received as the Lord, but he shall not abide more than a single day, or if there be need, a second likewise; but if he abide three days, he is a false prophet."* These apostles/prophets are described as *ones sent;* they are on their way to establish new house churches as did Timothy and Titus when *sent* by St. Paul.

Appoint Bishops: *"But if ye have not a prophet [sent one]... Appoint for yourselves therefore bishops and deacons worthy of the Lord, men who are meek and not lovers of money, and true and approved; for unto you they also perform the service of the prophets and teachers Therefore despise them [bishops] not; for they are your honorable men along with the prophets and teachers."* It should be noted here that in early Christianity bishops were chosen only by members of the diocese with no mention of Apostolic succession. No teaching of first Christianity is more illuminating of its later development than is the *Holy Tradition* that, after the first generation of Diocesan "Presidents" (Later termed Bishops) were appointed by the first Apostles and Disciples, all later bishops and deacons were elected by faithful Parishioners. Today, we are denied this right.

In order to offer some context between the Didache and House-Churches the term "priest" does not appear in the Didache nor in the House-Church described by St. Paul in 1Corinthians 11, or by Pliny, c.111 AD (Second Century House-Churches). Neither Jesus' Apostles nor Disciples would have identified themselves as a priest, who alone was capable of personally offering sacrifice to God. Only in the third century do we find the new and revolutionary concept that only Sacerdotal Priests who "Act in the place of Jesus" may pronounce the words of consecration. This belief is not contained in the Deposit of Faith or The New Testament.

GENDER AND COMMUNAL EQUITY

In his book, *The Birth of Christianity,* John Dominic Crossan[9], an ordained priest from 1957 to 1969 and perhaps the most renowned scriptural scholar, provides a section on the Didache and the place of women in the Church, which is paraphrased here. We recall that during the session on *"Women and the Historical Jesus"* presented in the Society of Biblical Literature meeting (1996)...Deborah Rose-Gaier discussed *"The Didache: A Community of Equals."* In this presentation she elaborated on the Didache's sections 1.1- 6.2 and 4.1 in which the term "'my child," is contrasted with the Old Testament's patriarchal use of "my son" Proverbs 5. From the Didache [Rose-Gaier] speaks about household relationships with a striking lack of anything about wives and husbands, concluding there is no prohibition against women as trainers, baptizers, eucharistizers, apostles, prophets, or teachers, so it must be assumed that these functioning roles within the community were open to women. Apparently, a fuller understanding of House-Church norms established by Apostle/

Prophets such as Timothy and Titus who were the first *ones sent* by Paul, and later Apostles/Prophets, *ones sent,* in the Didache.

Women Deacons mentioned by Pliny, who spoke for the house-church in 111AD, were both leaders and speakers for their House-Church. However, in his letter to the Corinthians Paul congratulates the President for following the *traditions* passed on to him requiring women to remain veiled if they pray or prophesy in church, asserting it is the *"custom* with us."1 Corinthians 11:2 Paul then says "women are to remain quiet at meetings since they have "no permission to speak...they must keep in the background as the *Law* itself lays down." 1 Corinthians 14:34

Apparently St. Paul reveals here his patriarchal indoctrination as a youth by Rabbi Gamaliel the Elder, this *law* did not come from Christ. Jewish Law is solely contained within the 613 commandments of the Torah, the first five books of the Old Testament. No such commandment exists in these 613 commandments prohibiting a woman from teaching in the assembly.[10] However, from the Talmud 200 years later the *Mishnah* will develop rabbinical *opinions,* described as Jewish *oral* law, not infallible Torah Law. Oral Law at the time of St. Paul represented only Judaism's *traditional* understandings [by rabbis] of matters not contained in the Torah's written Law; therefore it is not Jewish Law *per se.* It is interesting and informative that Paul describes his *tradition* as Law while in the same letter to the Corinthians he says, "To those who have no Law, I was free of the law myself, though not free from God's Law, being under the Law of Christ." 1 Corinthians 9:21. Later Paul says, "The law will not justify anyone in the sight of God." Galatians 3:11 It is not unusual today for one rabbi to disagree with another regarding the Mishnah. Without a doubt women were House-Churches leaders. We also know that all Jews did not accept *Oral* Jewish Law, which was rejected by both Sadducees and Essenes.

The simplicity of early Jewish-Christianity which we have described above will soon change. As the first generation of believers are forced to depart the Holy Land they will face new challenges - without a pope.

CHAPTER EIGHT

AN INFALLIBLE MONARCH?

"At first not all Western bishops believed the bishop of Rome, or even the Popes, were superior to other bishops in authority."
— *The History of Catholic Christianity.* Anthony Gilles

"The institution of the Pope and his curia has grown over time increasingly into a seat of concentrated power. Yet there is nothing to indicate that Peter was to have a successor."
— *National Catholic Register*, Alain Woodrow, 11/14/97

There is no record in the Deposit of Faith that anyone succeeded Jesus' brother St. James as leader of Christianity following his death in 62 AD, a time when Christianity was spreading beyond the Roman Empire only five years before St. Peter's death. The suggestion that St. Peter believed himself to be the monarchial leader of Christianity as later popes assert, is historically untrue. Addressing his fellow Christian leaders [Elders] St. Peter said, "To the elders among you, I appeal as a fellow elder, a witness to Christ's suffering...Be Shepherd's of God's flock that is under your care...not lording it over those entrusted to you, but being an example to your flock." 1 Peter 5:1-3. And, St. Paul assured us that no apostle had authority over him, he merely asked Christians to "respect those above you in the Lord." Paul later confronted Peter to his face, asserting that he was "manifestly wrong" for siding with Judaizers who demanded circumcision for Gentile converts. Galatians 2:11f

St. Peter, this writer's patron saint, was selected as my intercessor Saint and advocate during my Sacramental Conformation. He was the epitome of all apostles and highly revered when he preached in Rome as well as in other communities across the Empire, from Antioch to Babylon to Britain and Gaul before his death. Upon returning to Rome in 67 AD, he and his wife Perpetua who traveled with him from the beginning of his mission, were executed. Some historians believe their daughter, Petronella, was born after the death of Jesus.

Catholic historians acknowledge that in the early centuries local bishops did not believe the bishops of Rome were superior to other bishops, albeit during the chaotic hundred years following the death of the apostles, Rome, the center of the Empire, became the most esteemed Christian Church. Along with such esteem, Bishops of Rome sometimes assumed an unwarranted posture of authority over other bishops, bringing about conflict between the Roman Bishop and other autonomous bishops. This challenge of other bishop's independence was rejected by Apostolic Father St. Ignatius of Antioch, a student of Apostle St. John, who in c.106 wrote, "You do nothing without your bishop, you must follow the bishop as Jesus Christ follows the Father" Letter to the Smyrnaeans; St. Ignatius acknowledged both Peter and Paul were equals during their time in Rome, both were independent bishops. St. Ignatius informs the Roman Christians during a time when Rome had several bishops that he has no authority over the other bishops in Rome: "I do not command you, as Peter and Paul did" Letter to the Romans Ch. 4, thereby acknowledging the equal authority of individual bishops.

Later, conflicts of authority began after 190 AD when St. Irenaeus became the first to support only bishops of Rome. Irenaeus had come to believed other churches should follow Rome; writing, The "...Church founded and organized at Rome by the two most glorious apostles, Peter and Paul...the faith comes down to our time by means of the successions of the bishops...The blessed apostles, then, having founded and built up the Church [Rome] committed into the hands of Linus the office of the episcopate." Irenaeus, Against Heresies 3.3.2: However we now know historically the Roman church was active before either Peter or Paul went there. It is known Peter encountered Christians when he first arrived in Rome years earlier in 42-50 AD.

PAPAL CONFLICT

Speaking of other Apostles St. Paul writes, "As far as I can tell, these arch-Apostles have nothing more than I have."

—2 Corinthians 11:5

In the next century many heated disputes between bishops of Rome and other bishops arose with each threatening to excommunicate the other. Most notable, as late as 226 years after Jesus, in 256 AD came the heated conflict between Pope St. Stephen and Bishop St. Cyprian of Carthage who, asserting his apostolic authority demanded heretics be re-baptized. But Stephen, attempting to assert the authority of St. Peter to "bind and loose" Matthew 16:19 claimed the apostolic authority of Peter when he declared it unnecessary to re-baptize repentant heretics. Threatened with excommunication by Pope Stephen, St. Cyprian upbraided the Bishop of Rome and goes on to say that Stephen's apostolic tradition is a "Tradition of men," and that the rest of the churches of the world agree with his, Cyprian's, apostolic tradition. This was a classic example of confrontation between independent bishops. Such confrontations continue today in the Eastern Orthodox churches.

As this disagreement continued, St. Cyprian was supported by Bishop Firmilian of Cæsarea, Bishop Dionysius of Alexandria and Tertullian. Cyprian replied, "neither does any of us set himself up as a bishop of bishops, nor by tyrannical terror does any compel his colleague to the necessity of obedience; since every bishop... has his own proper right of judgment, and can no more be judged by another [pope] than he himself can judge another."[1] In the end, bishops were autonomous in their position on teaching authority. This autonomy of bishops is clearly revealed by their personal selection of which books may be read in their churches. Following Cyprian's rebuke, Pope Stephen retreated and Papal Infallibility did not become an issue until Siricius unilaterally assumed the title Pope in the fourth century c 385AD. Many Catholic scholars insist St. Peter was not viewed as a Monarchial leader during his missionary travels. A scholarly article by Catholic historian Vynette Holliday explaining why St. Peter's Apostolic travels did not consist of Monarchial leadership in Rome or other communities where he preached; this discussion it may be read on the international Catholic website *Catholica*.[2]

EARLY CHRISTIANITY 30–325 AD

Note: Later we will elaborate on historical events supporting this book's position that the concept of a Monarchial Pope appeared only late in Christianity, long after the Deposit of Faith was closed. Below is a secular discussion that may assist a modern Catholic's understanding of this historical question.[3]

"It seems that at first the terms "episcopos" and "presbyter" were used interchangeably. The consensus among scholars has been that, at the turn of the 1st and 2nd centuries, local congregations were led by bishops and presbyters whose offices were overlapping or indistinguishable. There was probably no single "monarchical" bishop in Rome before the middle of the 2nd century...and likely much later." Other scholars and historians disagree, citing the historical records of St. Ignatius of Antioch and St. Irenaeus who recorded the linear succession of Bishops of Rome (the popes) up until their own times. They also cite the importance accorded to the popes in the ecumenical councils, including the early ones. [Authors correction, St. James was not a pope as defined today]

"In the early Christian era, Rome and a few other cities had claims on the leadership of worldwide Church. James the Just, known as "the brother of the Lord", served as head of the Jerusalem church, which is still honored as the "Mother Church" in Orthodox tradition. Alexandria had been a center of Jewish learning and became a center of Christian learning. Rome had a large congregation early in the apostolic period that Paul the Apostle addressed in his Epistle to the Romans, and according to tradition Paul was martyred there.

"During the 1st century of the Church (*ca.* 30–130), the Roman capital became recognized as a Christian center of exceptional importance. Clement I at the end of the 1st century wrote an epistle to the Church in Corinth intervening in a major dispute, and apologizing for not having taken action earlier. However, there are only a few other references of that time to recognition of the authoritative primacy of the Roman See outside of Rome. In the Ravenna Document of 13 October 2007, theologians chosen by the Roman Catholic and the Eastern Orthodox Churches stated: "41. Both sides agree...that Rome, as the Church that 'presides in love' [not authority] according to the phrase of St Ignatius of Antioch (*To the Romans*, Prologue), occupied the first place in the *taxis*, and that the bishop of Rome was therefore the *protos* [influence, honor] among the patriarchs. They disagree, however, on the interpretation of the historical evidence from this era regarding the prerogatives of the Bishop of Rome as *protos*, a matter that was already understood in different ways in the first millennium."

"In the late 2nd century AD, there were more manifestations of Roman authority over other churches. In 189, assertion of the primacy of the Church of Rome may be indicated in Irenaeus of Lyons's *Against Heresies* (3:3:2): 'With [the Church of Rome], because of its superior origin, all the churches must agree...and it is in her that the faithful everywhere have maintained the apostolic tradition.' In AD 195, Victor I, in what is seen as an exercise of Roman authority over other churches, excommunicated the Quartodecimans for observing Easter on the 14th of Nisan, the date of the Jewish Passover, a tradition handed down by Apostle St. John the Evangelist (see Easter controversy). Celebration of Easter on a Sunday, as insisted on by the pope, is the system that has prevailed."

As the Christian movement increased in cities and rural communities of the Empire we find vastly different positions taken by independent bishops of the time, not merely on the nature of Christ but on the origin of Judaism and its God.

CHAPTER NINE

OUT OF JUDEA

THE CHANGING LANDSCAPE

"Earliest Christianity, as I reconstruct it in the villages of Galilee and the streets of Jerusalem, is not Hellenized into Platonic dualism.
—*Birth of Christianity*, John Dominic Crossan.

"It is difficult to appreciate the predicament which confronted those Christians who first lived in a church bereft of apostolic leadership... Jesus disciples thought they were living in end times. They expected Jesus to come again soon, certainly within the lifetime of the twelve apostles. It wasn't long however before this expectation began to wane."[1]
—*People of God: The History of Catholic Christianity.* Anthony Gilles

The first epigraph above describes the Jewish-Christian movement founded by Christ and preached by His Apostles until the end of the first century, a time when the Jerusalem center of Christianity no longer controlled Christian thought. With Simon Bar Kokhba's defeat in 135 AD Judea was bereft of both the Apostles and the Apostolic Fathers who studied under them, leaving disorganization and confusion as explained in the second epigraph.

As the first century passed from the scene, the Mediterranean world was awash with pagan religions hostile to and in competition with emerging Christianity as it fled into the pagan world; dispersing as a virus across the Empire to Africa, Greece, Rome, Europe, Persia, even to Babylon and India. Christian-Jews were universally confronted by erudite pagan scholars well-versed in esoteric philosophies and Hellenistic beliefs. Polytheistic Pagans reared in a society indoctrinated with belief and tolerance of many gods brought new thoughts, beliefs and cultures into conflict with the tribal Jewish-Christian heritage, causing near insurmountable problems. Unknown by these foreign converts, Christianity was formed around and based upon the Jewish Old Testament that forecast the coming of a Jewish Messiah, the Christ, and exacerbating the problem of the New Testament not yet being gathered together and recognized as the only legitimate source of Christian scripture. Only late in the fourth century would the New Testament Canon be recognized, and during that time new and spurious Gnostic gospels identifying Jesus as the Son of a benevolent non-Jewish God, certainly not of the evil Jewish God that was believed to have created the world, and its evil. These foreign beliefs became popular during the second century when Christianity was quickly becoming a religion composed primarily of pagan converts who, as a result of the Jerusalem Council of 49 AD were not required to understand Judaism.

An impediment for modern Christian's understanding of the problems faced by second century Christians was the totality of pagan beliefs that permeated the Empire's pagan world. As the Roman Empire expanded across the Mediterranean their policy in general was to absorb the deities and cults of other peoples with the intent of preserving traditional social stability. Throughout the Empire deities other than Christianity's were accepted. For ordinary Romans religion was a part of daily life, each home had a shrine at which prayers to family deities were offered; and in addition to personal gods, the beliefs of all other gods and deities were worshiped or tolerated. This toleration was a hallmark of the Roman world: The Olympian gods, Cybele, Isis, Mithras and the Vestal Virgins who were the priestesses of the Goddess Vesta. While toleration of gods was expected, the Christians and Jews were different; failing to sacrifice and preaching against pagan sacrifices resulted in conflict. An instance recorded in the book of Acts describes the arrest and prosecution of St. Paul and Silas in Philippi when the slave master of a soothsayer, realizing St. Paul's preaching was devastating his income, had him dragged before the magistrate and prosecuted. Acts 16:16_

THE GNOSTIC THREAT

"The new religion of Christ the Lord, from the moment it moved out-side the Jewish milieu in which it was first preached, was thus immedi-ately brought up against the influence of world-wide religious activi-ties. In every city there were philosophical mystics and moral teachers ready, with their list of disciples and adepts, to see affinities between their own beliefs and teachings of the new arrival."[2]
—*A Popular History of the Catholic Church*, Carl Koch

"Orthodox Christian doctrines of the ancient world - and thus of the modern church - was partly conceived of as being what Gnostic scrip-ture was not."
—*The Gnostic Scriptures*, Bentley Layton

It was during the early years of the second century when Jewish-Christianity was first brought squarely into conflict with pagan Hellenism and its fondness for ascetic celibacy and the misogynis-tic fear of female temptation. Initially rejected by Christianity's' first generation, beliefs and practices began to change among sec-ond and third generation pagan converts who became Christian bishops, bringing with them a belief that Judaism was ruled by an evil and oppressive God *(Yahweh),* a god not associated with the risen Christ. Rejecting the Old Testament, these new bishops strove to separate Christ from His Jewish origins. This new gen-eration of leaders, identified as Christian Bishops by their follow-ers is difficult for today's Christians to reconcile; how could such diverse beliefs have entered Christianity? The answer is simple; there was no New Testament and the Old Testament was rejected by most bishops.

Gnosticism was founded on the belief that matter is evil; believing the human body was weak and sinful, and the soul is its prisoner. The soul's emancipation from this bodily prison may only be realized through *gnosis*. It would require two centuries

90

for Christianity to reject this Gnostic belief of Christianit. Broadly speaking it is the belief that Jesus only seemed to be human, and that his physical body was a merely a *semblance* without reality. For the Gnostics, Jesus was a God who merely appeared as a human. A residue of this gnostic belief would linger for three centuries, and for this reason it is helpful to understand some of the more important Gnostic Bishops of great importance, whom we will here briefly describe.

CERDO

"The Cerdonians were a Gnostic sect founded by gnostic Cerdo, a Syrian, who came to Rome about 137."

—*Cerdonians Encyclopedia*

Bishop Cerdo, a Gnostic-Christian Bishop from Syria, moved to the rising center of Christian philosophy in Rome. A magnet for neo-Christian philosophies, he quickly became an important Christian leader c.138 AD. Cerdo became the teaching-master of the Gnostic Marcion whom we will also discuss. Cerdo accepted only one statement from the Gospel of John 1:14, "The Word was made Flesh." Accepting this literally, that "Christ, the Son of the Highest God" appeared without birth from the Virgin and without any birth on earth as man.[3] Second century Gnostic teachers such as Cerdo were free to believe as they chose and introduced their followers to Gnostic beliefs, including new ascetic understandings of sexual relationships between men and women. It is believed Cerdo was first a follower of Simon Magus, who is recorded as having confronted St. Peter Acts 8:9-24; according to St. Irenaeus, "Cerdo was the one who took his system from the followers of Simon Magus at the time of Hyginus who held the ninth place in the Episcopal from the Apostles onward." A brilliant Gnostic philosopher, Cerdo taught there were two gods, one who was a vengeful god that demanded obedience while the other was good and merciful. Of these two gods Cerdo taught the Jewish God was the evil god of the Old Testament who created the world. He taught the god of Jesus was merciful, a superior God who came to be known only through his son, Jesus. Here, with

this description of two Gods we find the introduction of panthe-
ism into Christianity for the first time, thus separating Christ from
Jewish-Christianity that professed, *"Hear, O Israel: The Lord our
God, the Lord is one"* Deuteronomy 6:4, and like the later Gnostics
Cerdo rejected the resurrection of the dead.

Historian St. Irenaeus tells us Cerdo was excommunicated by
Hyginus, but at that time in Rome such an excommunication would
have been meaningless in that Bishop Cerdo's followers competed equally with Hyginus. In all likelihood Cerdo simply ignored
him. By the third century, Cerdo and his followers were gone.
However, in fairness to Hyginus, and later Pope Pius I, c.144-156
who excommunicated bishop Marcion, they were correct. Cerdo
and Marcion were excommunicated because they were *Docetic.*
Docetic Christians believed Jesus never had a physical body, he
merely appeared as a human; however, they were not excommunicated because they preached the superiority of ascetic celibacy,
which was by then becoming popular among many Christians.
Cerdo reveals the ignorance of pagan understanding of Judaism
and Jesus' human nature in the second century.

VALENTINUS

*"Valentinus followed the Docetist heresy, suggesting that Jesus' mortal
body was simply an illusory emanation of the ultimate reality."*
—*New World Encyclopedia*

Bishop Valentinus was born in c.100 AD and died in Alexandria,
the center of Hellenistic Christian belief. He was a Gnostic
Christian who founded his movement in the second century AD.
His influence was widespread and not just within Rome, it spread
from Egypt through Asia Minor and Syria and ultimately through
Northwest Africa. Of all the ancient Gnostic beliefs, Valentinus'
were the most complicated. Please bear with us as we present
a brief synopsis of his confusing beliefs and a link for those who
wish to pursue this ancient system.[4]

According to Irenaeus, the Valentinians rejected Judaism and
thus created a new Heavenly Hierarchy, believing that in the
beginning there was a *Pleroma,* also known as the "fullness," an

indescribable Supreme god. At the center of the Pleroma was the creative Father, *Bythos.* Valentinian identified the God of the Old Testament as the *Demiurge,* the imperfect creator of the material world. Man, the highest being in this material world participates in both the *spiritual* and the *material* nature. Any Christian reading Valentinus' teachings today will think it absurd that such a belief could ever have been accepted.

The work of redemption as Valentinus saw it consisted in freeing man from the material world. St. Clement of Alexandria wrote that the Valentinians regarded Catholic Christians "as simple people of faith, believing gnosis is [already] within themselves. Through this seed of gnosis found within them, they may by nature be redeemed when their *gnosis* is as far removed from faith as the spirit is from the physical."

Valentinus proudly proclaimed his Gnosticism and emerged as one of the greatest spiritual guides in the Christian world during a time when Christian Gnosticism flourished in Rome, "Claiming that only he and his disciples had understood the extent of the invisible transformation of the entire creation, announced to mankind only by the brief ministry of Christ on earth. Ordinary believers [He believed] were content to live according to...banal ethical injunctions contained in the Gospels."[5] He denigrated the New Testament. For those who have difficulty believing Valentinus could have actually threatened Christian beliefs we must understand he was more popular than the Pope. Tertullian tells us that Valentinus was a candidate for the office of Bishop of Rome, only losing the election by a rather narrow margin,[6] during a time when the Bishop of Rome who, elected by a minority of Roman citizens *and* exerted no authority over other bishops, indicating how well entrenched Gnosticism was in the second century.

MARCION

"Marcion, a wealthy Christian ship owner, came to Rome in about 139 and brought with him a controversial interpretation of the Jewish scriptures."

—The Marcionite Movement

Bishop Marcion was ordained Bishop by his father, the Bishop of Sinope (Turkey). Later in Rome, c.140 AD, as a bishop-teacher it soon became apparent Marcion preached an ascetic gospel that rejected marriage. As a young man he studied under Apostolic Father St. Polycarp, who himself had studied under Apostle St. John, and upon discovering his ascetic teaching Bishop St. Polycarp later called Marcion a "Satan" to his face. Therefore, we know that some students of the Apostles remained alive at that period and clearly understood Marcion's mandatory asceticism to be spurious. Cerdo and Marcion, who followed Cerdo were the first churchmen to preach complete asceticism in Rome, thereby dissenting from the Apostles and contrary to the Deposit of Faith which had closed half a century earlier.

As a Gnostic, Marcion taught the body was to be rejected as a stumbling block to salvation because Jesus' death was only a hallucination. Jesus, he claimed, had no physical body. He considered the God of the Old Testament to be evil; therefore he rejected the Old Testament and accepted only a shortened version of Luke's Gospel that was in circulation at the time. "For Marcion the present age was the visible world, subject in its entirety to the rule of the evil 'Creator-God', to whom the true *God of Love* was unknown... Marcion gave this harsh Dualism of Spirit and matter a marked dimension - asserting the evil creator God was the God of Jewish Law. His sinister power was shown less in the tensions of body and spirit than in the dire constraints of society....Mankind lived 'under the [Jewish] Law'. It was to unlock those heavy bars that Christ had suddenly appeared"[7]

This brief explanation does little justice to the charismatic Marcion and his theology that was effective during the formative years of Christianity where he gained a large following among Christians. Some of Marcion's followers were so fervent in their belief they became martyrs for those doctrines. Claiming they were the true Church, his followers asserted that those Disciples of Christ who did not marry had already attained the world beyond and the resurrection. Clearly, Marconi's theology represents another early influence of Dualistic Gnostic belief derived from Greek-Hellenist speculation, into whose world Christianity was quickly moving in the second century. During this time, some

94

Christian writers would succumb to Gnosticism; it had already appeared among Christians in Alexandria, Egypt.

For these reasons Marcion was excommunicated by the tenth Pope, Pius I, c.144-156 AD, and in return Marcion excommunicated Pius, who himself supported ascetic celibacy. Marcion went on to form Marcionite Christianity that lasted until the third century. There were other important Gnostic bishops who are recorded as having great followings, such as Theudas, and Nicola Cerinthus and Carpocratess, but these were typical of Gnostic movements in Rome and other areas, which eventually became dominant in the second century.

MONTANUS

"The words of Montanus and the two prophetesses (Priscilla & Maximilla) were regarded as sacred. This reverence for their leaders, and apparent disregard for the insights of the bishops attracted a lot of hostile attentions."[8]

—Montanus and the New Prophesy

Montanus, who perhaps became the most successful of all heterodox ascetic Christian teachers claimed to speak for God, and needs some understanding because it was his beliefs that captured the mind of Patristic Father Tertullian. Montanus, a new Christian convert from Phrygia, Turkey had first been a eunuch priest of the goddess Cybele. After converting he began to utter astounding prophesies and this same gift apparently fell upon two prophetesses who were his missionary associates. These prophets did not speak as a messenger-prophet of God, i.e., "thus saith the Lord," but described themselves as being possessed by God who spoke directly through their mouth, "I am the Father, the Word and the Paracleat [Holy Spirit]." And, "Montanus claimed not only to have received a series of direct revelations from the Holy Ghost, but personally to be the incarnation of the *Paracleat* mentioned in the Gospel John 14:16.[9]

Montanus was accompanied by two women, Prisca, sometimes called Priscilla, and Maximilla, who likewise claimed to be the embodiments of the Holy Spirit that moved and inspired them. As they went about, "the Three" as they were called, spoke of ecstatic visions and urged their followers to fast and pray so they might share these personal revelations. His preaching spread from his native Phrygia, (where he proclaimed the village of Pepuza as the site of the New Jerusalem) across the contemporary Christian world, to Africa and Gaul." Of course, this new revelation violated the Deposit of Faith that ended only fifty years earlier when the last Apostle had died.

The Montanist's were puritanical in the extreme. Virginity and ascetic chastity was paramount, second marriages were not allowed and martyrdom was sought after. After abandoning the Church, Tertullian himself divorced his wife, violating the Sacrament of Matrimony; his Hellenistic-misogynistic writings had the negative affect of denigrating women to the point they were not allowed to touch the Altar Cup or other Sacramentals. Only in recent years has the Vatican begun to allow females to serve as acolytes at the Altar.

THE COMING THREAT

Thus far we have mentioned ascetic celibacy, but it must be noted that excommunication of these Gnostics had nothing to do with their ascetic Platonic philosophy. Ascetic celibacy was wrongly accepted because Christ had said, "Let them accept who can." These bishops were excommunicated not because they were ascetic celibates, but merely because they rejected the Jewish nature of Christ and His Jewish God at a time in the early second century when Jesus of Nazareth was still known by many to be a Jew.

But, as we will see, in the third century another threat will befall Christianity, a threat that will acknowledge Christ's Jewish humanity while continuing to preach ascetic celibacy. Attempting to denigrate Christ's Jewish nature, the next generation of Christian leaders desired to set Hellenistic-Christianity free from a stumbling block, The Old Testament. This threat will come from the Patristic Fathers._

CHAPTER TEN

THE PATRISTIC FATHERS

This syncretized Hellenistic-Christian belief would later spread widely among the uninformed Christian community. Its effects on later Christians was commented on by Philip Schaff in his exhaustive History of Christianity, "The Alexandrian fathers furnished a theoretical basis for this asceticism in the distinction of a lower and higher morality, which corresponds to the Platonic or Pythagorean distinction between the life according to nature and the life above nature or, the practical and contemplative life...Here was a source of serious practical errors, and an encouragement both to moral laxity and ascetic extravagance. The ascetics, and afterwards the monks, formed or claimed to be moral nobility, a spiritual aristocracy, above the common Christian people; as the clergy stood in a separate caste of inviolable dignity above the laity, who were content with a lower grade of virtue. Clement of Alexandria, otherwise remarkable for his elevated ethical views, requires of the sage or gnostic, that he excel the plain Christian not only by higher knowledge, but also by higher, emotionless virtue, and stoical superiority to all bodily conditions; and he inclines to regard the body, with Plato, as the grave and fetter of the soul." This philosophy is taught of priests by the Vatican today; it is the legacy of the Hellenistic-Christian belief-systems which dramatically influenced third century Christians.

—Anti-Nicene Christianity, Vol. II, Philip Schaff,

"The Christian faith [today] views itself as preserving the Jewish heritage in its integrity, that is to say, of the relationship between the Old and the New Testaments...tensions that occur within the narratives and teachings of each of the two Testaments had to be explained

and smoothed over as well. Some of the strategies that the church
fathers used in order to harmonize the texts of Scripture were them-
selves scriptural, such as allegorization, which Patristic thinkers widely
employed to read the Old Testament in light of the New."[1]

—*Scholasticism and Patristic Roots*

From the end of the first century until the end of the second
century, Christianity expanded from Jerusalem to Britain in the
west to Babylon in the east, and from North Africa to the Black
Sea in the north. During this time they spread the Christian faith
through Christian House-Churches in rural areas where illiteracy
was prominent. The lack of communication between dispersed
communities proved a problem when generations changed and
non-Jewish converts became dominant. However, in major cities across the Empire, erudite polytheistic philosophers became
enamored with the risen Christ and sought to understand Him in
light of their lifelong ascetic indoctrination, introducing two problems. First, as the generations changed isolated illiterates became
dependent on Gnostic-Christian leaders who were the only liter-
ates in many areas. The second problem came with the conversion
of brilliant philosophers, true scholars who as followers of Plato
were not pantheists. Plato accepted the belief of an unfathomable creator which he termed the "One," but Patristics viewed the
Old Testament tribal foundation of Christianity as inadequate to
explain the true nature of Christ, who they accepted as a divinity.
The problem these Hellenists struggled with was tribal Judaism
from whence Jesus came, and from Jewish animus of Hellenistic
asceticism since Alexander. This posed a great problem for their
lifelong support of Plato's ascetic philosophy. While the shallow
Gnosticism that first affected Christianity ultimately fell by the
wayside, some Gnostic beliefs would continue with this new generation of Christian leaders, the Patristic Fathers.

THE PATRISTICS

The Patristic Fathers are today deemed by the Vatican to be
the most prominent Christian theologians after the Apostolic
period and the death of St. John, the last living apostle. During the
second century, Christianity in the pagan world began to manifest

itself in variant ways when Hellenistic-Christianity came to dominate Christian belief across the Empire. After 170 AD the Church remained a marginalized and illicit religion, but one becoming an important movement tolerated by emperors and gaining converts among intellectual pagan scholars, who became influential teachers in major centers of Christianity. By then the Old Testament had come to be recognized by scholars as a valid part of Christ's Jewish tradition, but Jewish Laws requiring priestly marriage were contrary to their life-long Hellenistic beliefs, and desiring to obviate Old Testament restrictions they individually selected, or rejected New Testament writings of their choosing, along with influential gnostically-inspired writings supporting their ascetic views, neither of which were considered more authoritative than the other. This change would put the two Testaments into serious contradiction.

As Christians today attempt to understand the often contradicting positions taken by individual Patristics, it is necessary to realize that no central authority such as a pope existed in the beginning. An analogy that may make some sense for Americans would be to imagine New York City with only two Authoritative theologians such as Billy Graham and the revered Catholic preacher Cardinal Fulton J. Sheen, each preaching a Christianity based on their private understanding. These Patristic bishops should not be viewed merely as ministers of their individual Dioceses, but rather as competing philosophers such as Graham and Sheen would have been within their purview of authority; both considered theological "Rock Stars" by their followers. While few Patristics were not originally from Rome, most eventually found their way there.

Though devout and pious men, they struggled with the problem of associating Christianity's Jewish roots with their Hellenist philosophies and their vision of a celibate hierarchical priesthood above the average Christian. The first Patristic to solve the problem of Old Testament restrictions was Tertullian. He insisted that since the Jews had rejected the Christ the Old Testament it was no longer in force and must be interpreted *spiritually*, thus providing a new *philosophical interpretation* that would forever change Catholicism's view of sex.[2] With this new interpretive license supporting ascetic philosophies contrary to apostolic teaching came lasting change.

Before identifying the nullification of Christian doctrines instituted by the Patristics, we will briefly introduce important Patristics who became Hellenist-Christians at the time of their conversion from Hellenism.

Justin Martyr

In explaining Justin's teaching, "...it is necessary to distinguish in them between poetry and truth."
—New Advent Catholic Encyclopedia

Renowned today as the most intellectual of the Patristics, St. Justin the Martyr was a celibate pagan philosopher from Palestine prior to his conversion to Christianity. He arrived in Rome c.162 AD. As a young man he first became a student of various philosophical schools, becoming first a Stoic then a Pythagorean, a Platonist, and finally becoming a Christian philosopher in Rome. He founded a theological school in which one of his students was Tatian, who later started his own theological school and founded a Gnostic sect, the Encratites who fanatically rejected wine at Eucharistic meetings, substituting water in its place. Tatian's sect also rejected marriage for all Christians, a movement sweeping Christianity.

Justin was essentially a Christian-Platonist who seemed to feel uncomfortable with the reality that the transcendent Jewish God Yahweh had actually entered into the affairs of humans – he taught the *Word* (Jesus) of St. John, not the Holy Spirit to be another "flesh enrobed" God,[3] thus revealing his Hellenistic pantheism. Described as an "impenitent intellectual," he always made a point of wearing the somber robe of the professional philosopher. Historian Peter Brown[4] describes him as presenting Christianity as a religion distinguishable from all others by the stringency of their sexual codes. Justin, speaking of his celibate Christian followers, men and women who as Disciples of Christ since their youth: "continue in their immaculate purity...it is our boast to be able to display such persons to the human race." This was a time when Hellenist-Bishops began to preach celibacy for *all* Christians.

Justin mentioned the term "Gospels" twice in all his writing, referring to them as "Memorabilia of the Apostles," but his desire to eliminate conjugal love within Christian marriage has no place in the Gospels. He was intense, as indicated by his writings in *First Apology*, "Either we do not marry except to rear children or we refuse to marry and we exercise complete self control. Further, to convince you that we do not have secret rites or licentious sexual intercourse, one of us sent to Felix, the governor of Alexandria, asking him to permit a surgeon to take away his [the Christian's] testicles. For the surgeons there said they were forbidden to do this without the permission of the Governor. When Felix was not at all willing to sign, the youth remained by himself, and found his own and his associates conscience sufficient. [To perform the castration]" Clerical castration among future priests in order to escape female temptations will become widespread.

Justin was the first truly intellectual Hellenist to exert a lasting influence on Christian theology, yet he simply could not intellectually accept Christianity's Jewish beginnings. As Justin claimed, Jesus had brought to Christianity "The Law over against a Law that made the one before it to cease [Jewish Law]."

While Justin exerted long lasting influence on Christian theology he was unable to accept the teachings of the Old Testament. During this time a growing number of Hellenist converts such as Justin began to introduce anti-Semitic bias clothed in philosophical terms. The animosity of these new Christian writers toward Christianity's Jewish roots is well described in Justin's *Dialogue with Trypho the Jew,* 160 AD. Justin wrote to Trypho, "The custom of circumcising the flesh, handed down from Abraham, was given to you as a distinguishing mark, to set you off from other nations and from us Christians. The purpose of this was you and you only might suffer the afflictions that are now justly yours; that only your land be decimated, and your cities ruined by fire, that the fruits of your land be eaten by strangers before your very eyes; that not one of you be permitted to enter your city of Jerusalem. Your circumcision of the flesh is the only mark by which you can certainly be distinguished from other men...as I stated before it was by reason of your sins and the sins of your fathers that, among other precepts, God imposed upon you the observance of the Sabbath mark." While Justin condemned circumcision he supported castration, perhaps failing to understand that Jesus of Nazareth, as all Jewish men, was circumcised.

The theological landscape was changing at the time Justin left Palestine for the capital of Rome in 162 AD. By Justin's time another center of asceticism, one removed from Christianity's' Palestinian origin and from Athens, had arisen in Alexandria, Egypt.

ALEXANDRIA EGYPT

Nearly 200 years after St. Paul, among Christians in areas heavily influenced by Hellenistic philosophy, such as Alexandria in Egypt, there appeared misogynistic teaching in the third century. After Constantine in the fourth century mysogeny was to be found in other areas, as Christian philosophers arose who continually confronted what they believed to be an incomplete explanation of Christianity's beginnings. They attempted to find compatibility between Christianity and the pagan philosophies that ruled their intellectual world. For pagans, Christianity seemed far from intellectual and unfortunately, a part of pagan philosophy demanded celibacy for religious leaders and was said to be beneficial for all Christians. As Christian philosophers investigated these belief systems, pagan celibacy proponents would change the view of some toward both men and women and marriage. Where did these Christian philosophers come from? Certainly not from the house churches with their married couples of Paul's day. Here we examine the origins and effect of such philosophies on Christianity.

During the third century as the Church began to grow in acceptance and build worship centers, House-Churches were giving way in major cities. Philosophers appeared, many with new and different views of Christianity's beginning. This faulty understanding often resulted from their wish to obviate Christ's Jewish beginnings because, by that time great theological confrontations with paganism existed in all areas and Jewish beliefs were fading among both Christians and pagans. Even though women lived with and supported their husband-priests in Church ministries during the first two centuries, a misogynist strain of theology began to appear, condemning the "female threat to celibacy." This early misogyny will be found to originate early on with non-Jewish converts such as Philo of Alexandria, who brought with them an admiration for the Greek practice of consigning women to second class citizenship, not suitable for inclusion into their male-dominant society.

Women were so disenfranchised from Greek male society that the poetess Sappho formed a colony of women on the island of Lesbos in order to institute a society of women both married and unmarried. Slowly, Greek misogyny now centered in Alexandria began to rub off on Christian philosophers. Several reasons have been advanced by commentators for this late appearing strain of misogyny because it went far beyond the Biblical admonitions from St. Paul against women preaching in Church, and against Christian-Jewish roots. Though perhaps unmarried, St. Paul accepted women disciples, and he most certainly accepted marriage for all Christians, including the Apostles, of this there is no doubt. Many see the rise of this misogyny to be a creeping loss of Jewish identity as the Church moved into Greek-Hellenist areas; mystical pagan thought and misogyny sanctioned celibacy in much the same way Gnostics had the previous century during St. Paul's time, when he preached against it.

In the next chapter we will present writings against women, along with the influences that gave rise to them. Misogynistic writings definitely offered support for future attempts to control the priesthood through celibacy. Their reasons were contrary to the foundations of Christianity replete with women disciples. Regarding women, it should be pointed out that many early Patristic writings such as these below were left by venerated Patristic Church Fathers. However, while historians continue to source these writings as authorities, they are now known to often be in gross theological error, some heretical, as judged by current Church teaching.

BISHOP CLEMENT OF ALEXANDRIA

"The Gospel, as Clement reads it, not only restricts sexuality to marriage but, even within marriage, limits it to specific acts intended for procreation."

—Adam, Eve and the Serpent; Elaine Pagels

"'...deliver us from error and from this use of generative organs... When Salome asked the Lord: 'How long shall death hold sway? He answered: 'As long as you women bear Children. Then the Savior Himself said 'I Came to undo the works of women', meaning by this 'female,' - 'sexual desire,' and by birth the corruption of death.'"

—Clement, Stromateis. 3

In 200 AD the Stoic philosopher Titus Flavius Clement, later a Christian Bishop, Clement of Alexandria, began to actively preach a new variant of Christianity. In order to clearly understand the "truth" of Christianity he initially sought out "Christian" teachers from Sicily and Syria, among them Tatian a Gnostic student of Justin. Finally he attached himself to Pantaenus, a brilliant philosopher known as an "ornament of the Stoic school [Alexandria]... [Clement] ultimately succeeding Pantaenus as master of his school. He instinctively returned to the stoic view, along with Platonic metaphysics."[5] Clement's teacher Pantaenus was originally a Stoic who earlier studied the writings of Philo, whose philosophies were incorporated into his school. Clement, as Philo before him, believed philosophers such as Plato and Socrates should be considered equal to Jewish prophets like Elijah and Isaiah. Clement was born the son of wealthy pagan parents from Athens, the womb of pagan Hellenism, and converted only after traveling widely throughout the Empire in search of the true philosophy; to this end he spent many years pursuing different beliefs. He was celibate at the time of his conversion.

Hellenistic philosophy is quite evident in Clement's writings, which are replete with quotations from Greek poets and philosophers. Both of these philosophies were incorporated into his Alexandria School of theology. In this Christian school for the instruction of converts Clement united Greek philosophy and Cabalist asceticism with Christian doctrine in much the same way Philo earlier attempted and failed with Judaism. Such teachings became particularly effective and damaging during a time when wide disagreement and theological confusion existed among different Christian communities scattered across the Empire. For more than a century, Christianity had little cross communication because of persecution.

In Alexandria of 200 AD "The intellectual temper was broad and tolerant and many races mingled...Plato was the most favored of the old masters." By Clement's time in 200 AD Alexandrian Christianity was in this mix; Alexandria was, in addition, one of the chief seats of that peculiar mix of pagan and Christian speculation known as Gnosticism. Valentinus also taught there as a highly respected Hellenist-Christian Bishop before establishing his school in Rome. "Clement always took the Valentinian image of the "redeemed person...The role of Gnostic teachers within the Catechetical Schools of Alexandria placed the views of Valentinus and his followers in the foreground of his concerns."[6] As difficult as it may seem to have been, Clement attempted to combine the philosophy of Plato who, while a dualist, also believed in a single unfathomable creator that he styled, the *One*.

Clement did believe in what he termed Gnosticism within Scripture. There was a difference however in Clement's Gnosticism. Clement's belief was based not on *secret* gnosis as others had preached but upon a spiritual gnosis. His spiritual gnosis combined paganism with Christian belief and faith. He nearly succeeded. Earlier gnosis' claimed to possess new historical information concerning Jesus, Clement's gnosis on the other hand was mystical, it came from a new spiritual insight he believed could be found by blending Plato's teaching of the Logos with that of St. John's Logos (Word). Not surprisingly, Clements attempt to combine Plato and St. John in order to describe Jesus to pagans didn't quite work out. While Clement's was a new and malleable concept, he believed average uneducated Christian converts from paganism would come to accept his beliefs.

TERTULLIAN

"Do you know that you are Eve? The judgment of God pronounced upon your sex lives on in this age. You are the gateway of the devil, you desecrated that fatal tree, you first betrayed the law of God...you deserve death and it was the son of God who had to die."

—Tertullian, *de cultu feminarum 1.1.2*

A major figure in ancient Catholic theology was Tertullian, 197 AD, "The father of Latin theology." Initially a Stoic, he was born in Carthage of pagan parents and became the most prominent lawyer for those seeking defense in pagan courts. It is debated whether he later became a priest but it is known his writings were highly respected, often to the consternation of other Christian-Hellenist philosophers. A theological narcissistic, he was not a "dualist" as others were, insisting instead on rigorous control of the body because he believed bodily sensations could directly control one's physical sensations. Some important Patristics such as St. Jerome supported him, while others could be extremely confrontational. It was Tertullian who first wrote that, since the Jews had rejected the Christ, the Old Testament must be inter-preted only in a *spiritual-allegorical* manner.

"Tertullian's handling of the place of the law of the Old Testament in the life of the Christian was allegorical. Having vir-tually removed the burden of a legalistic Old Testament religion he introduced a legalistic New Testament. He agrees that the burdens of the law which even the fathers of old could not bear should be dispensed with."[7]

Tertullian was both narcissistic and malleable in his beliefs. After two decades of impressive theological support of the church, he changed his theological beliefs. Ultimately he left the Church to become a follower of Montanus and the prophetess Priscilla and Maximilla. His rigorism became extreme and his anti-clerical-ism reached the point of invective in support of what he believed to be the priestly role of the layman. As described earlier, this sect accepted new revelation after the Deposit of Faith, new revela-tion spoken by the prophetesses. Without doubt Tertullian was a

Hellenistic misogynist who influenced later clerics, and today few apologists are cited authoritatively as often as Tertullian.

ORIGEN – THE HELLENISTIC FOOT SOLDIER

"Origen goes still further, and propounds quite distinctly the catholic doctrine of two kinds of morality and piety, a lower for all Christians, and a higher for saints or the select few."

—*History of Christianity,* Schaff

In Alexandria where Justin and Clement taught, intellectual speculation remained rife among philosophers, pagans, Jews and Christians, on the superiority of asceticism for religious leaders. Born in this matrix, Christian philosophers such as Justin and Clement exerted an influence on our famous scripture scholar, Origen. Although Origen strongly disagreed with other scholars of his day on which books should be included in the New Testament, his translation of the Old Testament into six languages was brilliant, and would be an invaluable asset to later scholars. That being true, one wonders how he could have taught as he did. There seems no doubt Hellenistic Christian philosophers in Alexandria drew heavily from apocryphal Christian literature that abounded in their day. Origen, however, was well versed in all Christian literature, which, though not defined as "scripture" was in circulation, and much of the current New Testament was generally accepted along with Apocrypha of the philosophers.

Origen was a key player during his time for promoting the Hellenistic penetration into Christianity, a penetration which so clouded the original teachings of the Apostles it would require centuries to correct. He was born of Christian parents in the center of Christian Hellenism, Alexandria c. 185. Ultimately he succeeded his mentor Clement of Alexandria as head of the theological school originally begun by the Stoic convert Pantaenus. During his lifetime he became a key player in the Christian-Hellenist axis between Rome, Alexandria, and Antioch that actively propagated heterodoxy among Christianity. He traveled widely. In 212 AD he went to Rome and became a life-long comrade of Hellenist Anti-Pope Hippolytus, who unsuccessfully preached *cultic purity* (celibacy) for priests. This term was later appropriated by Pope Damasus who, as we will note below, used the term in an attempt to emasculate the priesthood via celibacy. Three years later in 215 AD Origen was invited to Palestine to preach in Jerusalem and Caesarea. This invitation came from the bishops in that area. Origen was widely admired by bishops who actively sought his scholarship. Again in 230 AD he traveled to Greece, preaching there and once again in Judea, making disciples in each diocese over the years. The virus spread. Ultimately Origen established a school of theology in the Holy Land which he patterned after Clement's theological school in Egypt, thus establishing a Hellenistic theological base in the womb of Christianity.

Following Justin's viral anti-Semitism, along with his Hellenist peers Origen continued to castigate Judaism. "Concerning Israel's rejection [of Christ], Origen promoted a punitive suppressionist approach in which the people of Israel were forever 'abandoned because of their sins.' He also declared, 'And we say with confidence they will never be restored to their previous position. For they committed a crime of the most unhallowed kind, in conspiring against the Savior of the human race in that city where they offered up to God a worship containing the symbols of mighty mysteries.' According to Origen, 'The Jews were altogether abandoned...so that there is no indication of any Divinity abiding amongst them." [8] Origen's statements repeatedly reappeared during the Inquisitions of the Middle Ages.

Two centuries after his death, Origen was condemned for having taught reincarnation of the soul, a belief he acquired from Plato. Reincarnation contradicted the Deposit of Faith as explained in the Book of Hebrews. Here with these Christian-Hellenist philosophers we find an axis of cooperation which endured for decades after Justin. Between Origen, Clement, Justin, Anti-Pope Hippolytus, and the vast number of students they affected, a definitive shift toward not merely ascetic celibacy but other heterodox as well. These men, while devout and well intentioned were ascetic, self-important and puritanical in the extreme. They sought a return to a self-imagined pristine beginning of Christianity. They were wrong. As philosophers before them, they envisioned a divine law of their own making; repentant sinners were not to be readmitted lest they sin after baptism. They had no concept of Jesus' words, "Yes, if you forgive others their failings, your heavenly Father will forgive you yours; but, if you do not forgive others, your Father will not forgive your failings either." Matthew 6:14 They also saw chastity as being superior in the same manner as did their previous pagan mentors.

Concerning Origen's self-castration, Vatican apologists make no mention of the Hellenistic pension for religious castration, stating simply, "Apparently concerned with his ability to resist the temptations of sex Origen castrated himself in a misguided attempt to follow Jesus teaching: 'there are eunuchs who have made themselves that way for the sake of the Kingdom of Heaven.'" Matthew 19: 12

Origen held highly unorthodox views of the Deposit of Faith, views heavily influenced by both Clement and Justin. He stated the literal resurrection of Jesus was "Preached in the Church for the simple minded and for the ears of the common crowd who are led to live a better life through their belief." [9] Later the misogynist St. Jerome condemned Origen for his position on Christian resurrection, "You, heretic, say 'body' and do not mean 'flesh' at the same time, for you wish to deceive the ears of the ignorant." However, one point of Hellenistic doctrine on which they both agreed was ascetic celibacy.

One may understand from these early Christian philosophers that while mandatory celibacy was not yet required, its foundation was being laid.

Hellenistic philosophy continued to exert great influence on many Church writers who wrongly blended their celibate philosophies with orthodox Christian belief. Infant Christianity proved to be fertile ground in which to plant the seed. It is difficult to quantify the totality of negative impact against marriage imbued into Christianity from brilliant Hellenists, beginning with the Patristic Fathers and lasting until today. They were Hellenists-Christian philosophers with an ability to exert a deviant influence on Christian theology. These men and many others brought with them a foundation of Hellenism that prized celibacy and many priests were seduced into accepting chastity, thus resulting in later assertions that our first priests were all celibate. The Genesis of these seductions is to be found in pagan philosophies, not within Orthodox Judaism or the Deposit of Faith.

From our Catholic Encyclopedia we take this glowing compliment on the positive effects of Hellenism, "Nevertheless, the great majority of the Christian philosophers down to St. Augustine were Platonist. They appreciated the *uplifting influence of Plato's psychology and metaphysics*, and recognized in that influence a powerful ally of Christianity in the warfare against *materialism* and *naturalism*,"[10] including the practice of ascetic celibacy. Still, it would be two centuries before mandatory celibacy became law.

ASCETICISM'S *FAIT ACCOMPLI*

"St. Jerome, 419AD, was the most ardent advocate of celibacy... Jerome, according to the same author, regarded St. Peter as a lesser saint that St. John because Peter was married and John wasn't. St. Jerome considered marriage an invention of Satan and encouraged married couples who converted to Christianity to renounce their marriage vows: 'How many there are who, by consent between themselves, cancel the debt of their marriage, eunuchs of their own accord through the desire of the kingdom of heaven.'"[11]
—Mandatory Celibacy and Sexual Ethics in the Latin Right Catholic Church

During the time span from 160 AD when St. Justin Martyr proposed priestly castration as armament against the seduction of women until the first celibacy law of 385 AD, the Christian movement that began as a Jewish sect when all Christians were married, had now morphed to where a majority had succumbed to Plato's ascetic philosophy. No longer was castration necessary, priests were simply denied the Sanctifying Grace of Sacramental Matrimony established by Christ, as infallibly defined at the Council of Trent: *"All Sacraments of the New Covenant were instituted by Jesus Christ."*[12] As the Church approached mandatory celibacy requirements, it was no longer simply an efficacious practice proposed by pagan converts in the second and third century, it was by then becoming a misogynistic demand.

St. Gregory – St. Ambrose - St. John Chrysostom - St. Jerome

Following Emperor Constantine's acceptance of Christianity, Hellenistic efforts to change the priesthood increased. St. Gregory of Nazianzum 389 AD wrote "Fierce is the dragon and cunning the asp; but women have the malice of both."[13]

St. Ambrose, c.397, from Rome and later Bishop of Milan insisted on celibacy when he wrote, "Remember, God took the rib out of Adam's body, not a part of his soul, to make her. She was not made in the image of God, like man... The Ministerial Office must be kept pure and unspoiled and must not be defiled by coitus."[14] Ambrose was a personally devout man who did not object to remarriage for widows, but continued to preach that widowhood was similar to virginity and therefore to be esteemed above marriage. The Vatican teaches the same today.

St. John Chrysostom c.407 AD, Bishop of Constantinople, wrote eight anti-Jewish polemics[15] which were so virulent they were extensively used by Germany's Nazi party to justify Hitler's anti-Semitic holocaust. In addition to his anti-Semitism, Chrysostom was classically misogynistic. "It does not profit a man to marry. For what is a woman but an enemy of friendship, an inescapable punishment, a necessary evil, a natural temptation, a domestic danger, delectable mischief, a fault in nature, painted with beautiful colors?" Today this man is considered both a Saint and Doctor of the Church, "The whole of her body is nothing less than phlegm, blood, bile, rheum and the fluid of digested food... If you consider what is stored up behind those lovely eyes, the angle of the nose, the mouth and the cheeks you will agree that the well-proportioned body is only a whitened sepulcher."[16]

Chrysostom's first teacher was the Stoic Libanius, a friend of pagan Emperor Julian the Apostate, who is quoted as saying Chrysostom had been destined to become Libanius' successor, "If the Christians had not taken him from us." Chrysostom's two closest associates over his career were St. Gregory of Nazianzus c.374 AD, the son of a bishop and Gregory of Nyssa c.394 AD who, though married, promoted celibacy. All these men, regardless of the piety, brilliance, and theological contributions they may have made, taught Hellenism which promoted misogyny, celibacy, and anti-Semitism that did not come from the Deposit of Faith. It's way past time for us Catholics to face up to our history.

St. Jerome, c.420 AD, who worked surprisingly well with women who were religious (nuns) and wrote the Latin *Vulgate* translation of the Bible said when speaking of marital sex not specifically intended to procreate, "All intercourse is impure."[17] This comment offers insight into the contentious nature of pro-celibate advocates' intentions before mandatory celibacy was successfully imposed. This statement was contained in a letter concerning his bitter theological opponent, Jovinian. We have this vignette from Pagels' research into the Patristic Fathers, "Eventually another debate arose in the Christian community between Jerome and Jovinian concerning abstinence. Jovinian rejected the belief that celibate people, or people who abstained from food or wine, were holier than those who married or who enjoyed such foods. To him, so long as a person remained faithful to their baptismal vows, they could expect reward in heaven. Jerome argued bitterly against his opponent, describing the main conflict as such: 'He [Jovinian] puts marriage on a level with virginity, while I make it inferior he declares that there is little or no difference between the two states. I claim that there is a great deal. Finally... he has dared to place marriage on an equal level with perpetual chastity.'"[18] Jerome taught one morality for priests and a lesser morality for average Christians.

Jovinian, c.405 AD, had earlier been a monk who ultimately rejected asceticism, believing sexual abstinence was no better than partaking of food with the right disposition. Jovinian's writings proved to be quite powerful and effective in defense of marriage, for which he was branded a heretic by Pope Siricius, who himself had abandoned his wife and children in order to assume the papacy.

The argument by Jerome here against Jovinian is identical to that of Anti-Pope Hippolytus against Pope Callistus in 222 AD, who permitted both priestly marriage and second marriages following the loss of a spouse. Where Hippolytus failed, Jerome and the later Patristics ultimately succeeded. During this era, all Patristics favored celibate priests who by their time were being coerced into accepting chastity in many areas where a man could not be ordained otherwise. A familiar scenario exists today.

SUMMARY

We will stop here with our investigation of Patristic Fathers because things only worsened with the next few generations. Anti-Semitism, misogyny and mandatory celibacy became more thoroughly pronounced. Uncontrovertibly, historians agree that celibacy had its origin and roots in paganism from ancient societies, not from Jewish Christianity, but from yellow-capped Lammas from Tibet, ascetic hermits of Egypt, the Astarte cult of Syria, primitive worshippers of Dodona, priests of the goddess Cybele and her eunuch companion Attis, and the Vestal Virgins of ancient Rome. All of which would ultimately influence Hellenism and later through Hellenism influenced those Hellenist-Christian philosophers of whom we write.

Fortunately, these men who originally promoted celibacy had no authority over the Universal Church during their day, but it is widely known by Church historians that such a theology had already influenced most dioceses to promote celibacy as a means of setting themselves apart from and above the Laity and more importantly, establishing Christian priests as equal to the ascetic pagan priesthood. Clement taught that the communication of *true gnosis* is bound up with and limited to Holy Orders (Ordained priests) and this did lead to an increase of priests who accepted the vow of celibacy in their area; much the same way as today. It will be remembered, however, that these local impediments were not official Church teaching until 385 AD. Initial attempts to impose celibacy were merely illicit. After 450-500 AD, during the Dark Ages, these local anomalies attempting to impose celibacy would largely fail, especially in rural areas, but sporadic attempts continued in major dioceses by some Popes and bishops until celibacy was universally reestablished during the Lateran Council of 1139 AD.

Retrospectively, this misogynistic development seemed more than odd since no organized religion in human history was so influenced by women as supporters, organizers, prophets, teachers, and Christian leaders. Nothing so pro-woman had existed in

113

the foundations of Judaism, not even the women whose names appeared in the titles of Old Testament books. As we leave this discussion a point must be made that will later be explored in depth. All arguments for celibacy put forth above were based on Hellenist philosophy, not Canon Law as it is today. We have yet to see a Christian Theological warrant for mandatory celibacy. Where did these laws come from? We shall soon see.

CHRISTIAN-PAGAN CASTRATION

Since we have introduced the subject of Christian castration sanctioned by St. Justin, the practice should be further examined for its pagan roots. We have no elaboration or explanation from Justin of why his Christian friend felt his conscience sufficient to perform self-castration with the assistance of his associates, but we may look elsewhere for answers. Among the first sources of theological castration that began to appear before Christ is attributed to the cult of goddess Cybele and her companion Attis.

At the time of Justin, the goddess Cybele was viewed as the deification of the earth mother whom Zeus impregnated as she slept. From this seed was born a hermaphroditic demon who so terrorized the other gods they deemed his castration necessary. From his dismembered testicles grew an almond tree which, when eaten by the goddess Nana, impregnated her, producing a boy, Attis, with whom the goddess Cybele then fell in love. This made Attis the grandson of Cybele.

Attis, unaware of Cybele's love, fell in love with a human princess and so incensed Cybele she drove Attis insane with her jealously. Attis' madness was so severe he castrated himself and bled to death as he sat under a pine tree that protected his soul but left his flesh to decay. With this turn of events Cybele became so distraught with grief that Zeus came to her assistance, resurrecting Attis as a eunuch. So enamored then was Attis with Cybele that after his resurrection he became her companion and servant, as a eunuch.

Modern Christians unable to fathom such myths should not view them simply as aberrations; they were commonplace in the first century AD. The cult of Cybele and Attis grew wildly before Jesus' day and enjoyed a large following replete with celibate emasculated priests. However, differing from most celibate priests of that day these priests performed group castration rituals in order to emulate Attis and gain acceptance into the priesthood of Cybele. After castration, their testicles were then sacrificed upon the altar of Cybele. So ghastly were these rituals that Emperor Claudius, 41-54 AD, placed a prohibition against it, insisting future pagan high priests should be Roman citizens and could not be castrated. This did not bring an end, however, to all Cybele cult castrations. Thereafter, bulls were castrated for testicular sacrifice to Cybele. It becomes apparent from this episode why Governor Felix refused to allow Justin's Christian friend to be castrated. The Emperor had forbidden religious castration.

We introduce this subject because such practices were well imbued into the Hellenistic consciousness of that day. An inscription of 160 AD during Justin's time records how one Roman follower of Cybele, Carpus, transported a bull's testes from Rome to Cybele's shrine in Lyons, France for sacrifice. We have no direct evidence of Justin's castration.

Hellenist castration practices would continue. About one century later there arose in Rome a Christian sect that practiced self-castration, the Valesii. Little is known of this shadowy group who believed castration was necessary to their salvation. Disturbingly, it is reported they considered it their Christian duty to castrate male visitors to their monastery, including the young. Condemned by the Church little is known of them.

Later we will describe the heretical Christian sect led by Montanus who Tertullian came to follow. Both were peers of Justin. The history of Montanus identifies him as originally, before converting to Christianity, a priest of Cybele who, St. Jerome described as a *semivir* (half man, half woman) and *abscissus* (a cut one).[19]

Much later after the Patristic Fathers other such aberrations arose. In the 16th century, the *Skoptzy,* a Russian sect of castrated priests proselytized among the peasantry, promising converts that redemption would follow their sterilization.

"The fact that there are 72 eunuchs to be found in the list of Catholic Saints indicates the special place castration has earned in traditional Christianity."[20]

CHAPTER ELEVEN

LASTING CHANGE BEGINS –
THE GNOSTIC LEGACY

"In the remarkable fifty years that stretched from the generation of Marcion, Valentinus, and Tatian to that of Tertullian and Clement of Alexandria...I have been concerned with recapturing the distinctive flavor of that period in the history of Christianity which distinguished it from all subsequent centuries."
—*The Body and Society,* Peter Brown

In recent decades imminent historical scholars have described changes in Christian beliefs during its formative centuries, changes that remain with us today. Examining these changes, it is with gratitude that I cite Peter Brown's book *The Body and Society.* Confining his research to history alone and avoiding polemical discussions, Brown introduces us to an understanding not previously available. Here I will rely on his cogent description of these changes.

"Put very briefly, this was a time when leading figures in the scholarly and ecclesiastical worlds [Patristics] had come to look backward in anger on the Christian past...To them, it was the writing of major Christian authors - from the Apostle Paul in the first century to Augustine of Hippo in the fifth - that appeared to have foisted on the churches of the modern West attitudes toward women that tended permanently to demean them, and attitudes toward the body that had led, over the centuries, to a permanent suspicion (if not outright hatred) of sex.
—*The Body and Society,* Peter Brown

As we enter that period of change from the time of St. Justin Martyr's writings c.160 AD, who was first to introduce apologetic literature supporting Hellenistic-Christianity, until Augustine c.400, we will find the ascetic origins and source of infallible papal doctrines that have today returned the Church to its scandalously debauched Medieval priesthood, a time when St. Peter Damien presented his *Book of Gomorrah* to Pope Leo IX and pleaded for reform of the failing priesthood. At the turn of the first to the second century, the only Christian leader designated by Christ, His brother St. James the Just, was dead and only two Apostolic Fathers (Those who were "hearers" of an Apostle) were left. St. Ignatius of Antioch and his young friend St. Polycarp, they were independent bishops ruled over by no Church authority. At the end of the first century Jerusalem was no longer the center of Christianity, and Rome, the center of the world was attracting Christian leaders with vastly differing views to this center of influence, introducing conflicting philosophies by those who wished to define Christianity.

This was a time of expansion when the numbers of pagan converts entering Christianity increased without their understanding its Jewish-Christian foundation. The writings of St. Paul carefully instructed his disciples, "The Spirit clearly says that in later times some will abandon the faith and follow deceiving spirits and things taught by demons. Such teachings come through hypocritical liars, they forbid people to marry and order them to abstain from certain foods, which God created to be received with thanksgiving by those who believe and who know the truth...Have nothing to do with pointless philosophical discussions and *agnostic* beliefs of *the 'knowledge'*, which is not knowledge at all." 1Timothy 4:1, 6:20. Early in the second century, however, Paul's teaching was largely rejected by "agonistic" philosophers who introduced the pantheistic belief of two Gods. An evil Jewish God was introduced as a foil of the benevolent God of Christ. Looking back to earlier Hellenistic myths for an understanding of Jesus of Nazareth, Gnosticism revisited earlier mythical gods and saw the *Christ* who merely appeared to be human, and to a benevolent heavenly hierarchy that would later be rejected by the new generation of Platonic and Stoic philosophers. While individually different Gnostic teachers conflicted with each other, they would firmly establish an ascetic Hellenistic philosophy.

GNOSTIC CONFLICT

Although Christianity had established outposts across much of the Empire from Persia to Western Europe, the Christian movement remained primarily in the Eastern Mediterranean area until late in the second century. During that period many Gnostic converts became Bishops capable of establishing individual and differing belief systems, which is best illustrated by the conflicting views of Marcion and Tatian.

Early Christian groups and communities followed the "spiritual leader" of their own choosing, leaders they expected to exude a charismatic superiority above the laity and to possess the "divine gift" of teaching. The Gnostic Marcion fulfilled all expectations. A wealthy ship owner, he was ordained by his bishop father and is known to have bought himself into an elevated Church status with huge sums of money from his shipping business. Firmly established as an independent bishop, Marcion conceived his own scripture, *Gospel of the Lord,* a gospel based on selective writings from the Gospel of Luke that was then in circulation, but considered merely another version of Christ's teaching. Marcion believed there could be only one true gospel, all others being fabrications by pro-Jewish elements determined to sustain a devout worship of *Yahweh,* believing these same pro-Jewish elements to also have corrupted the Pauline epistles. Drawing many followers to his ascetic teaching Marcion taught a strident dualism of spirit and matter, teaching the evil "Creator God" was the God of Jewish Law that intended to constrain society during this "present age," thus separating humans. And, believing Christ "surprisingly appeared" merely to free humans from Jewish Law, Marcion, a *Docetic*, taught Jesus of Nazareth appeared in human form only to set humanity free from Jewish Law.

Throughout the Mediterranean world Marcionites first settled in close knit sectarian communities, all of whom renounced marriage in a manner similar, some suggest, to the early American "Shakers." Thriving by taking in children from poor families unable to sustain themselves, Marcionites endured for centuries, ulti-

118

mately establishing themselves near populated areas where they continued to succeed.

Tatian however, an ascetic Christian-Bishop d. 180AD, was first a student of the Patristic St. Justin Martyr, and later a follower of Valentinus; a peer of Marcion they differed greatly. Although both required complete sexual abstinence, their meaning of abstinence was quite different. Differing from Marcion's belief that the evil "Creator God of the Jews" was the problem, Tatian approached salvation differently. Tatian's belief in the union of weak humans with the Holy Spirit permeated his teaching. He believed: "Man is not, as the croaking philosophers say, merely a rational animal... Man alone is in the image and likeness of God: but by "man" I mean not one who performs actions similar to those of animals, but one who has advanced beyond such mere humanity - to God Himself...For the Spirit of God is not with all, but takes up its abode with those who love righteousness , and intimately combined with the soul... [such ones] have attached themselves to that cognate Spirit."[1] For Tatian, all sex was animalistic and contrary to the will of God.

Tatian's followers came to be known as *Encratites* (Continence) who were famous for challenging all differing Christian beliefs. The Encratites declared the Christian Church must consist of men and women who were "continent" in the strictest sense. They had constrained to have sexual intercourse with each other. And to this basic continence the Encratites demanded ascetic dietary restraints, the abstention from meat and from drinking wine. "These abstentions were intimately linked to the constitutive act of sexual renunciation: for the eating of meat was held to link human beings to the wild, carnivorous nature of animals, as intercourse linked them to the sexual nature of brute beasts. Furthermore, wine was a known source of sexual energy - 'for wine imparts warmth to the nerves, sooths the soul, recalls pleasure, engenders seamen, and provokes to Vinery.'"[2] There were some among the Encratites' disciples who ascribed Adam and Eve's original loss of the Spirit as being directly linked to a sexual act. A true ascetic, for Tatian there was no difference between adultery and marriage.

Other than being an Assyrian and student of Justin Martyr in Justin's Alexandrian School for Catechumens little is known of Tatian. He was, however, an important Christian and renowned in many areas. Tatian wrote *Diatessaron,* described as a "harmony" of the four Gospels, but he puts the text in a new and different sequence. Believing the four gospels differ from one another, Tatian resolved what he considered to be "contradictions" by omitting what he believed to be contradictory. His "harmony" does not include Jesus' encounter with the adulteress John 7:53– 8:11, a passage he believed to be a spurious later addition to the Gospel of John. This harmony became the standard text for the gospels in Syriac-speaking churches down to the 5th century, attracting many Christians.

During the second, and even into the third century, Gnostics such as the competing prophet Mani (Manichaeism) of Iran and other Gnostic sects established missionary movements surpassing the first generation Christians. As St. Paul said, "So then faith comes by hearing, and hearing by the word of God" Romans 10:17. For these Gnostics the heretics were those who professed Christ to be merely a human man, and until the third century they were the most successful missionaries across the Roman Empire.

APOCRYPHA, ASCETICISM AND WOMEN

It was from such men as Marcion, Titian and other writers, many of who remain unknown, that the Christian landscape was changed with apocryphal acts, gospels and epistles. Primarily from Syrian sources these writings began to *change* the teachings of Christ who taught, "A man must leave his father and mother and cling to his wife, and the two shall become one body." The Gnostics believed that married "intercourse linked them to the sexual nature of brute beasts." Christianity, with no central authority capable of understanding and challenging the Hellenistic-Gnostic Apocrypha, the Deposit of Faith began to change. Until the New Testament was recognized late in the fourth century and mythical Gnosticism exposed, apocryphal writings dominated the Christian landscape. This is an important change that many modern Christians have come to understand. To better illustrate these changes over time, no apocrypha demonstrates its lasting influence than *The Acts of Paul and Thecla.*

Toward the beginning of Christianity's succumbing to the ascetic movement an illustrative incident occurred in Turkey. A priest of the shrine of Saint Thecla expanded the original version of a second century apocryphal book, *The Acts of Paul and Thecla.* This book describes the rejection by a woman, St. Thecla, of her betrothed lover, Thamyris. Originally written in the second century when many Christians continued to expect the imminent return of Jesus, some withdrew to asceticism and prayer to await His return. It was these devout ascetics who began a semi-Gnostic strain of complete sexual abstinence. This abstinence was not intended merely for priests, it was directed to all Christians. The story of Thecla was originally written during the period in which the Stoic convert St. Justin Martyr wrote.

These "acts" presents St. Paul and a female companion, Thecla, as they travel from city to city preaching, "those who seek salvation must observe a life of perpetual virginity," and with virginity the abandonment of marriage. Thecla, a noble virgin, described as a wealthy woman listened to Paul's "discourse on virginity" from her window, and being enraptured with Paul's message she abandoned her suitor, Thamyris, shaved her head, baptized herself and became the follower and co-worker of Paul. Highly influential, this apocryphal book spread widely across the Empire gaining many adherents.

The rejected lover Thamyris sought relief from the local governor for what he termed "A new teaching, bizarre and disrupted to the human race...We know that [Paul and Thecla] deprive young men of their intended wives, and virgins of their intended husbands, by teaching, there can be no future resurrection, unless you continue in chastity and do not defile your flesh."[3] However, a century later in the fourth century the aspect of women such as Thecla associating with St. Paul as an associate preacher would be intolerable, requiring a different explanation of her "false" teaching.

That a book of the nature of Paul and Thecla would first appear at an early time in the second century should not be viewed as unusual. Judaism and Christianity had separated and Christianity

121

was slowly developing a priesthood that would erect a wall of division between clergy and laity in the Church, and most prominently, against women. What is informative in the book is its continued importance over nearly three centuries during the formative years of Christianity. It spans the century of change since the Gnostics of the early second century until the Sacerdotal Priesthood began to develop in the fourth century. In 160 AD clerics, most of who were married were encouraged, but not required to practice celibacy, but at the beginning of the fifth century when the new expanded version of Thecla's teachings appeared, priests would be required to abandon their wives and practice ascetic celibacy. Still, the Acts of Paul and Thecla continued to have a place within Christian circles at a time when the New Testament made no mention of Christian priests.

Other changes came, the father as family head responsible for selecting a suitable husband for his daughter had passed. Christianity was experiencing rapid growth while keeping their distance from the outside world. Marriage to Jews, pagans and heretics were shunned, resulting in many virgin daughters unable to find a suitable husband, prompting many young women to choose perpetual continence to the delight of their revered clergy; and supporting universal continence for all Christians other Apocrypha appeared enticing young men to remain celibate. Appearing before 200 AD the apocryphal *Acts of John the Evangelist* became widely popular as it describes perpetual chastity, not merely for females but for all. A powerful book that influenced Christianity, it circulated widely, introducing perpetual celibacy for males in the same manner as the young man in the Acts of John who prayed to Christ, "Thou who hast kept me also till this present hour pure for Thyself and untouched by union of a Woman; Who, when I wished to marry in my youth, didst appear to myself and say...John, if thou weren't mine, I should have allowed thee to marry,"[4] thereby describing Christ as an Hellenistic ascetic

CHAPTER 12

LASTING CHANGE COMPLETED – THE PATRISTIC LEGACY

"They are described as Fathers of the Church — wrote John Paul II in his Apostolic Letter 'Patres Ecclesiae' (1980) – ascribed to those saints who with the strength of their faith, and the profundity and richness of their teachings, have influenced and changed the course of the first centuries.
The fourth and fifth centuries were the golden age of patristic writing."
—*Fathers of the Church*

THE PATRISTIC PHILOSOPHERS

The landscape of Christianity was changing once more during the third century. From c.150 AD until the late in the fourth century the arrival of Platonic and Stoic scholars would replace Gnostic asceticism with true Hellenistic asceticism, as it remains today. With the arrival of Patristic philosopher-bishops' Gnostic myths of a "flesh covered" Christ, a new Heavenly Hierarchy would be replaced by a more scholarly mythology. Understanding the original philosophies of Plato and the Stoics allows us to understand the origin of our modern ascetic doctrines.

Stoicism. "The underlying principle of Stoicism was based on a "natural Law" which Stoics taught regulated and controlled all persons and events. In order for humanity to be happy it was necessary to be in harmony with this natural law. Stoics were a practical people, and while not given to speculation for its own sake they had a well-conceived system to explain the world and its ways. "For Stoics, God was an integral force *within* the world which held the world together and directed its operation.

Pantheism played no part in Stoicism. God was a rational spirit which produced material creation and subsisted *in* this creation. God was not separate from the world, He was the vital *soul* of the world...that is, they believed everything was part of one and the same ultimate *substance*: God."[1] Therefore, God is not transcendent! As absurd as these beliefs may be for modern Christians, try and imagine how pagans imbued during their life with these beliefs viewed the New Testament. For Stoics the ultimate goal was to become godlike through the practice of virtues such as intelligence, justice, bravery and, especially, self-control.

Stoic teaching believed the motivating force behind creation was the *Logos*. This Logos, which they define as God the creator, was the actual "stuff" of God existing in all matter. The only way to obtain harmony with nature and thus God was to become attuned to this Logos.[2] This term, *Logos,* with a fuller Christian meaning was used by St. John; it   appears in the New Testament as the *"Word"*(Logos) John 1:1 "In the beginning was the *Word*"

Platonism. Plato, c. 350 BC, was the most influential philosopher affecting pagan thought of Christ's time and his thinking was in nearly every philosophical system then in vogue. Plato was convinced of the impossibility of reforming the human character and therefore distinguished between the philosophical (elite) mind of some, and the "brutish" mind of the masses. Consequently, he predicted a better fate lay in store for the elite. Contrary to the Stoics who were *monotheists* (All is one), Plato was a monotheist who believed God and the world to be separate. God was the absolute and ultimate transcendent reality, above and beyond the world of the senses...In order to 'arrange' the world, he did not believe in creation from nothing, thus God employs a "craftsman" known as a *Demiurge;* a concept prominent in Valentinus' heavenly hierarchy.

Plato was convinced that the Supreme Being was hard to find and impossible to describe to the masses. They must therefore be content with visible gods and heavenly bodies. For Plato the world was simply a changing shadow based on the real world which exists in the mind of the *One,* and remains unchanging. In other words the further removed we are from the One the more materialistic we are.

124

"The single pagan thesis that underlies all the rest is that at the hierarchical top of the universe there is an abstract entity - variously called the *Infinite Spirit,* the *First Principle,* the *Original Mover* or the *One* - in whose spiritual substance all other spirits participate (or exist), including the human soul. In other words, God, for the pagan world was an "it," and the thought of a loving God was not only unthinkable, it was repugnant making it difficult for pagan scholars to worship a Jewish carpenter. "How can one admit," asks Porphyry in his *Against the Christians* (frag. 77) "that the divine should become an embryo, that after his birth he is put in swaddling clothes, that he is soiled with blood, bile, and worse things yet?"

One must imagine how Jewish-Christianity would have received these philosophies following three centuries of occupation by the Greeks, but understanding them will assist in understanding the Patristic Fathers.

PATRISTIC PHILOSOPHERS WEAKEN GNOSTICISM

"The patristic early fathers called the Gnostic writings textually inferior because they contained blasphemies and heresies. But perhaps the very texts against which they felt they must vigorously defend the faith were simply providing another lens for viewing fledgling Christianity. For the young Christian church with its patristic views and an emerging male hierarchy, Mary Magdalene presented something of a conundrum."[3]

—Meera Lester, *Textual Inferiority or Just Different*

Things had changed since the time of House-Churches when the Eucharist was a communal worship service often led by women such as those of 111 AD whom we discussed, and women such as Priscilla, a co-worker with Paul, and wife of Aquila, who taught Apollos Acts 18:26 Romans 16:3; 1 Corinthians 16:19; 2 Timothy 4:19. One wonders why the wife Priscilla is always named first. We remember in *Romans* Paul mentions Phoebe, a "minister" or "deacon" from Cenchreae Romans 16: 1. We have Junia Romans 16:7 who is a relative of Paul whom he describes as an "Apostle." There was also Mary and the mother of Rufus, both prominent members of the Roman church Rom 16:6, 13, and Chloe, who was a "leader" of a church community in Corinth 1 Cor 1:11. The earliest Jerusalem church met in the house of Mary, the mother of John Mark Acts 12:12. All this occurred at a time when there were no Christian priests as defined today.[4]

But still, the Patristics cherished St. Paul's preaching: "Let women *learn* in silence with all subjection, *I* do not give permission for a woman to teach or to tell a man what to do because Adam was formed first and Eve afterwards, and Adam was not led astray, but the woman who was led astray fell into sin. Nevertheless, she will be saved by childbearing." 1 Timothy 2:12 (We have pointed out that in that instance Paul spoke as a Pharisee whose tradition opposed women teachers. It was not a Jewish Law, neither contained in the Torah nor preached by Jesus. However, by the end of the fourth century St. Ambrose wrote "Remember, God took the rib out of Adam's body, not a part of his soul, to make her. She was not made in the image of God, like man...The Ministerial Office must be kept pure and unspoiled and must not be defiled by coitus."[5] Since the first century the seduction of women had increasingly been viewed as the first threat to salvation.

Within fifty years after Thecla first appeared, the Church was no longer a Jewish sect when Jesus "appears and speaks" to a young man as recorded in the apocryphal *Acts of John* saying: "John, if thou wert not mine, I should have allowed you to marry."[6] Appearing at a time when the New Testament was not recognized, this popular teaching was quite different from Jesus Himself who said, "For this reason a man will leave his father and mother and be united to his wife, and the two will become one flesh" Matthew 19:5

During this century of change followers of the ascetic preacher Tatian had gone so far as to contend the Christian church must consist of men and women who were not only continent, they were to abstain from meat and from wine. The eating of meat was held to link human beings to the wild carnivorous nature of animals, as intercourse linked then to the sexual nature of brute beast. Further, wine was known as a source of sexual energy which imparts warmth to the nerves and engenders semen[7], a belief that lingers today among some Christians. Additionally,

charismatic Gnostic teachers had successfully developed followers whose principle doctrine held the human soul initially possessed faith in one God, but lost it with the fall of Eve, a result
of the alien "animal" world into which the serpent first led Eve.
This belief, that the fall of Eve originally separated man from God
would be expanded by the Patristics.

APPROACHING THE FOURTH CENTURY

An incident described by Peter Brown in *Body and Society*
occurred late in the third century explaining a new situation in
Christianity; no longer was religion merely for the old. For the
first time in its history Christianity had become a religion of the
young, not merely for the old. About 295 AD parents, Aurelius and
Aurelia, mourned the death of their unmarried daughter Ammia
with ancient phrases "How is it you died...already before the brid-
al crown...snatched out of time, deprived of the marriage bed?"
An answer came within eight days when Ammia appeared in a
dream, "Weep not afflicted father, or thou mother, to die is common, but my Savior, Christ has joined me to the righteous. At the
Presbyter's hand I received baptism, virginities lawful prerogative;
I came to heaven a pure virgin...having life eternal among the holy
ones...My slothful father and sluggard mother sought to frighten
me...For by espousing my virginity to Christ I brought them sor-
row insufferable."[8] For two centuries Gnostics had successfully
instilled a fear of sex, not merely fornication, but sex of all nature,
including marriage. At the turn of that century marriage itself was
threatened in some areas, primarily in the Latin west.

No longer was it expected of the parents to protect their
children from falling into fornication by marrying them off at an
early age; nor was it solely the responsibility of the father. Fearing
sexual sin parents, from their children's pre-pubescent youth,
taught them to be the "keeper" of their own soul. But in many
areas, even in large communities, Christianity was a marginalized
and often a persecuted minority. The prohibition of marriage to
Jews, pagans or heretics limited young men and women. It was
a time when the *Acts of John,* promoting male celibacy became
an onerous burden, severely limiting opportunities for youthful
marriage. Again, in this environment young girls often choose

perpetual virginity that was strongly encouraged by the clergy. Many young men in areas where bishops demanded celibacy increased the priesthood. This was also a time when church hierarchies encouraged celibacy for all. Bishops supporting celibacy six years later during the Synod of Elvira, Spain, where ascetic celibacy was observed by that dioceses' independent bishops, the Synod's canon 33 enjoined celibacy upon all clerics, married or not, and all who minister at the altar. At this council, thirty-four of its eighty-one rulings were on matters regarding marriage and illicit sex. A full one fourth of all their edicts instituted greater control of women in the Christian community.[9] However, not being a universal edict this isolated Synod had no effect on other dioceses, but times were changing.

This change among the young and increasing pressure from ruling clerics brought about a new template for Christian leaders. Following Origen's model of powerful men with public skill and leadership as Christian leaders, a new acceptance of celibacy became necessary in most dioceses in order to secure leadership and authority among Christians. Only a man capable of having shown "virginal continence" in his personal life should possess such power.[10]

In major communities virginity was brought into the service of its bishops, but where Origen's support groups had been selected from "spiritual" men and women, the selection of women would by then be unimaginable by powerful bishops. Bishops treated their own subservient priesthood as men of rank such as later feudal lords. Bishops would not treat women as partners in Christ. "Virgins," who now submitted to clerical leadership were from well-to do families, a crucial matter. Their wealth was to be used only for the Church, both for helping the destitute and securing the bishops' authority among his competitors, as would any politician today. For Bishop Cyprian of Carthage "The virgins [who were] warned in his preemptory manner came from the wealthy families. It was a crucial matter to Cyprian that the considerable wealth should be used only to support the Christian poor; it must not be brought to bear in any way to put pressure on the clergy."[11]

Brides of Christ

"Now concerning Virgins, I have no message from the Lord."
—St. Paul to the Corinthians. First Corinthians 7:25

Within two decades after the Elvira Council, Constantine legalized and accepted Christianity in order to bring this growing and important movement into his service, as expressed by Bishop Athanasius in his letter to the Emperor Constantius II, *Apologia ad Constantium,* "The son of God, our Lord and Savior Jesus Christ, having become man for our sake...that we should possess upon earth, in the state of virginity, a picture of the holiness of angels. Accordingly, such as have attained this virtue the Catholic Church has been accustomed to calling *the Brides of Christ*...For indeed, this holy and heavenly *profession* is nowhere established, but only among us Christians." Control over the marital prospects of these young women was absolute, and often devious, but, "However much Christian authors wrote, in Platonic terms, of the innate love for virginity that stirred at the bottom of the heart of every Christian child, such children were seldom free agents."[12] She was no longer a woman nor was she a nun; she had become a "sacred vessel dedicated to the Lord."

Initially it was difficult for bishops to protect and control adolescent girls of marriageable age from protective families who were capable of nullifying their daughter's vow. However, mature dedicated women who were often from wealthy families or were wealthy widows, came to be thought of as controlling wealth prized by these bishops and considered by all Christians as precious. Many women with ascetic *professions* emerged in the upper class where there wealth and prestige made an impact on the Christian church, thus establishing an authoritative position of importance in a patriarchal society, but still relegated to womanhood. So important and valuable were these "sacred vessels" that the Christian Manichaean polemists of North Africa attacked the Roman clergy, pointing out that while they claimed marriage was instituted by God, what they preached most fervently was virginity: "You always strive to out-do each other in pursuing girls to adopt this vocation, to such an extent that in every church there is almost a greater number of virgins than married women."[13]

This change will assist women who wish to establish a "presence" of importance.

LOOKING BACK

During the period from 70 AD when both Christians and Jews dispersed, until 160 AD when Justin Martyr introduced Hellenistic-Christian apologia, both experienced traumatic change. Jews were somewhat more fortunate. Since the Babylon Captivity of c. 500 BC Jews were established in the *Diaspora* (Dispersed) and remained under leadership of the rabbis, thus maintaining their ancient beliefs in a different environment. By the end of the first century, however, the first generation of Jewish-Christian leadership had changed. Only a few Apostolic Fathers who had "heard" one of the Apostles remained. The Apostles were gone and non-Jewish converts were now admitted into Christianity with no understanding of Christianity's Jewish foundation.

At the beginning of the second century, after the Deposit of Faith was closed, Platonic asceticism had been rejected by Apostolic Fathers such as Bishop Ignatius of Antioch, the third bishop of Antioch after St. Peter; he was a "hearer" of Apostle St. John. Sentenced to death in the Roman Arena, Ignatius wrote eight letters to Christian communities as he traveled to Rome. One letter was to his young bishop friend Polycarp. Repeating the teaching of Paul, Ignatius condemned those who boasted of their asceticism when he wrote "Speak to my sisters that they love the Lord, and to be satisfied with their husbands both in the *flesh* and *spirit*. In like manner also, exhort my brethren, in the name of Jesus Christ, that they love their wives, even as the Lord loves the Church–If anyone can continue in a state of purity [celibacy], to the honor of Him who is *Lord of the flesh*, let him so remain without boasting. If he begins to boast, he is undone; and if he reckons himself greater than the bishop, he is ruined. But it becomes both men and women who marry, to form their union with the approval of the bishop that their marriage may be according to God."[14]

Here, shortly after the Deposit of Faith had closed, St. Ignatius preaches Christ's teaching on celibacy: "let those accept who can", for both men and women Matthew 19:12, while at the same time demeaning the belief that asceticism of the *flesh* is superior to marriage. Additionally, by identifying the *flesh* of Christ, which we are to honor, he also demeans Gnostic beliefs that Christ is a god clothed in human flesh. The term "priest" does not appear in Ignatius' writing, nor will we find the term priest associated with Christianity until late in the third century when ascetic beliefs permeated Christianity. But Christianity was to change by the end of the second century when women were taught to reject the flesh, becoming "brides of Christ" and men were to thank Christ in prayer for "Thou who hast till this present time kept me pure for thyself"

By the end of the first century the Apostles had traveled throughout the Empire and beyond, spreading Apostolic teaching while following Jesus' admonition: "Teach them to observe all things whatsoever I have commanded you" Matthew 28:20. This mission was accomplished as St. Paul explained: "This good news must be preached! How then shall they call on Him in whom they have not believed? And how shall they believe in Him of whom they have not heard? And how shall they hear without a *preacher*? And how shall they *preach* unless they are sent? As it is written: 'How beautiful are the feet of those who preach the gospel of peace, who bring glad tidings of good things!' So then faith *comes by hearing*, and hearing by the word of God" Romans 10:14-17.

By the end of the second century the "preachers" had changed. Gnostics such as Montanus, formerly a castrated priest of Goddess Cybele, Tatian from Assyria, Valentinus of Rome who had nearly become Pope, and Mani of Iran, and others, had established missionaries across the Empire that dwarfed the previous apostolic missionaries of Christ. So much so that ascetic beliefs became secure, until the Patristics arrived with their scholarly asceticism separating Christ from the Old Testament. Until 385 AD the ascetic "law for celibacy" did not exist and many clerics remained married men. In an earlier time the Bishop "Polycrates of Ephesus 200 AD belonged to a family in which he was the eighth Christian bishop, in which 'the traditions of St. John were yet fresh in men's minds'"[15] But later, we will find Pope Siricius was required to abandoned his wife in order to accept the Papacy in 384 AD.

At the end of the fourth century other changes had occurred. Based solely on documents such as the *Didascalia* and *The*

131

Apostolic Constitutions, which in turn were based on apocryphal literature of the second century; ascetic celibacy will become an "Ancient Christian Tradition."

CHAPTER THIRTEEN

APOCRYPHA BECOMES TRADITION

"Didascalia Apostolorum (or Didascalia) is a Christian treatise which belongs to the genre of the Church Orders. It presents itself as being written by the Twelve Apostles at the time of the Council of Jerusalem, however, scholars agree that it was actually a composition of the 3rd century, perhaps around 230 AD. The earliest mention of this work is by Epiphanius of Salamis, who believed it to be truly Apostolic. The author is unknown, but he was probably a bishop. The provenience is usually regarded as Northern Syria.[1]

—Wiki Encyclopedia

The epigraph above describes a document composed in the third century, two hundred years after Christ, by an unknown author. Today it is considered the most plausible document supporting the alleged *tradition* of apostolic celibacy during the life of Christ and His Apostles. From our youth as Catholics we are taught the Apostles' abandoned conjugal relationship with their wives, freeing them from all earthly responsibility in order to "Act in the place of Jesus" as celibate men. Today the Vatican assures us this Apostolic *discipline* began the priestly *tradition* of sexual continence, insisting this discipline is *not an impediment* to the Doctrines of Christ. However, it is only natural that a question is asked by those seeking the origin of our faith: what historical proof, not contained in the Deposit of Faith, supports the truth of Apostolic celibacy? Having diligently searched for historical documentation and finding none contained in the Deposit of Faith it was illuminating to read a transparent history of the Didascalia, presented by Peter Brown in his book *The Body and Society*. There we find that this ancient document that would change

Christianity developed over a period of two centuries, from 160 AD until its completion c. 375 AD before reaching its present form, as described below by Brown.[2]

"It is difficult for a modern reader to enter into the intensity of the *didaskaleion,* of the small study-circles of male and female disciples that would gather for years on end around a single spiritual guide."[3]. Initially, these widely dispersed "study-circles" began during a time when the New Testament was not yet recognized and separated from other writings, or believed to have any sacred authority over the sea of apocryphal Acts, Gospels and Epistles composed during the second and third centuries, which were accepted at the time by most Christians to be as authoritative as the New Testament. With no clear understanding of which "Christian" literature was most authoritative and informative, the "...well to do Christians of the second century took it for granted that their spiritual growth depended on close, face to face consultation with beloved teachers. A Christian bishop traveled regularly from Cappadocia to Palestine 'in order to deepen his spiritual life, by setting at the feet of the great Origen...many serious Christians were convinced that only through prolonged, intimate contact with a spiritual guide, and not through the somewhat jejune preaching of the clergy in church would the 'dead coals of sacred learning come to glow again.'"[4] Providing a vehicle for ascetic teaching, no commentary better describes the confusion among various study-circles that ultimately led to the intrusion of Apocryphal beliefs confronting us today.

For modern Christians to gain insight into these Didascalia study-circles is to compare the growth of Protestantism through its *"scripture alone* Bible study circles" as they strove to more clearly understand their views of Christ's teaching based only on the New Testament. Having rejected most Sacraments, which they considered to be a tool of Vatican authority controlled only by the Catholic hierarchy, Protestants disagreed with Catholicism. And, just as "Christians had disagreed profoundly with each other since the days of St. Paul," so too would later Protestant leaders such as Martin Luther, Joseph Campbell and John Calvin, all of whom accepted "Scripture alone," these men would differ from each other's beliefs as did the Christian "study-circles." While

Protestants preached "Salvation by faith alone," based on their understanding of New Testament texts, Didascalia study-groups would belabor the text of Apocrypha such as *The Acts of Paul and Thecla* calling for all Christians to remain virgins, even to the act of abandoning sex with their spouses. We are now taught the Apostles abandoned sex with their spouses, a belief now rejected by historians who believe St. Peter and his wife Perpetua produced a child, Petronella, after the death of Jesus and were imprisoned and executed in Rome thirty seven years after the crucifixion of Christ. Today we are asked to believe both Peter and Perpetua mutually agreed to accept ascetic chastity.

Originally conceived by pagan teachers before Christianity appeared, the *didaskaleion* study-circles were first used by the Gnostic Valentinus c. 137 AD with great success. Becoming the most popular spiritual guide in Rome he nearly became Bishop of Rome. But, "It was, indeed, Justin, a man accustomed to the intellectual in fighting of pagan schools of philosophy, who may well have been the first to introduce the notion into Christian literature." It was only natural that competition between spiritual guides and their competitors such as the Patristics Clement of Alexandria, Origen and Anti-Pope Hippolytus who vilified Pope Callistus c.222 AD for admitting married men into the priesthood. Hippolytus was a driving force of Hellenist ascetic teaching. Ultimately it would be powerful clerics such as the Patristics who claimed to speak for the "Great Church," often alleging heretical beliefs of competing leaders. Ultimately establishing the "Christian norm" throughout the Church these competing groups, all working from the same apocryphal literature, became "powerhouses" of Christian culture and thought during the second and third century. "As the Christian *Didascalia* matured the "competitive spirit" of individual Christian teachers (sages) allied with pre-existing pagan and [Hellenistic] Jewish sects [such as Philo of Alexandria] to introduce alien doctrines into the Church."[5]

With arrival of the Gnostics, and later the Patristics in the third century, all strove to separate Jesus of Nazareth from His Jewish origin, and from women. Some relied on apocryphal writings such as The *Gospel of Thomas* which said: "Simon Peter said to them, 'Let Mary [Magdalene] leave us, for women are not worthy of life'.

In this Apocrypha Jesus said 'I myself shall lead her and make her male.'" This became an important text in many areas. Ultimately the Didascalia and their leaders would prevail, primarily by separating Jesus of Nazareth from His Jewish nature when He taught: "Have you not read that the creator from the beginning made them male and female, and that He said, 'For this reason a man must leave his father and mother, and cling to his wife, and the two shall become one body.'" Matthew 19:4 Thus, study-circles introduced ascetic Apocrypha into the New Testament. From such second century Apocrypha women were often denigrated, as was Eve, by men, who would cite: "For it is semen, when possessed of vitality, which makes us men, hot, well braced in limbs, heavy, well voiced, strong to think and act...Women by contrast were failed males, the creator had purposely made one half the whole race imperfect, as it were, mutilated."[6]

After 200 AD the role of women had changed somewhat. Encouraged to be continent and urged to remain widows after the death of their first husband they were welcomed into Christian *Didascalia* study groups. However, the biological fact that menstruation occurred disqualified them from participating in rituals or approaching the Eucharistic Altar, because it was impossible for women to control their biological time table. During the second and third century a strict division between the clergy and the laity did not prevent "dedicated women" of means from participating in the Didascalia with celibate men. However, in 320 AD Emperor Licinius, fearing the seductiveness of females, harassed the Churches in the Eastern provinces. By law he enjoined men from appearing in company with women in houses of prayer, and forbade women to attend sacred schools of virtue or to be instructed by bishops. By that late date women were marginalized and the Didascalia was essentially complete and accepted as authentic Christian history.

The *Didascalia* is presented today as an *orthodox* source of early Christianity, and is described as "Church Order composed according to recent investigations in the first part, perhaps even the first decades of the third century, for a community of Christian converts from paganism in the northern part of Syria...and [it] forms the main source of the first six books of the

Apostolic Constitutions."[7] [These six books] which, are taken verbatim from the Didascalia and presented as legitimate Christian *traditions,* including *"The Doctrine of the Twelve Apostles...* [containing] The Epistle of Pseudo-Barnabas...in which Clement of Alexandria, Origen, the author of the *Apostolic Constitutions* had quoted or embodied fragments of it in their works."[8]

These three Church documents were completed c. 375 AD and include the earliest ascetic beliefs from the original Didascalia that are rarely known today by the Catholic faithful. They were ascetically inspired teachings that would later become doctrines of the Catholic Church denying Sacramental Matrimony for clerics of all rank, and misogynistic disenfranchisement of women from the Eucharistic table. So the question is answered, there are no suggestions, overt or covert, contained within the Deposit of Faith that the Apostles abandoned their wives, thus violating the Sacrament of Matrimony as it is infallibly taught today. Only by reaching into second and third century Apocrypha will the Church find "proof" of Apostolic celibacy. While these beliefs were accepted by many Christian leaders of the second and third centuries, they were individual beliefs not official Church Doctrines of that time. These changes will later lead us to three conflicting infallible papal doctrines that transformed the Christian Church. As we proceed we will identify several papal changes inserted into the Deposit of Faith from second century Apocrypha nullifying the teachings of Christ.

A brief chronological review of these changes may assist those who are reading of these second and third century changes for the first time.

AFTER **100 AD**

"After 100 AD, Christianity lost the sunny rapture of its first days. It denied its Jewish heritage and, instead, allied itself with the alienated intelligentsia of the declining Greco-Roman world. For centuries, Greek philosophers had warned healthy men and women that their bodies were, in reality, a tomb. Now, with the increasing spread of Christianity, between the second and third centuries, what had been a

137

countercultural dream of a few unsettled souls became the icy night-mare of entire populations."

—*The Body and Society.* Peter Brown

As Christianity dispersed across the Roman Empire during the second century they carried with them Jesus' teaching permitting any Christian who wished to freely accept celibacy "for the Kingdom of Heaven" to remain unmarried, "let those accept who will." The phrase *"Kingdom of Heaven"* defies brief explanation, but it does not mean a place somewhere away from here i.e., the eternal abode of God. Fundamentally it means the reign of God in this world which God created and "so loved." Both of these teachings will be changed. With the second century intrusion of ascetic philosophies these teachings of Christ would be the first and most important changes. As we enter the second century we find: "The North African Tertullian, c. 160 – c. 225, writing of the apostles, indicated that he was *obliged* to believe that...the apostles were continent."[9] With Tertullian's comment here we find the first recorded instance of a Patristic interpreting the New Testament in a manner expressing his own ascetic view. We know that all married Apostles honored their wedding vows.

For the first time in Christian literature the *Didascalia Apostolorum*, written in Greek in the first half of the 3rd century, mentions the requirements of chastity on the part of both the bishop and his wife, and of the children being already brought up when it quotes 1 Timothy 3:2–4 as requiring that before someone is ordained a bishop, enquiry must be made "whether he be *chaste*, and whether his wife also be a believer and *chaste*; and whether he *has* brought up his children in the fear of God".[10] With this requirement the entire family, including the children of a newly ordained "president" *(episcopos)* were compelled to practice ascetic chastity for life. No such requirement existed in the Deposit of Faith.

And later, "The consequence of the requirement from higher clerics who lived in marriages to abstain permanently from sexual intercourse with their wives was [also] prohibition for those who were single of entering a marriage after ordination. *The Apostolic Canons* of the *Apostolic Constitutions* decreed that only lower clerics might still marry after their ordination. Bishops, priests, and deacons were not allowed." [To marry][11]. These documents were advanced by later ascetic bishops in support of their ascetic beliefs, "Jerome referred in *Against Jovinianus* to marriage prohibition for priests when he argued that Peter and the other apostles had been married, but had married before they were called and subsequently gave up their marital relations."[12]

However, "There is record of a number of third-century married bishops in good standing. They included: Passivus, bishop of Fermo; Cassius, bishop of Narni; Aetherius, bishop of Vienne; Aquilinus, bishop of Évreux; Faron, bishop of Meaux; Magnus, bishop of Avignon. Filibaud, bishop of Aire-sur-l'Adour, was the father of St. Philibert de Jumièges, and Sigilaicus, bishop of Tours, was the father of St. Cyran of Brenne."[13]

THE APOSTOLIC CONSTITUTIONS

"The Apostolic Constitutions is a Christian collection of eight treatises which belongs to genre of the Church Orders. The work can be dated from 375 to 380 AD. The provenience is usually regarded as Syria, probably Antioch. The author is unknown. The Apostolic Constitutions contains eight treatises on Early Christian discipline, worship, and doctrine, intended to serve as a manual of guidance for the clergy, and to some extent for the laity. It purports to be the work of the Twelve Apostles, whose instructions, whether given by them as individuals or as a body. Books 1 to 6 are a free re-wording of the Didascalia Apostolorum."
Apostolic Constitutions, Wikipedia[14]
—The Search for the Origins of Christian Worship[15]

With acceptance of the Apostolic Constitutions, "The Great Church" of Constantine formally accepted the ascetic belief that the "body is the prison of the soul," threatening one's salvation as first introduced by the Gnostics. In fairness to those leaders who accepted this teaching it should be noted they were merely man-made doctrines (Authoritative Doctrines), not infallible doctrines that would have disproved the concept of Church or Papal infallibility. For over three centuries the superiority of ascetic philosophies taught by hierarchical Church leaders became a means to climb the ecclesiastical ladder, requiring only that they not be married or were prepared to abandon their spouse. Many however, chose to remain in a lower rank that permitted marriage. Anti-Catholic accusations over the centuries have gone so far as to teach this belief threatens one's soul, wrongly criticizing faithful Christians who merely followed their leaders as do Protestants and Jews, as well as Catholics.

We must remember as we go forward that Jewish-Christians also followed their leaders, as St. Paul taught: "Be respectful of those above you in the Lord" During the time of Christ the literacy rate for Jews was less than five percent and most worked for minimum wage. Normal salary for a day laborer was 1-3 sesterces a day while the salary of a Roman soldier was 900,000 sesterces per year.[16] Primarily, those who were literate were so because they had studied for the Jewish priesthood, such as St. John. During the influx of pagan converts in the second century it should be noted that they too were highly illiterate and poor, and as such followed their converted Hellenistic leaders, but their faith was in the resurrection of Christ who had said "let those accept who can." Therefore it is grossly unjust to condemn someone who attempts to follow the teachings of Christ with a good conscience and faith, as do faithful Catholics today.

The faith of the Christian laity, who faithfully followed their bishops or their "study-circle" leaders, is not an issue in this book. The faithful did not read scripture, they followed their leaders. It is the error of three Infallible Doctrines later instituted by the popes that will transform Catholicism and lead us into the worldwide scandal of today.

CHAPTER FOURTEEN

THE FIRST ASCETIC PAPAL DOCTRINE THAT TRANSFORMED THE CATHOLIC CHURCH

*"In 1324 Pope John XXII condemned this idea[Papal Infallibility]
as the work of the devil and then set about ignoring the dogma of
infallibility."*

*"In 1800, papal infallibility was still generally rejected except in Italy
and Spain. Pope Gregory XVI (1831-46) was the first pope to claim
that popes were infallible. His encyclical, Mirari, also viewed freedom
of conscience as "a false and absurd concept," indeed a mad delusion.
According to him, freedom of the press could never be sufficiently
abhorred."*

*"Dogmas were proclaimed at Vatican Council I on July 18, 1870... the
dogma of papal infallibility, means that the pope is incapable of error
when he makes ex cathedra decisions on matters of faith and morals.
However, virtually all matters, including political, social and economic,
can be framed in terms of faith and morals.... The bishops were at that
moment, according to Küng, reduced to mere lackeys of Rome, and
this arrangement continues to this day."* [1]

—History of Papal Infallibility

CHANGE BEGINS

"In antiquity, the Apostolic Constitutions were *mistakenly supposed* to be gathered and handed down by Clement of Rome,
the authority of whose name gave weight to more than one such
piece of early [apocryphal] Christian literature. The Church seems
never to have regarded this work as of undoubted Apostolic

authority."[2] Ancient beliefs die slowly; during the fifty years since Constantine accepted Christianity and the Apostolic Constitutions appeared, much changed in the Church.

We recall the first recorded attempt by local Church leaders to *mandate* ascetic celibacy occurred nearly 300 years after Christ in the far western reaches of Christendom, at the local Council of Elvira, Spain in 306 AD. The Elvira Council banned both married priests and marriage to Jews. One may recognize the Hellenistic influences of this small group of bishops that spurred this isolated incident. At this time bishops were independent and often selected only celibate men. This council of Elvira occurred only 30 years after the Hellenistic-Christian axis between the Patristic Fathers in Alexandria and Rome. In addition to this attempt demanding celibacy, the council also determined that if a woman guilty of adultery should kill the baby she is denied salvation. A female catechumen who strangles her illegitimate child may only receive the Eucharist on her deathbed and, apparently, they also had a problem with pederasts (ephebophiles) when they decreed, "To defilers of boys, communion is not to be given even at death."[3] Many modern priests would shudder to believe this last edict should ever be instituted by the current Pope.

No Pope was aware of the Elvira decrees since there was no Pope in office or authority from 304 AD when Pope Marcellinus died until 308 AD when Marcellus I ascended; during that time the Diocletian persecution attempted to decimate Christianity. Although this local action in Elvira had no effect outside of their area, other things were quickly happening by then. Constantine became emperor within seven years and soon legalized Christianity. Later persecutions would follow Constantine's death but the genie was out of the bottle with this newfound theological supremacy. With acceptance of Christianity the quest within the Church for authority began in earnest as the number of new converts who wished to become "'priests" grew exponentially. Bishops of Rome found themselves ensconced at the center of Imperial power and the struggle among clerics for this powerful office became intense.

NICAEA

The first ecumenical council empowered to issue infallible decisions demanding ascetic doctrines binding on all Christians occurred 300 years after Jesus. This council was called by Emperor Constantine – only nineteen years after that local council in Elvira first imposed celibacy in their area. There is little record of *Pope Sylvester I,* other than the gifts conferred upon the Roman Diocese by Constantine.

During this Council Spanish clerics once again attempted to push their agenda with a proposal for universal celibacy. While that attempt failed overwhelmingly, a crack in the Deposit of Faith appeared. It was ruled (fallibly) that married men could be ordained but could not later marry *after* ordination, revealing early attempts to set the clergy apart from and superior to the Laity in the same manner as their competition, the pagans. Apparently, at that early date the Council's efforts were not so much to gain control over the priests, but to elevate their political-social status and set them apart as semi-divine personages of importance in a largely pagan world where religious leaders had been, and remained, celibate. Priests with such credentials could be valuable papal ambassadors throughout the growing Empire as representatives of the Vatican.

Incidentally, following the lead of Governor Felix who refused to allow castration of Justin Martyr's Christian friend, Nicaea also banned the ordination of eunuchs. This must have been a continuing problem considering it was the first canon. Canon 1: "If anyone in sickness has undergone surgery at the hands of physicians or has been castrated by barbarians, let him remain among the clergy. But if anyone in good health has castrated himself, if he is enrolled among the clergy he should be suspended, and in future no such man should be promoted."

Lastly, before leaving this Nicaean Council it will be informative to examine a historically contentious event that occurred during this council and swayed the vote away from mandatory celibacy. This event is described in literature[4] surrounding Bishop *Paphnutius* from Upper Thebais in Egypt. Bishop Paphnutius spoke eloquently against the mandatory celibacy proposal of the Spanish Bishops. This incident is presented here to record the understanding among many Christian leaders of the fourth century who believed ascetic mandatory celibacy had no theological basis in Christianity. "Paphnutius declared in a loud voice, that too heavy a yoke ought not to be laid upon the clergy; that marriage and married intercourse are of themselves honorable and undefiled; that the Church ought not be injured by an extreme severity, for all could not live in absolute continence: in this way (by not prohibiting married intercourse) the virtue of the wife would be much more certainly preserved (viz. the wife of a clergyman, because she might be injured elsewhere, if her husband withdrew from her married intercourse)...This discourse made so much more impression, because he had never lived in matrimony himself, and had had no conjugal intercourse...and left to each cleric the responsibility of deciding the point [personal celibacy] as he would." It was only upon this impassioned plea of Paphnutius' that mandatory celibacy failed. Paphnutius, a favorite of Constantine who much revered his piety, had earlier lost an eye to Roman torturers and later was to become a martyr for his faith.

This historical event is important because it sheds light on future attempts by Popes who would again seek to justify ascetic celibacy as an ancient tradition.

DAMASUS AND THE LAW

It would be a half a century after Constantine before we find truly significant traces of change being evidenced by future Popes. Bishop Damasus I[5] is to be noticed because he was born the son of a priest in Rome, Antonius, and mother Laurentia. Born in 305 AD he grew to maturity with the rise of Constantine and witnessed important changes within the hierarchy. From childhood "he was raised in the service of the Church" and would himself become an early agent of change when he preached "cultic purity" (a term first coined by Anti-Pope Hippolytus). It is also alleged Damasus insisted St. Jerome, whom he commissioned to translate the Vulgate Bible change the word *wife* to *sister* in his translation. 1Corinthians 9:3-6

Church belief played a role in Damasus' selection over his papal contender Urisinus. Urisinus, professing *Arian* beliefs had opposed the Nicaean declaration proclaiming Jesus and God were one. Both papal claimants were elected simultaneously by competing Roman political-theological factions and power was up for grabs. The situations remained tense and within one month 137 supporters of Urisinus' were killed in the basilica where they fled for protection. After three days of rioting peace was restored by Roman officials. Arians opposing Damasus later lodged accusations of murder and fornication against him and it is accepted that he provided lavish and vulgar entertainment in the papal quarters. St. Gerome termed Damasus, who also ran Rome's city brothels, *matronarum auriscalpius* (ladies ear-tickler.). Ultimately demonstrating Damasus' Imperial support, these accusations of fornication were squashed by Emperor Gratian himself. In future rivalries such allegations and counter allegations of one candidate against another would become commonplace.[6] There were no "good guys" in this power struggle.

SIRICIUS AND INFALLIBLE CELIBACY

Even with the Roman Emperor's Imperial acceptance of Christianity sixty years after Emperor Constantine legalized Christianity in 313 AD, the Church continued to be challenged by powerful pagan religions governed by ascetic priests and philosophers; Stoicism, Mithraism, Vestal Virgins and priests of Goddess Cybele and her eunuch companion Attis remained more highly venerated across the Empire than married Christian priests. Renouncing fleshly temptations – primarily sex – pagan priests and philosophers had established a distinction between a lower and higher morality. Pagan priests were seen as a spiritual aristocracy above the common man who must be content with a lower grade of virtue. How, pagans asked, can a Christian preacher who engages in the fleshly temptation of marital sex communicate directly with the divine? Although Constantine appointed many Church officials to important governmental positions of authority, fully two-thirds of Rome's power brokers remained pagan leaders, and were viewed as a threat to the Church.

This feared pagan threat became a reality following an event in 365 AD with Emperor Julian's failed attempt to vanquish Christianity and reestablish Rome's ancient pagan religions.

145

Seizure of Church property and assassinations had failed, but following Julian's death the lingering fear of another pagan revival and the desire to elevate Christian priests to the venerated level of rival pagan priests remained. Reacting to this threat the first papal attempt to impose universal celibacy on the priesthood was instituted by a Roman cleric, Siricius. A Roman by birth, Siricius had been one of Pope Damasus I's deacons, having before that served Pope Liberius as reader and then a deacon. Although Antipope Ursinus again put himself forward, Siricius' election was unanimous and was confirmed with evident satisfaction by Roman Emperor Valentinian II, probably to cut short any intrigues in the Urisinus camp. As a young Deacon, Siricius had married and was therefore required to abandon his wife in order to become pope, and with this newly bestowed authority Siricius immediately imposed a new law upon the universal priesthood, laws requiring all clerics cease sexual intercourse with their wives. This was a revolutionary change because Siricius' predecessor Pope Damasus I was the son of a Roman priest.

Having forever been permitted to marry, one can only imagine the trauma experienced by priests and their wives who were forced to abandon conjugal love with their life-long spouse in order to remain priests, and apparently no thought was given to the fact that such a demand violated the Sacrament of Matrimony established by Christ, where, as Catholics are taught today, each spouse is granted the right of marital intercourse. Only in later centuries do we find Church apologists asserting priests and their wives "freely chose" to forgo marital intercourse when in fact, violation of this law meant expulsion from the priesthood. Moreover, future priests were denied marriage. Still today this "freely chosen" vow of celibacy for priests (Canon Law 1037) continues to deny priests, including St. Peter today, the individual freedom of choosing either marriage or celibacy as Christ permitted. In other words, this law denies the sanctifying grace of matrimony granted by Christ. Today, St. Peter would be ineligible for the priesthood — because he was married.

Papal Infallibility

The First Ascetic Papal Doctrine That Transformed the Church

"Those who argue against the issue of papal infallibility Evidence a basic confusion, since it must always be phrased this way: 'Have two popes disagreed when officially teaching on faith and morals'"
—*Catholicism and Fundamentalism.* Karl Keating

Having been reared in a small town where Catholicism was tolerated, but considered by most to be a false religion, this writer wished to discover the reason why Protestant friends were upset with Catholic beliefs, primarily the teaching of Papal Infallibility. Attempting to find the origin of these differences I was thrilled to read Karl Keating's book from which the epigraph above is taken. Keating's book so inspired me with his historical understandings of false allegations directed at my Church, that I too was inspired to look back into our history. Over many years of study I became supportive of all Catholic Doctrines until the priestly abuse scandal brought back questions I had dismissed in my support of the Church. That event led me back to earlier questions and to this book. I still consider Keating to be the most effective Catholic apologist and continue to respect his work. Having now come to understand a history of the Church that disagrees with Keating's, I continue to respect him and other Vatican supporters who I believe have been denied the true history of early teachings which changed the Church. My first disagreement is that the idea of an Infallible Papal Monarch being the only human capable of speaking infallibly for God on matters of Christian faith and morals does not exist in Christianity. Moreover, it is the Papacy that has led the Church into repeated international scandal.

For those who are unfamiliar with Papal Infallibility we must first understand the Vatican's formal definition of Papal Infallibility as described in Dr. Ludwig Ott's authoritative book: *Fundamentals of Catholic Dogma.* This book provides an in depth explanation of all infallibly defined Dogma from the Deposit of Faith.

"The Pope is infallible when he speaks ex cathedra." (De fide). Vatican Council I defined: "The Roman Pontiff, when he speaks ex cathedra [From the chair of Peter]- that is, when in discharge of the office of Pastor and Doctor of all Christians, by virtue of his supreme apostolic authority, he defines a *doctrine* regarding Faith and Morals *to be held by the Universal Church* – by Divine assistance promised to him in Blessed Peter, is possessed of that infallibility with which the Divine Redeemer willed His Church to be endowed in defining doctrines regarding Faith and Morals; and therefore such definitions of the Roman Pontiff are *irreformable* of themselves, and not in virtue of the consent of the Church."

We mention only in passing that infallible Ecumenical Council definitions require the Pope's acceptance, thereby nullifying Jesus' teaching that all bishops are equally graced with authority to bind and loose: *"I tell you solemnly, whatever you bind on earth shall be considered bound in heaven; whatever you loose on earth shall be considered in heaven."* Matthew 18:18. The question we raise is: Did this gift end with the death of Peter and the Apostles?

THE APOSTOLIC ORIGINS OF PRIESTLY CELIBACY

"The early centuries of the Church had no law on celibacy as it is now understood in modern times, i.e., a law stating as a primary condition for admission to the Orders the obligation to renounce marriage."
— *The Apostolic Origins of Priestly Celibacy*. Christian Cochini, S. J.

"Thirty years after Nicaea, the Synod of Gangra, Spain, 355 AD, agreed with the Nicaean Council by ruling priests would still be allowed to marry before ordination. Canon No. 1 of that Synod stated, 'If anyone shall maintain, concerning married presbyters [bishops], that it is unlawful to partake the oblation when he offers it, let him be anathema."
—New Advent Catholic Encyclopedia

The primary focus of this book is the false concept of modern Papal Infallibility that developed over the first three hundred and fifty years after Jesus' death in 30 AD, when Pope Siricius first declared himself Pope in 389 AD. With this development many changes occurred, and because of changes which we have described, this writer believes it important for the reader to keep in mind the Deposit of Faith was completed with the death of the last Apostle in the first century. Infallibly proclaimed by the Church, there has been no new revelation from God since Jesus' death, nor may the teachings handed down by Jesus and the Apostles be altered or amended. This important teaching was well described by Pope John Paul II in 1965: "Guarding the Deposit of Faith is the mission which the Lord has entrusted to the Church and which she fulfills in every age."[7] The most illuminating Vatican *apologia* on this matter is by Vatican apologist Christian Cochini, S.J., in his book, *The Apostolic Origins of Priestly Celibacy*. An important book, "The work of Father Cochini, S.J., about the origin of celibacy in the Catholic Church has a history of its own: a version was submitted, in May 1969, to the board of examiners of the Institut catholique de Paris presided over by Jean Cardinal Danielou." An impressive and knowledgeable scholar, we will quote Cochini's comments from his book on Apostolic celibacy and his presentation of Pope Siricius' text as it was contained in Siricius' response to Spanish Bishop Hemerius.

CHANGE

With the death of Emperor Julian "the Apostate"[8] in 363 AD his attempt to restore Rome as a Pagan state had failed, and in 375 AD the new Roman Emperor Gratian published an edict that all subjects should profess the faith of the bishops of Rome and Alexandria, revealing the importance of the Hellenistic church of Alexandria, Egypt; but concerns of another uprising led by powerful pagan leaders in Rome remained a threat to the Church, and for Pope Damasus I when he was elected in 366 AD. Until his death in 384 AD Damasus, during the reign of Gratian became an important supporter of the newly developing *Apostolic Constitutions* that were formally accepted by the Church c.380 AD, only four years before Damasus' death and the instillation of Pope Siricius as his successor. Beginning back in c.230 the acceptance of the *Didascalia Apostolorum,* composed by Hellenisticly inspired "study-circles" and first introduced into Christianity by the converted Stoic, St. Justin Martyr. These ascetic beliefs made dramatic inroads with the support of a growing number of ascetically inspired bishops. With the acceptance of the Apostolic Constitutions the circle was complete. "The Apostolic Constitutions contains eight treatises on Early Christian discipline, worship, and doctrine, intended to serve as a manual of *guidance* for the clergy, and to some extent for the laity. The structure of the Apostolic Constitutions can be summarized: Books 1 to 6 are a *free re-wording* of the Didascalia Apostolorum"[9] which arose from second century Apocrypha.

Unhappily for those who wished to elevate all clerics to the semi-divine prominence of competing pagan leaders, and present all Christian clerics as important ambassadors-at-large in the Roman Church, problems continued. Although most clerics had come to accept the onerous demand of their bishop to remain sexual chaste, all did not go well, and in one way or another most continued to keep their wedding vows as St. Paul had taught when he spoke of marriage and virginity: "Since sex is always a danger, let each man have his own wife and each woman her own husband." 1 Corinthians 7:2. Only five years after introducing the Apostolic Constitutions distress with the law's apparent inability to limit sexual intercourse between clerics and their wives had failed, bringing great distress to Spanish Bishop Hemerius who sought assistance from Pope Damasus. We recall it was the Spanish bishops who first failed in their efforts to institute mandatory celibacy during the Council of Nicaea fifty years earlier. Unfortunately, Pope Damasus died before responding to Bishop Hemerius.

As the matter stood at the time of Damasus' death the Didascalia *authoratively* taught elements of *The Acts of Paul and Thecla, and The Gospel of Peter* containing the *Docetic* belief that Jesus "felt no pain" on the cross. The demand of ascetic celibacy (At this time celibacy, sexual chastity and virginity were synonymous terms) was merely a "*genre* of the Church Orders" imposed and enforced by individual bishops. These demands were contrary to the freedom of marriage given with Christ's Sacrament of Matrimony, or to marry or to remain chaste as taught by Jesus when He spoke to His 70 "other" Disciples, whom he was sending out to preach "The Kingdom of God is at hand" Luke 10:9, Speaking to them regarding choosing marriage or celibacy He said, "It is not everyone who can accept what I have said, but only those to whom it is granted...Let anyone accept who will." Matthew 19:11 It should be noted here that Jesus also describes His twelve Apostles as "Disciples" Matthew 10:1. The demand of clerical celibacy at Siricius' time was merely a fallible "Church Order," not an infallible Church Doctrine. But that would soon change for the first time in Church history.

Some believe Damasus composed a reply to Bishop Hemerius but died before it was issued; leaving the matter in the hands of his successor Siricius who, in keeping with his desire to impose priestly celibacy, which he declared to be an ancient *discipline instituted by the Apostles*, composed and issued a response to Hemerius on February 10, 385 AD. Siricius' response was issued as a *Directa* decretal, an authoritative papal teaching *"to be held by the whole Church."* We will cite Cochini's personal comments from his book and his presentation of Pope Siricius' text in his response to Spanish Bishop Hemerius.

Today it is acknowledged by Vatican apologists that the Didascalia and the Apostolic Constitutions were not, as taught in the early centuries, actually composed by the Apostles, and therefore can be supported only as "Orally transmitted traditions" handed down over two centuries. As Cochini describes it: "The fabrication of the 'pseudoapostolic constitutions...Their authors, most of whom remain unknown, wanted to respond to the need for collecting and establishing written norms of Christian life and ecclesiastical disciplines that were, until then, only part of various traditions...yet they offer a very interesting outline of the discipline that prevailed at the time they were written. They were collections of norms *set by the Apostles."* With this historically unsustainable depiction of first century Apostolic Christianity it becomes apparent why mandatory celibacy can be defended only as *Orally* transmitted norms first recorded in the Didascalia two hundred years after Christ c. 250AD. Realizing today that most bishops of the second century were married, and that the Ecumenical Council of Nicaea permitted marriage 160 years earlier, ascetic Apostolic celibacy cannot be defended as an historical truth, therefore apologists are reduced to defending celibacy as a "discipline" that nullified the Sacrament of Matrimony as it existed in the Deposit of Faith.

As we read Siricius' Decretal we begin when: "Siricius answered in the name of his late predecessor because the question had not been asked to the *person* of Siricius, but to the *representative* of Peter." With this understanding, "the *Directa* Decretal begins with the affirmation of the *presence and action* of the Apostle Peter on the Roman See in the person of his successors." Having identified the *Directa* Decretal as a response, not from himself but from St. Peter, Siricius states, "We carry the burdens of those who are laden: rather, *Blessed Apostle Peter is carrying them for us*, and we firmly trust that he protects and guards us in all things, as we [popes] are *heirs* to his function." As we begin our understanding of Pope Siricius' *Directa* Decretal we recognize he intends to speak for Peter, ex cathedra, from the chair of St. Peter. At that time in Church history the New Testament passage in Matthew 16:18 where Jesus spoke: "So now I say to you: You are Peter and on this rock I will build my Church...I will give to you the keys to the Kingdom of heaven: whatever you bind on earth shall be considered bound in heaven; whatever you loose on earth shall be considered loosed in heaven," was considered in Rome as *cart blanche* authority for the pope to speak infallibly for Peter, under the guidance of the Holy Spirit. Only in a much later time would the Church come to acknowledge, as they do today, that papal "binding or loosing" had no authority to alter or nullify *revelations* of Christ's infallible teaching contained in the Deposit of Faith. Recall, during an interview with the Catholic weekly *Our Sunday Visitor* Cardinal Joseph Ratzinger (later to Pope Benedict XVI) was asked a question on the possibility of new Revelation from God after the death of Jesus. He was quite emphatic on this point as he answered, "No, Jesus was Revelation." The mistaken belief that popes can alter the Deposit of Faith continues to confuse the laity.

Following Cochini: "Fifteen points are studied...Two of these points unveil a background of numerous married deacons, priests, and bishops. We recall in this respect that remarried men were not permitted to receive Orders (VIII, 12), a fact that confirms *indirectly* the compatibility of monogamous marriage and the priesthood." Here Cochini refers to those clerics who were forced to violate the Sacrament of Matrimony in order to remain priests. Continuing: "However, they were expected to live in a state of perfect chastity, of perpetual continence with regard to their wives, even if the latter were still alive... [However] It was against violations committed by some men that Pope Siricius took a firm position in chapter 7 of his *Directa* decretal when answering the question of Bishop Hemerius: 'Let us talk now about the very holy clerical Orders. As...we have seen that in your province they are trampled underfoot...We have indeed discovered that many priests and deacons of Christ brought children into the world, either through union with their wives or through shameful intercourse.'"

Thus far, Pope Siricius speaks as the bishop-teacher of his diocese in agreement with a fellow bishop. It is accepted by all that in such situations it is possible for a Pope to speak in error as a mere human without guidance of the Holy Spirit. In this instance he speaks in error of his *personal* views supported only by the newly issued *Apostolic Constitutions,* which were formally instituted only five years earlier as *authoritative*, not infallible Church teachings; he has not yet spoken ex cathedra as the Infallible Monarch from the chair of Peter. This however will change.

As Siricius continues to expound on the supremacy and necessity of priestly celibacy he writes: "This is why, after having enlightened us by His coming, the Lord Jesus formally stipulated in the Gospel that He had not come to abolish the law, but to bring it to perfection; this is also why **He wanted** the beauty of the Church, whose Bridegroom He is, **to shine with the splendor of chastity**, so that when He returns, on the Day of Judgment, He will find Her without stain or wrinkle, as **His Apostles taught."** With this papal pronouncement Siricius inserts a new doctrine ["Some new Doctrine"] into the Deposit of Faith.

Today, no celibacy apologist dares state that either Jesus or His Apostles *required* or *taught* sexual abstinence for any Christian; Cochini himself states "The early centuries of the Church had no law on celibacy as it is understood in modern times." Cochini relies only on the Didascalia Apostolorum which he candidly describes as "pseudo- apostolic constitutions" in his explanation of Siricius' authority. Nowhere however did Jesus, who granted free choice of marriage or celibacy *require or teach* that *He wanted* the beauty of the Church, whose Bridegroom He is, *to shine with the splendor of chastity.* To suggest otherwise is simply untrue. Jesus continually taught that "a man must cling to his wife." St. Paul followed this teaching of Christ when he taught "The husband must give to his wife what she expects [sex], and so too the wife to the husband. The wife has no rights over her own body, the husband has them. In the same way, the husband has no rights over his body, the wife has them. Do not refuse each other except by mutual consent, and then only for an agreed time, to leave yourself free for prayer: then come together again in case Satin should take advantage of your weakness." 1 Corinthians 7:3-5. To reject these teachings of Jesus and Paul is to alter the Deposit of Faith.

With this ex-cathedra statement Siricius inserts *his doctrine* of celibacy into the Deposit of Faith and therefore changes the Doctrine of Christ permitting all Christians the freewill choice of celibacy or the Sacrament of Matrimony.

Soon, we will examine Church Dogma concerning the insertion of "Some new Doctrine" into the Deposit of Faith. But, for now, let us return to the apologist Karl Keating's epigraph above describing the only method of determining if a pope has ever disproved papal infallibility: " *Have two popes disagreed when officially teachings on faith and morals?'"* If we are to consider Christ as our first infallible pope, Siricius has disproved papal infallibility. Only truth is infallible and infallibility does not later change or contradict itself. Therefore, should *any* pope issue a Papal Doctrine that alters a Doctrine of Christ the entire concept of Papal infallibility is disproven. Here Siricius does just that. It is beneath the dignity of debate to suggest that Siricius did not intend to speak *ex cathedra,* or infallibly from "The Chair of Peter."

Today the Church teaches this *Discipline* of continence was freely accepted by priests and their wives. In fact however, priests would have been laicized had they not complied. This was a law forced upon all clerics; their free-will played no part.

Finally, the most telling reason for Siricius' insertion of his ascetic doctrine is contained in his statement to Bishop Hemerius,

154

"If lay people *are asked* to be continent so that their prayers might be granted, all the more so [should] a priest...Which is why I am extorting, warning, supplicating: let us do away with this opprobrium that *even pagans hold against us*." Here Siricius clearly reveals his desire to elevate Christian priests to the venerated level of the pagans. That Siricius' inserted "some new doctrine" into the Deposit of Faith is beneath intellectual debate. With this act Siricius forever disproves the concept of an infallible Papal Monarch.

It is difficult for this writer to believe such alterations could have been inserted into the Deposit of Faith and go unnoticed until 1870 AD, which we will discuss. Not before Hellenisticly inspired "study-circles" sprang from the fertile ascetic ground of the third century do we find Church writings demanding sexual abstinence between a bishop and his wife. The first "official church" writings appear in 350 AD, stating, "But it is *required* that the bishop be thus: a man that hath taken one wife, that hath governed his house well...let him be *proved* when he receives the imposition of hands to sit in the office of the bishopric whether he be *chaste*, and whether his wife also be a believer and *chaste*.[10] Only with spurious interpellations of words or terms can someone attempt to force celibacy upon any cleric of the second century with literature originating first among pagan converts such as Valentinus in the second century, and secondly by the Patristic's "study-circles" of the third century.

DISCIPLINE VS. DOCTRINE

"As an apologist, I often find it necessary to explain that priestly
celibacy is not a doctrine of the Church. To the contrary: It is more
accurately described as a discipline. And, as such, it could theoretically
change—the Church could choose to ordain married men"[10]
—Catholic Answers

The epigraph above reveals modern efforts of Vatican apologists in defense of celibacy against accusations that *ascetic celibacy* is a Papal Doctrine. It is appropriate then to examine the Vatican's *Apologia* in defense of *mandatory* celibacy. First, we do not find celibacy *defended* as an ancient *Discipline* instituted by the Apostles until after the First Vatican Council of 1870 AD when papal infallibility was formally defined. Prior to that time no Church literature advanced mandatory celibacy as a Papally required doctrine.

Today Canon Law1037 defining priestly requirements states: "An unmarried candidate for the permanent diaconate and a candidate for the presbyterate *are not to be admitted* to the order of diaconate unless they have assumed the *obligation of celibacy* in the prescribed rite publicly before God and the Church or have made perpetual vows in a religious institute."[12]

Notice the term *Before God. The promise is not To God.* Under this Law St. Peter would be denied Ordination into the Priesthood because he was a married father. No pope has the authority to *require* someone to make a promise to God or man. Such a man-made requirement, demanding someone reject the Sanctifying grace of the Sacrament of Matrimony in order to accept another Sacrament, is illicit. Such a vow is meaningless in God's eyes. Incredulously, we grope through our intellect for any logic justifying the assertion that a disciplinary obligation is a free choice of itself; neither an "obligation" nor "required discipline" allow for a "free choice" as it was granted by Christ when He said: "Let him accept this who will" Matthew 19:12 How, we ask, does Siricius not nullify Christ's Doctrine when he states: "I am exporting, warning, supplicating: let us do away with this opprobrium that even the pagans can rightly hold against us?" Today this law would deny the Sacrament of Ordination not only to St. Peter but to all married fathers. Today, the admission of married Anglican priests is transparently an attempt to obfuscate (cover-up) Siricius' pseudo-infallible imposition of celibacy.

UNDERSTANDING SIRICIUS AND HIS INFALLIBLE DECLARATION

"Increasingly, clerics became a separate caste within society. Constantine exempted them from mandatory military and civil service, and Constantius exempted them from the burden of paying taxes. Bishops were established as judges competent to judge civil matters – and were eventually given offices within the imperial hierarchy.

Bishops came to be called 'most glorious' and priests and deacons 'illustrious'...Bishops took over the dress and insignia of imperial officers, such as the pallium and stole. Priests began to dress differently than lay people."

—*People of the Creed.* Anthony Gilles

As described above by Church historian Anthony Gilles, the Papacy became an organ of the Roman Government, whose laws, decrees and practices were enforced by Imperial edicts which later became the origin of Canon Law. Aside from the Roman Emperor, to whom the Pope was subservient, popes became the most powerful authority figure in the Empire. With such authority it can be understood why Siricius believed it within his power to institute an infallible Church Law. After three centuries of ascetic indoctrination and believing as he did, that priestly celibacy might actually have been instituted by the Apostles, he had no doubt that as spokesman for St. Peter, and capable of enforcing infallible Papal authority over Christianity world-wide, he mistakenly felt it his duty to "Do away with this opprobrium" of priestly sex. Understood in this manner it may be appropriate to have some sympathy for Siricius. Unfortunately for him, however, is the truth that all infallible Church doctrines must be infallible from the beginning, in the Deposit of Faith, no matter when it may later be infallibly defined by the Church. Mandatory celibates violates this truth.

VATICAN COUNCIL I, PAPAL INFALLIBILITY DECLARED 1870 AD

"Opponents of infallibility constantly assert that the Pope evoked the council solely to have papal infallibility proclaimed. Everything else was merely an excuse for the sake of appearance."

—*Catholic Encyclopedia.*

VATICAN COUNCIL I

Beginning c. 752 AD the Vatican controlled a majority of the Italian peninsula as a sovereign state governed by Popes who acted as sovereign monarchial rulers for more than 1,100 years. During

this time of European Papal Sovereignty, popes began to be identified as *monarchs.* In essence, the Papal States were as much
a sovereign European Nation as were England and France. Pope
Pius IX, 1846–1878 AD, presided over the Vatican retreat from
power and its previous holdings along with the decline of papal
respect across most of the continent. Additionally, the Church was
continually confronted by intense theological pressures throughout the world as a lingering result of the Reformation. By 1870 the
Vatican State had retreated to its present boundaries under the
protection of France. This Vatican retreat was complete when the
diminished Vatican State as it exists today in the heart of Rome
was granted by the newly formed Italian government.

Still, the Church remained the oldest continually organized
religious organization on earth with clerics around the world.
It was too late to recover lost holdings but a counterassault on
Vatican opponents was encouraged by some Cardinals and the
Pope's Jesuit advisors. Sensing a growing intellectual freedom
by Catholics, Pope Pius IX was assured by his advisors that a
re-assertion of papal authority with the Dogmatic definition of
Papal Infallibility was in order. Such a definition would dogmatically declare the Pope to have personal and individual authority,
requiring no support from the Cardinals or the Church in order
to issue infallible decisions *ex cathedra,* "from the chair of Peter."

While Papal Infallibility had been promoted as a pious belief
by few Catholics since Siricius in 385; it had never been publicly,
formally or dogmatically declared. Hence, a re-visit to the Deposit
of Faith was in order in an effort to quell opposition. When word
began to trickle from the council that such a definition was forth-
coming, citizens of Rome were abuzz. This council was deceptively
called in order to confront Renaissance materialism. The truth is
infallibility was the underlying political reason for this First Vatican
Council of 1869–1870 AD.

Pius IX, while being described by opponents as theologically
weak had worked his way up through the Roman political system
with support from the conservative political-theological clergy of
Rome in much the same way modern American politicians work
their way to the top: governor, senator, president. As with many
past popes he was a superb politician and dictatorial leader, but

one who was not well imbued with Dogmatism. However, Pius IX would serve longer than any Pope since St. Peter.

The opinion of this writer is that Pius IX was neither charitable nor pious. He became involved in one of the more personally despicable anti-Semitic acts of modern time. Under his pontificate it was illegal for Jews to raise a Christian child. Six year old Edgardo Mortara, the child of devout Jews, lay near death and in an act of charity Edgardo's Christian nurse baptized him. Upon later discovering this child's baptism Papal authorities removed the child from his parents and placed him with Pope Pius, as if adopted. Over continual objections lasting years, Edgardo's parents were forever denied the return of their child. At a tender age, Edgardo was placed in seminary, ultimately becoming a priest. It was this Pope who first dogmatically declared himself infallible.

"Pius IX believed, 'I am the Church.' In fact, during one of his many temper tantrums, he screamed at a Cardinal who asked him to submit to Church tradition, 'Tradition! I am tradition!'... He preached a world ruled by divinely appointed monarchs, and he acted in accordance with his preaching."[13] Pius IX is well described in historian and priest James Carroll's voluminous book, *Constantine's Sword: The Church and the Jews,* which traces the history of papal anti-Semitism.

During this first Vatican Council, strong opposition to the infallibility declaration among many liberal clerics from around the world was overcome by a conservative Roman-dominated council, and collegiality vanished. "It was not until the contest over papal infallibility outside the council grew constantly more violent that various groups and members of the council began to urge councilor discussion of the question of infallibility. And: "Bishops in the minority had constantly sought to block the matter." (Catholic Encyclopedia: First Vatican Council) Even many of the Pope's staunchest supporters only reluctantly agreed to this declaration because both theological and public attitudes of the time were tenuous at best. In that adversarial climate 60 Cardinals (including Americans) left the day before the vote, fearing such a definition would result in a worldwide firestorm of opposition, resulting from what many people could see as an attempt to "Deify" the Pope. That view prevails today.

In order for councilor politics to be more effective most of these debates were in private committees before the resolution reached the floor. These debates seemed to revolve around the Deposit of Faith which contained the source of all infallible declarations, defined or not. Previous to this council the bishops set agendas for discussion, but with this council total papal control was instituted. Cardinals were isolated in their committees and allowed to speak only at the conclusion of papal presentations. Written records of these committee meetings were forbidden. Moreover, *ad hoc* discussions were also forbidden. The control was summarized by Bishop Joseph Karl Hefele of Rotenberg, Germany. He was Professor of Christian History at the University of Tubingen. He said, "The longer I stay here the more clearly I see the duplicity behind my appointment as consultor concilii. That was just Rome's way of hoodwinking the public with the appearance of neutrality. In reality, I have no idea what I'm supposed to be doing here."

Perhaps the most scathing commentary on this First Vatican Council was issued by universally revered Catholic theologian Fr. Hans Kung in his book, *Infallibility? An Inquiry*. Fr. Kung served as official theologian for the Second Vatican Council 1962–1965. He writes, "So repressive were the agenda and official procedures; so one-sided and partisan were the selection of main theological experts and the composition of both conciliar commissions and the conciliar presidium; so numerous were the means of pressure (moral, psychological, church-political, newspaper campaigns, threatened withdrawal of financial support, harassment by the police) to which bishops of the anti-infallibilists minority were exposed; so varied were the forms of manipulation applied at the Popes behest, to advance the definition before, during, and after the Council...as painful and embarrassing as it may be to admit, this Council resembled a well-organized and manipulated totalitarian party congress rather than a free gathering of Christian people." As far as Fr. Kung was concerned the freedom of conscience during the First Vatican Council was so compromised it cannot be regarded as issuing an authentic or authoritative Catholic teaching under the direction of the Holy Spirit. The logical conclusion raised by Kung's assertion was as follows, "If

Cardinals, under duress, violated their conscience the infallibility declaration itself is licit." For this in 1979, Kung was forbidden from teaching theology in the name of the Church.

Today this Council and its illicit decree stands as an affront to Catholicism and, as then Bishop Carl Ratzinger was quoted as saying of Kung, "A predominately critical article should not, however, ignore the positive side of Kung's book... we affirmed he opened for discussion problems that must be reformulated... upon which the possibility of the survival of Catholicism seems to depend."[14] Reformulated? Only a new and legitimate council would have authority to reformulate this error on which the pope says, "... the possibility of the survival of Catholicism seems to depend."

Nevertheless, with such an infallible definition looming at this Council a private compromise was deemed necessary for passage, and ultimately agreement was reached. This compromise would protect the sanctity of the Deposit of Faith and persuaded recalcitrant Cardinals to support the vote. This compromise which *limits* papal infallibility and safeguards the Deposit of Faith was agreed to before Papal Infallibility was finally declared.

LIMITS OF PAPAL INFALLIBILITY – "SOME NEW DOCTRINE"

Few Catholics, much less non-Catholics, are aware that papal infallibility contains specific limits included as a means of protecting the immutable nature of our Deposit of Faith. This limiting clause was specifically inserted so that *some new doctrine* might not be added to the Deposit of Faith by later Popes, thereby foreclosing any future change in ancient beliefs handed down from the beginning. With that agreed to, the Papal Infallibility Declaration passed, along with this Papal infallibility *limitation*.

*"For the Holy Spirit was promised to the successors of Peter **not** so that they might, by His [Holy Spirits] revelation, **make known some new doctrine**, but that, by His [Holy Spirits] assistance, they [popes] might religiously guard and faithfully expound the revelation or **Deposit of Faith** transmitted by the apostles."[15]*
—The First Dogmatic Constitution on the Church of Christ. First Vatican Council.

Little did the Cardinals understand the implications and cogency of this decree. It is devastating to any proposed change in our original Sacraments, including the right of Priestly Ordination and Matrimony; it thereby nullifies the illicit changes made by Pope Siricius *before* this papal infallibility decree existed. Catholic teaching is clear: *"Sacraments are Christ's own gifts that provide us with His Grace... between the time He began His public life and the time He ascended into heaven, Jesus fashioned the seven Sacraments. When He ascended into heaven that put an end to the making of Sacraments...Sacraments give sanctifying grace; the Church cannot institute new Sacraments."*[16]

This Infallible Dogmatic Constitution of the Church declares that successors of Peter have never and will never receive new revelation in the form of "some new doctrine" not left by Jesus. We recall, as Pope Benedict XVI said: *"Jesus was revelation."* Therefore, it is infallibly declared and defined, Popes are to *"faithfully expound"* only that which was left to us by Christ.

At last now, not only are Sacraments defined by Trent to rest within the Deposit of Faith: "All Sacraments of the New Covenant were instituted by Jesus Christ",[17] they are unchangeable i.e., *irreformable.* Therefore, the Sacraments of Matrimony and Holy Orders are *immutable,* revealing mandatory celibacy requirements to be "some new doctrine." Since Dogma, either defined or undefined cannot develop, or be altered, we now have legal-theological evidence that mandatory celibacy is *some new doctrine* imposed first by Siricius and later by the Lateran Council of 1139 AD. This limitation is at the heart of this book. Still, we continue to find alterations made in order to accommodate political ends. Ironically, the Vatican I Council added, *"So then, should anyone, which God forbid, have the temerity to reject this definition of ours: let him be anathema."* In defiance of this Vatican I Council anathema, illicit celibacy remains as this book is written and consequentially, all popes since Siricius must take ownership of this illicit Papal Doctrine

CHAPTR FIFTEEN

DARK AGES

LOOKING BACK TO THE DARK AGES -
POPES AND ASCETICISM LOSE CONTROL

*"The Dark Ages begin at the time of the fall of Rome; in 476 A.D.
Rome's rule had lasted eight hundred years. In the place of Rome,
barbarian kingdoms arose and ruled the West. The Dark Ages were to
rule over Europe until about 1000 A.D., with the birth of the Middle
Ages and a recovery from artistic darkness as the lost knowledge of
the Greeks and Romans was rediscovered.*

—Our Ancestors in the Dark Ages

*"Convents, as the Council of Aix-la-Chapelle (836 CE) declares, were
rather brothels than houses of God. Infanticide of unwanted children
became common. Part of the monastic discipline was the letting of
blood in the hope of alleviating the effects of prolonged continence."*
—*History of Sacerdotal Celibacy in the Catholic Church.* Henry Lea

Consequences of the Dark Ages were traumatic and one must
examine the effects of that time before the Church moved into the
Middle Ages and the Renaissance when celibacy was imposed.
This was a time when the organizational Church in the West was
forced to make many changes in order to survive. These were brutal, dangerous, and near completely lawless centuries for a majority of the Western Empire when plague, starvation, and slaughter
were common. Over a period of 600 years the Vatican lost control
over clerics in most areas and nearly all parish priests began to
marry.

While the Eastern Catholic Church continued to grow with married priests, western civilization imploded. Before the rise of Islam in the 700s until near the end of the millennium, the Eastern Church in Constantinople, which differed vastly from Rome, enjoyed unparalleled wealth, literacy and respect. This continued until the fall of Constantinople to the Ottoman Empire in 1453 AD.

Twice, in 410 and 455 AD, Rome was sacked by Visigoths and Vandals. In 476 AD, the Western Roman Empire ended. This became a desperate time for Christianity. Urban population dwindled sharply and a feudal system of competing warlords arose. Parishes in rural areas became sparse while cities and castles were walled and guarded. Rome and the Vatican State itself would necessarily be concerned with its own survival, forcing the Vatican to become a political state first, and a servant of the Body of Christ second. During this time formal Church structures declined because pressures from feudal lords demanded undivided subservience of priests who survived in their feudal lord's often small and closely controlled fiefdoms. Travel and transportation between cities nearly vanished in some areas and during this age of illiteracy the parish priest was often the only person who could read. However, priestly education was sorely lacking and some priests were near illiterate themselves. In some western areas the Church was forced back into situations similar in many ways to the era of House Churches. During this time the first traces of post-Nicaean "heretical" Christians sprang up objecting to many Church teachings, wishing to return to their origins as they saw it.

Years later, during the Inquisition, many of these *deviant* Christians who saw errors in Rome would be brutally and unjustly tortured, martyred, and/or burnt at the stake for their beliefs – all authorized by our Popes. These Inquisitions, lasting more than 300 years, is a subject this writer hasn't the courage to relate to the reader, and those desiring more information will need to search it out for themselves. These un-Christian acts were authorized by our Popes. Absolutely no deviation from papal teaching was tolerated in any area under Church authority. Much of the Inquisition cruelty in the name of God was similar in many ways to that of the Muslim Taliban of today.

A major consequence of this time was the development of the Monastic tradition of celibate monks, begun at Monte Casino in 529 AD by the Benedictines. Benedict, as well as St. Teresa of Calcutta, 1919-1997 AD, are examples of Christians with the true gift of chastity. Both were Saints. Benedict's Monastic tradition of consecrated celibates had both positive and negative consequences on the Church. Negatively, the quickly spreading Monastic system caused the Church to turn inward as an isolated fortress in an island of darkness; but, a fortress often separated from the impoverished, illiterate laity. Rome's ability to communicate with and control the priesthood diminished for several centuries. By the same token it was the priests and monks that saved treasured classical literature, patristic writings, and Scripture itself. Chapter 22 of Benedict's rules stated, "Each monk is to have a separate bed and is to sleep in his habit, so as to be ready to rise without delay, and that a light shall burn in the dormitory throughout the night." Positively however, attempts by the Hierarchy to force celibacy on often destitute married priests all but vanished between 500-1000 AD, only to begin again during the late Middle Ages and the beginning of the Renaissance.

Just as the Vatican state filled the power vacuum left by the fall of Rome, so too emerging from the Dark Ages many bishops in areas devoid of meaningful Vatican authority quickly became lords of their diocesan realm. They were required merely to pay Vatican taxes. These taxes were in turn collected from priests, who in turn collected Simonist fees from the faithful. While nearly all these priests and bishops were married, an illicit power structure grew with Popes, bishops, and priests, each vying to secure their own earthly realm. This became an early cause of systemic moral failure within the hierarchy, much of which remains with us today.

While the above picture is valid, it must not be taken to include most of the parish priesthood. Always, within the core of the Church were saints of God who worked for the Kingdom and not for themselves. Without them, the Roman Catholic Church of today would not exist.

As the Church approached the end of the first 1,000 years and entered the heights of papal authority, those dangerous conditions all began to change as communication and control was reestablished.

1139 AD, THE LATERAN COUNCIL AND THE *COUPE DE GRACE*

"Take from the church an honorable marriage and an immaculate marriage bed, and do you not fill it with concubineage, incest, homosexuality and every kind of uncleanness?"
—St. Bernard of Clairvaux, 1135 AD

We decree that the selfsame thing is to apply also to women religious if, God forbid, they attempt to marry.
—Canon 8. Lateran Council

Here we again find an *infallibility assault* on the Sacraments of Ordination and Matrimony, an important epoch. Approaching the second millennium the Vatican had become a powerful European government of its own; to the point their authority was often unchallengeable by sovereign rulers. "Many priests and bishops had by then become degenerate, so much so that some married bishops protecting their own mercenary interests, treated the Church as a personal business, buying and selling bishoprics. No more was required than to 'lay hands' on the new bishop and complete the sale of a business with guaranteed income. We read, 'The Episcopal sees, as we learn...were given as fifes to rude soldiers, and were treated as property which descended as hereditary right from father to son...but we have evidence from other sources that corruption was wide spread and that few parts of the world failed to feel the license and venality of the times.'"[1] The Vatican was desperate to stem institutional bleeding.

IMPRISONMENT AND SLAVERY

The Church was imploding as a result of our failing priesthood and efforts to secure control over it and establish decorum would not be easy or pretty. Draconian measures were instituted, "...disabilities of all kinds were enacted...against wives and children of ecclesiastics. Their offspring were declared to be of servile condition, debarred from sacred orders and incapable of succeeding to their fathers benefices. The earliest decree in which children were declared to be slaves, the property of the Church... [and] similar penalties were promulgated later on against the wives, who by the fact of their unlawful connection...became liable to be seized as slaves... this is the first trace of the principle [not theology] that marriage of the clerics is ipso-facto invalid."[2] That brief statement of slavery in the Catholic Encyclopedia describes failed, desperate papal attempts of the ninth century to bring the priesthood into subservience. Individually they were:

Synod of Pavia, 1022 AD: Canon 4 – *"Children of priests shall be sold into slavery."*

Synod of Rome, 1049 AD: *"Wives of priests shall be taken as slaves of the Lateran Palace. (Wives of the time were seen as property of their priest-husbands, therefore property of the Church.)*

Synod of Melfi, 1089 AD: under Pope Urban II, *"Married priests who ignore the celibacy laws should be imprisoned for the good of their souls, and their wives and children to be sold into slavery and the money accrues to the Church of Rome."*[3]

The suffering and abuse these persecuted wife-slaves underwent is an historical truth. While the suffering and death of abandoned children is true, these accounts will not be found in apologetic Catholic literature. Even in the face of such crimes against the Body of Christ, priests continued to marry covertly and struggle against these terrible papal abuses that are today acknowledged by the Church to have been heretical. That century was a turning point in Christianity as the Hierarchy desperately attempted to salvage a failed *organization*. While Catholicism may still boast of being the oldest continuing religious organization on earth, it may no longer boast that it is organized as Jesus left it to us in the Deposit of Faith. It has changed.

Finally, even in the face of *"a whole literature of protest,"* control was later accomplished with this assault upon the sanctity of Sacramental Matrimony and Holy Orders. What must be noted above is a record of failed attempts by popes and bishops to impose celibacy over the first 1,000 years of the Church. While times have changed, celibacy remains. It should be noted that only a secular ruler may sanction the capture and sale of slaves.

This indicates the political power the Vatican State was able to wield at that time in Church history.

Ultimately, Pope Innocent II was successful and Siricius' doctrine of mandatory celibacy was reestablished during the second Lateran Council of 1139 AD when he merely reached back to Siricius' Infallible *Directa* Decretal, declaring the law to be "An ancient *tradition* first established by the Apostles," one thousand years after Jesus. This council culminated centuries of unsuccessful papal attempts to control the lower hierarchy through mandatory celibacy.

Canon 6: *Summary:* "Clerics living with women shall be deprived of their office and benefice."

With one fell swoop it was over. Live with a woman and you're fired. As the Catholic Encyclopedia above said, "*priestly marriage became ipso-facto null.*" Today, we simply call mandatory celibacy a vow, a promise, a practice, or a discipline. In those days Popes were more candid and no vow was sought.

Canon 7: *Summary:* "*Masses celebrated by members of the clergy who have wives or concubines are not to be attended by anyone.*"

In 1074 Pope Gregory VII had stated, "*The Church cannot escape from the Laity unless priests first escape the clutches of their wives.*"[4] A century earlier some bishops had foreseen problems that would ultimately ensue should mandatory celibacy be imposed. Italian Bishop Ulric of Imola argued, as had Bishop Paphnutius at the Nicaean Council, that the Church had no right to forbid marriage. Bishop Ulric said, "*When celibacy is imposed, priests will commit sins far worse than fornication.*"[5] Unfortunately, at that late date, more than a millennium after Jesus and more than half the time our Church has existed, mandatory celibacy was successfully imposed. After universal celibacy was achieved many later Popes such as Alexander VI, would simply keep mistresses. They were called *concubines*. It would be the next century after Pope Gregory before priestly marriage was imposed and in the interim other measures were available.

"Synod of Lillebonne [1080 AD] is worthy of note, for it affords us the earliest indication of a practice which subsequently became a stand-

ing disgrace to the Church [after Gregory's reforms]. The fifth canon declares that no priest shall be forced to give anything to the bishop or to the diocese beyond their lawful dues, and especially that no money shall be exacted on account of women kept. A tribute known as "collagium" [concubine tax] became at times a recognized source of revenue, in consideration of which the...ecclesiastics were allowed to enjoy in security the society of their concubines...this infamous custom continued to flourish until the sixteenth century, despite the most strenuous and repeated endeavors to remove so grievous a scandal."
—*History of Sacerdotal Celibacy*, Medieval Historian Henry C. Lea 1867

We see here a practice within the Church that lasted until after the Reformation.

1545 – PROTESTANT CHALLENGE SACRAMENTS, AND THE COUNCIL OF TRENT

"In the area of religious doctrine, the council refused any concessions to the Protestants and, in the process, crystallized and codified Catholic dogma far more than ever before. It directly opposed Protestantism by reaffirming the existence of seven sacraments"[6]
—Council of Trent

"By today's standards, Leo's plan was grossly unscrupulous. Catholics in that era, however, were accustomed to paying for spiritual benefit [Sacraments]"
—*People of God,* Anthony Gilles

During the 400 years after the Lateran Council, with control over the priesthood only tacitly secured until the Council of Trent in 1545 AD, things changed for the better for the popes, some of whom became military leaders, and for the worse for the priesthood. These changes led to the Reformation.

Western Europe emerged from the Middle Ages, during which civilization had nearly ended and meaningful communication with the Eastern Church with its truncated form of optional celibacy was almost totally useless. During this period literacy

169

vanished, intellectual growth and communications were often non-existent and "deviant" forms of Christianity sprang up. Across the continent, Europe was regrouping into nation-states that would challenge Vatican power. Highly nationalistic feelings began to influence the minds of all men, peasants and royalty. Voices from God-fearing churchmen against ascetic clerical abuse, and the sin they saw creeping further into the Church, had been raised at least a century earlier; dissidents remained in abundance. Two long simmering problems converged with Martin Luther - sinful Church leaders and secular European rulers who were hungry to shed the Vatican yoke in exchange for their own power and wealth.

Basically, nothing had changed. Imposition of Celibacy was out of control because; at a fundamental level a single man with no wife or family was easier to control. Powerful bishops and their families remained an untenable problem. Their huge family estates were handed on to family members. Some say Pope Boniface VIII, 1303 AD, provided nearly one quarter of Church revenues to his family. Popes saw married priests as men with divided loyalties. Of priests, theologian Erasmus of Rotterdam who supported a Catholic notion of free will said in 1525 AD, "I would like to see permission given to priests and monks to marry, especially when there is such a horde of priests among whom chastity is rare. I think the bishops would long since have given priests permission to marry if they did not derive more income from the taxes [culligium] on concubines than they could reap from wives."

Volume 12 of the *Old Catholic Encyclopedia* gives us an unusually candid view of the situation. "Gradually, a regrettable worldliness manifests itself in many high ecclesiastics...In the Papal Curia, political interest and worldly lives were often prominent. Many bishops and abbots (especially in countries where there were also territorial princes) bore themselves as secular rulers rather than servants of the Church... Luxury prevailed widely among the higher clergy, while the lower clergy were often oppressed." This is a polite way of saying the Church was under the control of a cabal of despotic clerics.

Still today, few Catholics realize Cardinals were once secular territorial princes who ruled their area as would a feudal lord. Rarely were they men of God. They were earthly barons, lords of their realm who operated sacramental filling-stations for a fee.

It mattered little that saintly preachers had tried to stem the tide of internal church failure. Throughout Italy, Catholic preachers denounced abuses in high places. The Franciscan John Capistrano, 1456 AD, preached penance and apostolic poverty to a morally indigent population, and Bernardino of Siena, 1444 AD, produced positive local effects. No matter, by 1498 AD, dissident Dominican priest Jerome Savonarola and his two supporting priests were publicly burned at the stake by Pope Alexander VI for preaching against clerical abuses. In some areas (Germany for example), greed and the quest for worldly secular power were too great to be overcome at this late date. During the Reformation, local princes (Cardinals) were often abetted by local bishops who would defy Rome and keep their church under tight control. By opposing the injustice of Rome's onerous financial demands, local bishops and princes were able to confiscate church property and relieve themselves from further payment to the secular Vatican State. Thus, the Reformation ensued, spurred by the illicit sale of Indulgences.

By the way, Luther was imminently correct in his initial objection to the selling of salvation through letters of Indulgence (Simony – a heresy).[7] Luther said correctly, "I had intended to say and to assent to nothing except what is contained primarily in Holy Scripture and then in the church fathers...and in Canon Law and the papal decrees."

Pope John Paul II later apologized for the Churches' personal actions against Luther at that time.

DETAILS OF TRENT – SACRAMENT OF ORDINATION

"Was not Pope Leo X a cultured atheist who used to tell his friends that 'Christianity was a profitable situation for Popes'?"
[Answer]: No.

—*That Catholic Church.* Fr. Leslie Rumble, Question 185

It is reported that Martin Luther's theological views began to change, not in Germany where he began as a pious monk, but during a pilgrimage to Rome in 1510 where he found, not other pious churchmen, but what he viewed as a corrupt and cynical system of authority. He felt theologically destitute.

In the beginning, this flap was correctly instigated by Luther as a means of confronting Rome concerning the *selling* of Letters of Indulgence. Priest John Huss (Jan Hus) was the first to publicly preach against the selling of indulgences that were initially bestowed upon contributors to the Crusades. He supported Wycliffe's belief that Biblical authority held superiority over papal teaching. Huss was burned at the stake unrepentant in 1415.

Without entering into a theological discussion describing Indulgences let us simply say it is not a Sacrament, merely a means of bypassing Purgatory, a place of waiting after death. Catholics teach the soul must temporarily abide there if they haven't fully atoned for earthly sins before entering the presence of God. Leo's indulgences even claimed to release dead relatives from Purgatory, but it was wrongly described as a place of torment similar to Hell. Here was apostasy of the highest order, as revealed by the powerful preaching of Pope Leo X's agent, Monk Johann Tetzel, "Don't you hear the voices of your dead parents and other relatives crying out, 'Have mercy on us, for we suffer great punishment and pain. From this you could release us with a few alms... we have created you, fed you, cared for you and left you our temporal goods. Why do you treat us so cruelly and leave us to suffer in the flames, when it takes only a little to save us.'"

Indulgences have nothing whatsoever to do with sin forgiveness, they presume one has already repented, confessed all their sins and consequently are in the state of grace. This incident however brought about the Protestant Reformation and is well recorded by Anthony Gilles in his book, *People of God*, an excellent Catholic apologetic (paraphrased): "Pope Leo X wished to complete construction on St. Peter's Basilica so that his family, the Medici, would receive the credit. Unfortunately Pope Leo was nearly bankrupt; therefore he devised a scheme with [Secular ruler] Prince/Archbishop Albert of Brandenburg who was in arrears on his financial obligations to Rome. Leo and Albert agreed to have Indulgences sold and split the money, 50-50, thereby settling both financial problems. For the purchase of Indulgences, Catholics would be presented with a papal document forgiving all sin and bypassing Purgatory, even freeing dead relatives from Purgatory with sufficient payment. It often became a public street carnival with liturgical peddlers singing a ditty. "As soon as the coin in the coffer rings, the soul from Purgatory springs." Many innocents believed their sins were forgiven, even future sins – for money.

This entire scheme was an utter lie. Indulgences do not forgive sins. Therefore both Pope Leo X and all associated with this scam were committing outright heresy. This author sees Leo X as a truly godless man who believed Jesus to be a myth. This opinion is held by the majority of secular historians. At age eight he was abbot of a wealthy monetary. By 13 he had been appointed either bishop or abbot sixteen times, yet never visited these dioceses or monasteries of which he was supposedly the spiritual head. He became a Cardinal 14 before eventually being ordained Pope at the age of 37 he was ordained Pope, despite never having been ordained to the priesthood.

To confront Leo X and "his Sacraments," Luther retreated to *Sola Scriptura* (scripture alone) as his sole theological authority and left the church, for which Pope Leo attempted to have him burned at the stake. Abandoning all Vatican authority, Luther sought other than Sacraments for his *justification* before God. Luther quoted St. Paul who, writing only of Old Testament Law, had said, "As we see it, man is justified by faith [alone] and not by doing something the Law [Jewish Law] tells him to do." Romans 3:28 Nonetheless, Luther's Bible translation revealed errors in Jerome's translation on key words such as *justification, penance*, and *Sacraments* which were all used to wrongly portray the efficacy of indulgences to unsuspecting Catholics. But in defending his new position, Luther equated Christian Sacraments with the Old Testament Jewish Law that Paul had preached against. Catholicism, asserting superiority of the New Testament *Law of Christ* responded, "We are justified by following Jesus' commandments and these commandments (Laws) include accepting His

Sacraments." Therefore, Sacraments were a central issue of the Reformation.

Whatever the other details, that solitary passage of scripture pretty much sums up the theological differences that surrounded the Council of Trent and the importance of Sacraments for Catholics – even today. The Reformers saw Sacraments as *works of the Law* that only ordained Priests in communion with Rome could administer. Thus giving Rome control over the illiterate masses that were often forced to pay Simonist fees for these God-given Sacraments and, as Luther rightly taught, "Paid for salvation." Today many Protestants hold only Baptism and the Eucharist as Sacraments; some only Baptism. Luther later refused to acknowledge five of the seven Sacraments while the Church continued to place all seven well within the Deposit of Faith. In whatever manner one may view this issue, Luther had a legitimate grievance with Pope Leo and with Monk Johann Tetzel.

The sanctity of the Sacraments, which were powerful papal tools when confronting secular rulers, were at risk. "*Sacramental Interdiction*" is an ecclesiastical censure that excludes from certain rites [Sacraments] of the Church individuals, nations or groups: "Pope Innocent III placed the Kingdom of Norway under interdict in October 1198. The same Pope also placed the kingdom of England under an interdict for five years between 1208 and 1213, after King John refused to accept the pope's appointee Stephen Langton as Archbishop of Canterbury."[8] These Interdicts were employed to bring rulers such as King John to their knees. We can imagine the pressure placed on the King by all Christians in England who for five years were denied Sacraments that the laity believed was necessary for salvation: even baptism of children was denied until the King capitulated.

Asserting Papal authority, the Council Infallibly Defined:

"All Sacraments of the New Covenant were Instituted by Jesus Christ" *(De fide)*

We belabor these decisions by the Council of Trent because they reveal an important point in support of this book and the truth it wishes to present – all seven Sacraments are unchangeably ensconced in the Deposit of Faith, as Doctrines of Christ, which Siricius' first ascetic Papal Doctrine of Celibacy nullified.

CHAPTER SIXTEEN

CONTRACEPTION –
THE SECOND ASCETIC DOCTRINE

"Later, effective birth control would arrive on the scene – but the Catholic Church in particular banned it because (some argue) it would result in enjoying sex (still seen as a major sin) without concerns about pregnancy."[1]

—The Ancient Roots of Our Judeo-Christian Sexual Prohibitions

All discussion of Catholic birth control should begin with Orthodox Judaism of the first century during a time when all Christians were Jews and Genesis 1:28, considered by Jews to be the first Biblical command stated: "Be fruitful, multiply." Following this first Biblical command from God, Jewish Talmudic literature prohibited male contraception, believing male semen to be the source of life; however, exceptions were made for women, permitting female contraception for health reasons such as danger to the mother and/or the potential child. Today this ancient Jewish law continues to provide exceptions for Orthodox Jewish couples in certain circumstances. For example, when the couples already have two children. This seems to be a most reasonable Rabbinical interpretation of the law, for after all, how is the word "multiply" to be understood? Has the law been fulfilled with only one child or would ten children be required? Apparently the number two was settled on. However, only brutal and dangerous contraception techniques were available at that time and rarely used; most ancient rabbinical texts refer to the use of "absorbents" such as a vinegar soaked sponge which was intended to act as an IUD. But, it must also be recognized that no effective or safe birth control technique existed.

Rabbi Meir Baal Haneis who lived side by side with Jewish-Christians for most of his life was also a supporter of Simon Bar Kokhba during his revolution against Rome in 135 AD. He was also a contributor to the formation of the *Mishnah,* which interprets ancient Jewish Law. Rabbi Meir identified at least three health reasons for allowing women to use a sponge soaked with vinegar as a means of contraception. Henry Daniel-Rops in his book, *Daily Life in Palestine at the Time of Christ* is an invaluable asset for Christians seeking to understand first century culture, society and practices for Christian-Jews allowed under Jewish Law. Daniel-Rops addresses the subject of contraception under "A Child of Israel." He says, "...it was licit to bring a midwife to assist her, to tie the umbilical cord and even, asserts the tractate Sabbath (18.3), to cut it. If there were danger to the mother, contraceptive practices were not only allowed but even recommended." (Yebamoth 12.6)

Rabbinical texts often varied, but factually, contraception was allowed in various cases during the Deposit of Faith. As described in Daniel-Rops' book, which is graced with both the *Nihil obstat* and an *Imprimatur*, indicating it violates no Church Dogma. This Jewish law to propagate applied to married Christian-Jews during the Deposit of Faith and required intent by couples to produce offspring. Today, both this "intent" to reproduce and conjugal consummation are required by the Church in order for a Catholic marriage to be a valid marriage. Unfortunately, this requirement of "intent" demanded by the Church today is an open-ended commitment, commanding continued production of children under any circumstances. Today 90 percent of Catholics ignore this law because absolutely no exceptions for health, finances or number of children are permitted. The Church forbids all use of contraception. Why? This Church restriction of today, enforced under pain of mortal sin, was unknown to Christian-Jews. Perhaps the simplest way to explain the beginnings of this Catholic law is an examination of the ascetic Hellenistic influences which we discussed.

Contraception first began to affect Christianity during the second century with the insistence that virginity was superior to marriage and that all priests should attain this superior spiritual

level, while the laity must be satisfied with a lesser level of sanctity. The ancient view that virginity was superior to marriage also
included the belief that procreation could not be used for pleasure or to express marital love; copulation was considered merely a duty that must be controlled, not for pleasure. The Church
position today is based on the natural law theory of Aristotle and
Augustine, both of which deem that all sex has as its ultimate end
procreation; love need not be a factor. Here we will merely cite
these Patristic beliefs which continue to affect Catholicism today.

Today, the first proposed objection to contraception
by Vatican apologists is from the Old Testament Gen 38:8. Jewish
law of the time could require a brother to marry the widow of his
deceased brother who died childless, thus providing offspring and
heirs for his dead brother's family and keeping his brother's property within the tribe. This tribal law continues today within Islam.
In this Biblical text a brother, Onan, realizing he could inherit both
his dead brother's and his father's estate, should his brother have
no heirs; violated this law. Scripture informs us he "wasted his
seed on the ground" when he slept with his sister-in law to prevent any heirs. This was apostasy and because it offended God,
"he brought about his own death." In this case Onan died because
he deviously violated a Jewish law which he had vowed to God,
requiring him to produce offspring for his brother; contraception
was merely his tool, apostasy and greed was his sin, "thou shall
not covet thy neighbor's house." In any case, this ancient law had
no application to Christians during the Deposit of Faith because
Jesus changed Jewish marriage laws – one man, one wife. Today
such a practice as impregnating one's sister-in-law would clearly
be considered adultery. This scripture, often used by Vatican apologists, is an invalid defense of contraception or celibacy.

THE PATRISTIC REJECTION OF CONTRACEPTION

*"Virtually all the major patristic writers from the first century to the
sixth insisted that virginity was a state greatly superior to marriage
and emphasized the propriety of keeping women in subjection; most
of them repeatedly expressed dread of women's seductiveness and
contempt for their mental or moral frailty. They recurred to the Fall [of*

177

Eve] again and again, and managed to interpret many other Biblical
texts as divine condemnations of the female sex."
—*The Troublesome Helpmate: A History of Misogyny in Literature.*
Katherine M. Rogers

Approaching the third century, Patristic Fathers held two sep-arate moral standards for Christians; priests should remain totally chaste, while the average Christian was allowed to procreate; so long as procreation was not for pleasure. Today the Church con-tinues to teach the Sacrament of Matrimony is inferior to the sac-rament of priestly Orders for celibate priests. The first Patristic objection to contraception came from Justin Martyr, c.160 AD, during the height of Hellenist influence of the Didascalia "study-circles" on Christianity, he said, "We Christians marry only to pro-duce children." While Justin could not directly oppose marriage itself for lay Christians, he considered marriage less spiritual than sexual abstinence, as the Church teaches today. Other Christians such as scripture scholar Origen, c. 200 AD, castrated themselves as a safeguard against the sins of sex. By 325 AD the Hellenist practice of self-castration among aspiring priests became so seri-ous that Canon 1 of the Council of Nicaea prohibited ordination of such men, yet the practice continued covertly for several cen-turies. Jewish Law prohibiting eunuchs from entering the Temple had existed for centuries

"The Gospel, as Clement reads it, not only restricts sexuality to marriage but, even within marriage, limits it to specific acts intended for procreation."[2] Bishop Clement of Alexandria c. 205 AD objected to the pleasure of marital sex so stridently that he preached, "If a man marries in order to have children he ought not to have a sexual desire for his wife...he ought to produce chil-dren by a reverent, disciplined act."

St. Jerome, translator of the Vulgate Bible, c. 400 AD said, "Do you imagine that we approve of any sexual intercourse except for the procreation of children?" He then took his procreation versus pleasure attitude to its logical conclusion: "He who is too ardent a lover of his own wife is an adulterer." His adversary, Jovian, who left the priesthood to marry was deemed a heretic.

Theologian Lactantius, c. 307 AD, condemning those who sought to avoid pregnancy because of poverty or health said, "Wherefore, anyone on account of poverty shall be unable to support children, it is better to abstain from relations with his wife." The "rhythm method" which the Church teaches today was unacceptable for Lactantius.

During his early life of debauchery, Augustine, c. 400 AD, fathered one child before converting and becoming totally committed to sexual abstinence, he then saw married intercourse as a great temptation to sin. "It is one thing to lay together [married] with the sole will of generating: this is no fault. It is another to seek [only] pleasure of the flesh in lying, although within the limits of marriage." Happily, he considered this merely a venial sin, not a mortal sin as is proposed today. Augustine's view of married sex was quite restrictive. He condemned the rhythm method that is approved today and considered sex the vehicle for passing on original sin. This belief is extremely close to that of the Gnostic Jewish belief system, Cabala, taught by Philo Judaea in 45 AD. The Cabalists considered absolute chastity necessary for holiness, believing the earth was in control of Satan and the procreation of children only furthered his reign. Augustine believed the male fetus received its soul 40 days before birth, the female 90; abortion prior to that was acceptable.

CONTRACEPTION BECOMES SIN

When did today's rigorous interpretation of contraception begin? We find no such interpretation until 130 years after Jesus, by Justin Martyr in 160 AD. Prior to that time only gnostic pseudo-Clementine writings appeared, claiming to be written by the third pope, Clement, who had died c. 98 AD. Clement himself makes no mention of contraception or virginity in his acknowledged writings. These apocryphal writings praising the virtues of virginity began to appear well into the second century. Those and similar Apocrypha were used later by Patristic Fathers during the second century when sex itself began to be seen as carnal, and all previous leniency was condemned. These writings are used by some apologists today to wrongly insinuate celibacy arose among the Apostles. Today, Conservative and Reformed

Jews note that sexual pleasure is permissible and contraception is sanctioned by rabbinical literature for both health and birth control. Protestants followed Catholic practice until 1930 when they declared it a matter of conscience. Today, our separated brethren, the Eastern Orthodox churches that split from us during the middle ages hold a similar view as do Jews today. The tradition of the Eastern Orthodox Church does not discern a moral difference between artificial or natural birth control methods such as the rhythm method.

The Vatican becomes apoplectic when it is suggested no difference exists between these two methods of birth control. Orthodox Church Fathers believe the Pauline texts in the New Testament do not strictly limit sexual intercourse to procreation. The Orthodox position on sexual intercourse is that it also constitutes an expression of love within the marriage contract. Today, asserting the "dignity of the very person" the Vatican lumps, contraception, infanticide and abortion together as one. It is strange indeed that both the Catholic Encyclopedia and Ludwig Ott's *Fundamentals of Catholic Dogma* fail to list contraception, chastity, or birth control as subjects; while Catholic literature is replete with writings on the virtue of monasticism and the superiority of sexual abstinence for our priests. Similarly, the Church also approves of married couples living together in sexual abstinence.

CATHOLIC CONTRACEPTION, A MODERN SCANDAL

It was not until the 20th century that the subject of mandatory procreation for Catholics under all circumstances became an international problem for the Church. In 1930 the Anglican Church was followed by all Protestant denominations in teaching contraception to be a matter of conscience. Upon this pronouncement by the Protestants, Pope Pius XI saw a threat to Church authority that must be defended, even though at that time unlimited reproduction was not an infallibly defined dogma of the Catholic Church. Sensing this challenge, similar to previous challenges by the Reformers, Pope Pius XI reacted swiftly with the issuance of a Papal Encyclical *Casti Connubii*, repeating several times that the conjugal act is intrinsically tied with procreation, identical to the position of the Patristics in the third century. Condemning all who accept such a position, both Catholic and Protestant.

Supported as an infallible pronouncement, this Encyclical (Papal Bull) issued by Pope Pius XI declared: "...any use whatsoever of matrimony exercised in such a way that the act [procreation] is deliberately frustrated in its natural power to generate life is an offense against the law of God and nature, and those who indulge in such are branded with the guilt of a *Grave sin*."

Here was a teaching threatening condemnation for all who disobeyed it, and it was assumed to be an infallibly Defined Dogma. It was not. There was a great outcry from Catholic faithful imbued with the mistaken belief that, when the pope issues an Encyclical, he speaks infallibly. This too is incorrect.

This looming scandal lay dormant until 1968 when contraception became a national discussion. Addressing this public discussion Pope Paul VI appointed a Papal Commission on *Population and Birth Control*. This commission was composed of 15 cardinals and bishops and 64 lay Catholic experts representing a variety of disciplines. One member, Thomas Burch, a professor at Georgetown University reported the pope had "...asked them to find a way to change the Church's position on birth control without destroying papal authority." With this papal request it must be acknowledged the pope did not consider the teaching of contraception, issued by Pius XI in Casti Connubii to be infallible dogma, otherwise he would not have considered such a commission to be capable of circumventing a previous infallible declaration.

After two years of study the lay commissioners voted 60-4 and the clergy voted 9-6 to change the position on birth control, even though some believed it could challenge papal authority. However, a minority report dissenting from the majority was issued by Vatican infallibility apologists and submitted to the pope. The following are quotations from the minority report.

"If it be declared that contraception is not sin in itself, then we should have to concede frankly that the Holy Spirit had been on the side of the Protestant Churches in 1930 [when Casti Connubii was promulgated] It should likewise have to be admitted that for half a century the Spirit failed to protect Pius XI, Pius XII, and a large part of the Catholic hierarchy from a very serious error.

181

This would mean that leaders of the Church, acting with extreme imprudence, had condemned thousands of innocent human acts, forbidding under pain of eternal damnation, a practice which would now be sanctioned. The fact can neither be denied nor ignored that these same acts would now be declared licit on the grounds of principles cited by the Protestants, which popes and bishops have condemned or at least not approved." This dissenting report was authored by Cardinal Karol Wojtyla of Poland, later Pope John Paul II.

It was solely on this minority report that Pope Paul VI issued another Papal encyclical, *Humanae Vitae*, in 1968, again infallibly asserting contraception to be a mortal sin. This then became a case of the Church defending a decision that was portrayed as infallibly Defined Dogma in order to protect papal authority. It is this Encyclical which today is proffered by Church apologists to be infallible, claiming it merely conforms to and supports a previous infallible pronouncement, Casti Connubii, issued in 1930. Addressing the reasons for the pope rejecting the commission's recommendations, and following only the minority report, Catholic theologian and historian Dr. August Bernhard Hasler said, "Thus it became only too clear that the core of the problem was not the pill, but the authority, continuity, and infallibility of the Churches' Magisterium."

INFALLIBLE DECLARATIONS

Confusion and misunderstanding surrounds this "infallible" Encyclical, *Humanae Vitae,* as does the fallible doctrine of mandatory celibacy. Neither Casti Connubi nor Humanae Vitae are publicly, solemnly and explicitly declared to be Definitively Defined Dogma; which Pope Paul VI realized in 1968. Whatever the Curia's declared intention may have been, a fatal flaw exists. Exemptions from this law, as presently required, were allowed during the Deposit of Faith when all Christians were Jews. Only in the second century when Hellenisticly influenced clerics began to denigrate the conjugal expression of love within a valid marriage do we first encounter this new doctrinal impediment to marriage being preached – it was "some new doctrine." Dogmatic Truths within the Deposit of Faith are the source of all infallibility. Infallibility is Truth and Truth does not contradict itself, nor can Truth develop, nor can natural law, which is science, contradict our first beliefs. Here again we find Authoritative Doctrines, which may be changed, portrayed as Infallible Definitive Dogma. Our present teaching of birth control laws violates the Deposit of Faith.

A CONSTITUTIONAL LAW

In 2012, this papal doctrine denying contraception exploded into American presidential politics with Republican presidential candidate Senator Rick Santorum's defense of the law. As a devout Catholic and political conservative, Santorum felt obliged to condemn as unconstitutional, government demands that Catholic organizations provide contraception insurance for employees. He lost. With over 90 percent of Catholics rejecting the contraception law, it is impossible for the public to know whether he was among those Catholic dissenters who rejected the law, or if he was bound for political and theological reasons to support the pope. Unfortunately for Mr. Santorum, his private position seemed meaningless.

The fear of having this papal doctrine exposed as illicit, and consequently undermining Vatican assertions of papal infallibility is so important that President Obama's administration clearly misjudged the extremes to which the Church will go in order to protect the papacy, despite the potential loss of billions of tax dollars funneled into other Church programs being at risk.

Concerned with potential Church rejection of progressive social issues such as the mandate requiring coverage of contraceptives in the Health Care plan, the Administration apparently believed that dramatically increasing federal funding for other Catholic affiliated organizations, both domestically and internationally, would mitigate Church opposition to the contraception mandate. The President's Administration miscalculated. Even with a fivefold increase for other Catholic affiliated charities since taking office and a total of $1.5 billion over the last two years,[3] the Church cannot afford to abandon the contraception law, and with it the belief in papal infallibility.

Understanding that to abandon the prohibition of contraception under any circumstance is to deny papal infallibility, Cardinal

183

Timothy Dolan of New York, who himself aspires to the papacy, and is head of the US Conference of Catholic Bishops, will never yield on this issue. Cardinal Dolan's effort to defend the pope at any cost now includes a financial attack on faithful Catholic parishioners.

In an effort to decimate a lay Catholic group,[4] Survivors Network of those Abused by Priests (SNAP), which reports on priestly sex abuse and cover-ups by bishops, Cardinal Dolan is prepared to invest millions of Church dollars into legal attacks designed to bankrupt the laities privately financed ability to defend itself. Money is not an obstacle when defending the papacy.

Today this contraception law has entered American politics. Unfortunately, the Vatican is not content with applying the law against contraceptive birth control only to the Catholic faithful. Pope John Paul II in his *Instruction on Respect for Human Life in its Origin and on the Dignity of Procreation* declared that Catholic teaching must become law. The pope's *Instruction* states: "Politicians must commit themselves, through intervention upon public opinion, to securing the widest possible consensus on such essential points. ..." They are expected to enact into law "appropriate legal sanctions" for violations of the contraception law. Today, this Church law denying contraception is on the brink of becoming a Constitutional Law.

While this papal doctrine's condemnation of "thousands of innocent human acts" remains in force, newly uncovered information revealing names and actions of Vatican officials, and the covert means employed to protect the concept of papal infallibility, were recently revealed in an article published by *National Catholic Reporter*. The extremes to which Vatican apologists will descend in order to protect the concept of papal infallibility is striking. This is a must read article for all Catholics who seek the truth.[5]

CHAPTER SEVENTEEN

THE THIRD ASCETIC DOCTRINE – THE PRIESTHOOD AND WOMEN

"The Vatican labels the ordination of women a 'grave crime' to be dealt with in the same way as sex abuse."[1]

—Mail On line. July 2010

The above epigraph made headlines throughout the Catholic world in 2010, only eight years after public revelations that celibate Catholic priests were guilty of sexually abusing vulnerable youths, a scandal that is decimating the priesthood world-wide. Confused and distressed by such an offensive allegation from the papal office, faithful Catholics could not understand such an offensive accusation being directed at devout religious women; this was a turning point for American Catholics. Understanding the abuse of women and children that has repeatedly occurred over the centuries since mandatory celibacy was imposed, this event has now created another class of victims. All priests, including those faithful priests who valiantly live out their sacrificial vow of chastity are now viewed by non-Catholic as no different than the abusers. These innocent priests are the victims of this scandal.

"The norms offer weak protection to innocent priests and deacons who are easy targets of groundless accusations."

—National Catholic Reporter. (NCR) Feb 20, 2004.

"The board of bishops must work harder to repair relations with priests, 'many of whom feel alienated from both the bishops and laity, because of the scandal."
—*Associated Press*, Rachael Zoll. December 14, 2007.

In the face of this tragic scandal Catholics were shocked to read the Vatican has identified the ordination of women to be as sinful as priestly sex abuse. How did this view of women come about?

THE PATRISTIC ERA

"Virtually all the major Patristics writers from the first century to the sixth insisted that virginity was a state greatly superior to marriage and emphasized the propriety of keeping women in subjection; most of them repeatedly expressed dread of woman's seductiveness and contempt for their mental or moral frailty. They recurred to the Fall [of Eve] again and again, and managed to interpret many other Biblical texts as divine condemnation of the female sex."
— *The Troublesome Helpmate: A history of Misogyny in Literature.*
Kathleen M. Rogers

Throughout this book we have attempted to identify the second and third century Patristic era as a definitive turning point in early Christianity, a time when Hellenisticly inspired scholars, the Patristic Fathers', converted to Christianity, bringing with them a lifelong commitment to ascetic Hellenistic beliefs which had no place in Christianity or Orthodox Judaism.With Justin Martyr, Clement of Alexandria, Tertullian, Anti-Pope Hippolytus, Origen, Gregory, Ambrose, and Jerome who translated the Latin Vulgate Bible, came Hellenistic teachings that St. Paul had so stridently preached against. There were others, but it was primarily these men who ensconced Plato's ascetic philosophy into the Church. It was also during this period that Tertullian was successful in theologically divorcing Jesus of Nazareth from His Jewish nature and the Old Testament, around which Christianity was formed. With this change came asceticism, misogyny and Anti-Semitism, much of which remains with us today. As we read through this epoch of change we discover the origin of today's Sacerdotal Priesthood and the expulsion of women from the Eucharistic table.

The greatest difficulty for the modern laity to grasp when considering the ordination of women is - Ordained Sacerdotal priests did not exist the beginning - and therefore did not consecrate the Eucharist. Today's definition of the priesthood did not originate in the Deposit of Faith. In first generation Christianity, the Mass was simply a communal meal as was the Last Supper. History now speaks to us; Jesus' had both male and female disciples at a time when meal preparation was a female role. Two *disciples* attending the Last Supper are firmly held by historians to have been women. St. Peter tells us of the first Jewish-Christian Mass, "They went to the Temple every day but met in their houses for the breaking of bread; they shared their food gladly and generously." Acts 2:46 No one today believed the Apostles employed a chef to cater their "upper room" Last Supper.

It is possible to understand the first century Christian "Mass" when St. Paul criticizes the lack of decorum at the Corinthian communal meal, where some became drunk. Upset with such decorum, St. Paul said: "I hear that when you come together as a community there are separate factions among you... The point is, when you hold these meetings, it is not the Lord's Supper that you are eating, since when it comes time to eat, everyone is in such a hurry to start his own supper that one person goes hungry while another is getting drunk. Surely you have homes for eating and drinking in. Surely you have enough respect for the community of God not to make poor people embarrassed...So anyone who eats the bread and drinks the cup of the Lord unworthily will be behaving unworthily toward the body and blood of the Lord." 1 Corinthians 11:18-27 With Paul's statement here concerning the "common meal," we understand the Eucharist was *the meal* prepared for the "Mass." More importantly, this communal *meal* was considered, through faith, to be the Eucharistic thanksgiving *Memorial*. There was no Sacerdotal Priest at this Corinthian Mass, only a President identified as a *Presiding Elder*. There is nothing in the Deposit of Faith associating any Christian with the term "Priest" as defined today, a term used only among the Levitical Jewish priesthood.

The First Appearance of Priests

The term "priest" first appears first in the *Didascalia* c. 250 AD, two centuries after Christ when it described "Presiding Elders" as "bishops", a term first introduced by Ignatius of Antioch c.106 AD with no indication of Sacerdotal power.

"You also then to-day, O bishops, are priests to your people and the Levites who minister to the tabernacle of God, the holy Catholic Church, who stand continually before the Lord God. You then are to your people priests and prophets, and princes and leaders and kings, and mediators between God and His faithful."[2] This was the first appearance of the term "priest" in Church literature.

In this voluminous third century Didascalia, the term "priest" appears 33 times. In each instance the term refers to the "bishop," who in all citations is merely *analogized* as a Jewish Levitical "priest." By this time in the third century, Christ's Jewish origins were well known, albeit He was by then viewed as the epitome of asceticism's triumph over the flesh. However, now analogizing bishops with Jewish "priests" there is no suggestion bishops possessed the Sacerdotal power of *consecration.*

The Absence of Priestly Power

In this voluminous Didascalia text the term "Eucharist" appears always in the context of consuming it with a "prayer of thanksgiving." The term "consecrate" does not appear in the Didascalia. The term "sacrifice" appears 28 times, always in reference to *Jewish Sacrifices,* such as: *"The Lord, by the gift of His grace, has set you loose and given you rest, and brought you out into refreshment [Ps 66.12 (65.12 LXX)], that you should no more be bound with sacrifices and oblations, and with sin offerings."* There is no reference in this newly developed "Church Orders" document to a "priest" consecrating the Eucharist. Only after that time was it taught that Ordained Sacerdotal priests must "consecrate" the Eucharist, or that the Mass is a "Sacrifice" rather than a "Memorial Thanksgiving." Christ instituted the Mass when, "He took the bread, and then when He had given thanks, broke it and gave it to them, saying, 'this is my body which will be given for you; do this as a *memorial* of me.'" Luke 22:19.

Following Jesus' request the "memorial prayer of thanksgiving" was originally celebrated precisely as described by house-church members in the *Didache;* as they "first *touch*" their "meal" (Eucharist) they individually offered a prayer of "Thanksgiving." Clearly the Sacerdotal Priesthood of today had not yet arrived by the middle of the third century as we read the third century *Didascalia.* Nowhere in his teaching does St. Paul indicate a Priest was required to "consecrate" the Eucharist of Christ. However, St. Paul *does* explain the term "priest" within the Christian context has nothing to do with the sacrifice of Christ. Writing to the Romans Paul explains: "God gave me this special mission. He has appointed me a priest of Jesus Christ, and *I am to carry out my priestly duty* by *bringing the Good News from God to the pagans, and so make them acceptable as an offering,* made by the Holy Spirit." Romans 15: 15-16 Paul here describes his priestly "offering" as *pagans made holy* by the Holy Spirit. Christ's sacrificial death on the cross ended all Christian sacrifice. Our weekly Mass is not another sacrifice, it is a "Memorial" of Christ's sacrifice, as He requested.

Here we find the first analogy of clerics with the term "priest." However, by the end the next century we find Siricius addressing all clerics as "priests" in his *Decretal* of 385 AD. Today, Vatican apologists retreat to Scriptural sophistry (*Eisegesis*) in order to obviate Christ's one-time sacrificial death. One Vatican apologist defines Christ's sacrificial death thusly: "I'd like to further examine the notion that Christ acts through the priest supremely through the celebration of the Eucharist. Without getting into a long apologetic, Catholic theology teaches that the Eucharist is the sacrifice of Christ that transpired on Calvary, *extended through time.*" Such eisegesis is beneath historical discussion. *Catholic Answers website.*

The Fourth Lateran Council 1215 AD Establishes the Sacerdotal Priesthood

"To turn to classical antiquity, Greece never possessed an exclusive priestly caste... [The] public priesthood was regarded as the privilege of the nobility. In Homer the kings also offer sacrifices to the gods.

The importance of the [Greek] priesthood grew with the extension of the mysteries, which were embodied especially in the Orphic and Eleusinian cults."
—Priesthood. New Advent Catholic Encyclopedia.

Seventy five years after Pope Innocent II re-established Siricius' law of celibacy the Church continued to struggle with the priesthood, many left the priesthood and by 1215 AD acceptance of the Eucharist had fallen noticeably among the Laity. Concerned, Innocent III assembled the Fourth Lateran Council in order to elevate the priestly image once more. This council was also called in response to an increasingly influential Christian movement, the Waldenses, who since 839 AD were tortured, exiled and martyred for rejecting the hierarchy, and a belief that all Christians could interpret the Bible. Facing these challenges Pope Innocent III acted.

In Dr. Ludwig Ott's authorative book, *Fundamentals of Catholic Dogmas,* he describes the Vatican's first definition of Sacerdotal Priests: *"The power of consecration resides in a validly consecrated priest only."* This statement is unsupported by first century Christian history. Ott further explains:

"According to [the Patristic] St. Justin 'the overseers of the brethren *perform* the Eucharist'...What is decisive in this matter is that *Tradition* always refers this *mandate* to the Apostles and their successors in the priesthood."

The *Tradition* Ott speaks of is the Didascalia. However, attempting to obfuscate the many non-ordained Christian leaders known to have presided over the Eucharist during the Deposit of Faith, Ott adds, "It may be *inferred* with a high degree of *probability* that the charismatically-gifted 'Prophets' of the primitive Church also *celebrated* the Eucharist. It does not contradict dogma to *assume* they possessed the sacerdotal powers on the ground of an *immediate* [non-ordained] Divine vocation just as the Apostles did." Here, Ott attempts to explain away the many non-ordained House-Church leaders who did "perform" the Memorial Eucharist, both men and women, yet were not "validly ordained priests."

In order to restore priests to their previously semi-Divine position first established by Siricius, the Council then required the laity to make a confession yearly and receive the Eucharist during Easter, under threat of excommunication.

THE JEWISH PROBLEM.

Before departing the Fourth Lateran Council we must note its residue of Hellenistic anti-Semitism. The Jews had been a problem since Lateran Council II when Usury [lending money] was "Stigmatized with the mark of infamy in Canon 13" Assaulting this *stigma,* Innocent acted. Throughout the Diaspora and since before Christ, Judaism had thrived on commercial and economic exchange, including lending money at interest. Therefore, Canon 67: *"The more the Christians are restrained from the practice of usury, the more are they oppressed in this matter by the treachery of the Jews"*; Canon 68: *"Jews and Saracens of both sexes in every Christian province must be distinguished from the Christian by a difference of dress. On Passion Sunday and the last three days of Holy Week they may not appear in public."* Canon 69: *Jews are not to be given public offices. Anyone instrumental in doing this is to be punished. A Jewish official is to be denied all intercourse [commercial] with Christians.*

Modern Christians must examine their conscience regarding the justice of Innocent's laws of the Fourth Lateran Council.

ON THE PRIESTHOOD AND WOMEN

"When the question of the ordination of women arose in the Anglican Communion, Pope Paul VI, out of fidelity to his office of safeguarding the Apostolic Tradition...reminded Anglicans...She [Church, infallibly] holds that it is not admissible to ordain women to the priesthood, for very fundamental reasons. These reasons include: the example recorded in Sacred Scriptures of Christ choosing his Apostles only from men."

In conclusion the Pope wrote, "I [Infallibily] declare that the Church has no authority whatsoever to confer priestly ordination on women and that this judgment is to be definitively held by all the Church's faithful."

—Ordinatio Sacerdotalis, (On Ordination to the Priesthood).
1994, Pope John Paul II

191

Ordinatio Sacerdotalis was issued by Pope John Paul II in response to what he believed to be another Anglican challenge should the Church not ordain women priests. We note in the epigraph above that the Pope appeals to Scripture, our first authority, thus claiming women's ordination would violate the practice of Jesus. A major contention of this book will be that the very term, Christian "priest," whether man or woman, did not exist in either Scripture or Tradition contained in the Deposit of Faith. While the venerable term "priest" is an ancient and honorable term, and perfectly acceptable for today's priests, the modern Vatican definition of a "Sacerdotal priest" as the only Christian capable of consecrating the Eucharist first appeared *after* the Didascalia Apostolorum of 250 AD. Therefore, the question is, did women disciples sometimes perform the same function as did male disciples, now termed "priests," before the concept of "Christian priests" arrived. We know women and men both "said the liturgy" during Mass in House-Churches.

St. Paul's greeting to husband and wife House-Church ministers and teachers: "Aquila and Prisca [Priscilla], with the *church* that meets in their house, sends you their warmest wishes." 1 Corinthians 16:19. Aquila and Prisca had been driven from Rome and later rendered hospitality to St. Paul on his first missionary visit to Corinth. They also accompanied Paul to Ephesus where *they instructed* the Jewish convert from Alexandria, Apollos, in their House Church 1 Corinthians 16. "They took him aside and taught to him the way of God more accurately." Identified by Paul in 1 Corinthians 4:6, 9-13 as an "Apostle" (Not selected by Jesus), Apollos later wrote the canonical New Testament book to the *Hebrews*. It is beyond question that Prisca "taught" the Apostle, Apollos. Paul acknowledged women such as Prisca as she "taught" Apollos in her House-Church. Questions concerning the important part women played as teachers were answered by Paul himself in his letter to the Romans when he wrote: "Greeting to those outstanding *Apostles* Andronicius and *Junia* my relatives and fellow prisoners who became Christians before me." Romans 16:6-7 The suggestion that Apostle Junia did not teach or offer the "Eucharistic" prayer of thanksgiving during the common meal in Church is beneath debate.

Recently the *National Catholic Reporter* (NCR) produced a series of scholarly reports describing titles of women leaders in the early church, *Early women leaders: from heads of house churches to presbyters*[3]

"The earliest references to local resident *leaders* in the Pauline churches are Philippians 1:1... [Where] Paul addresses his letter to the community at Philippi with their *episkopoi* and *diakonoi*...These are the terms that later came to mean 'bishop' and 'deacon.'" Later, Deacon became the first Church office one must achieve before becoming priests (presbyters). "In another letter from Paul Romans 16:1-2 he introduces to the letter's recipient, a woman named Phoebe, a benefactor who is also a *diakonos* of the church...Thus we know that women could hold this title at the time, and therefore the *diakonoi* [both men and women] in Philippi could be a mixed group. Should the *episkopoi* of Philippians be heads of house churches, as seems likely, it is not impossible that some of them were also women (for example, Nympha in Colossians 4:15). Within two years the Epistles of Timothy and Titus 1 Timothy 3:4 and Titus 1:7 '...seem to have had a single *episkopos* [Bishop]'" Women are explicitly included among the deacons in first Timothy.

THE DIDACHE

We continually return to the *Didache*; described as a book of instruction for Christian House-Churches and communities before the New Testament was written, it is the oldest Christian literature. The Didache instructs all present to individually offer a "Prayer of thanksgiving" before and after partaking the Eucharistic "meal":

"But as 'touching' the Eucharistic thanksgiving give ye thanks thus. First, as regards the cup: We give Thee thanks, O our Father... After the Eucharist when you are filled, give thanks this way: We thank you, Holy Father, for your holy name which you enshrined in our hearts, and for the knowledge." Within two centuries women would be forbidden to approach the Eucharistic table.

As it would remain in the third century there is no mention of a Sacerdotal priest, rather, the community permits all teachers to "Eucharize as they wish." Here again we find the "Common Meal" to be the first Christian liturgical worship. As previously mentioned in his authoritative book, *The Birth of Christianity,* Benedictine John Dominic Crossan[4] quotes from 'The Didache: *"A Community of Equals,"* concluding there is no prohibition against women as trainers, baptizers, eucharistizers, apostles, prophets, or teachers, so it must be assumed that these functioning roles within the community were open to women." Yet the Didascalia later prohibits women from approaching the altar.

Lastly, we call to mind the House-Church reported by Pliny the younger to Emperor Trajan c. 111 AD. We recall that he reported, "[The accused Christians] were in the habit of meeting on a certain fixed day before it was light, when they sang in alternate verses a hymn to Christ, as to a god; after which it was their custom to separate, and then reassemble to partake of food – but an ordinary and innocent kind [Mass in a house church]; I judged it much more necessary to extract the real truth, with the assistance of torture from two female slaves who were styled deaconesses, but I could discover no more than depraved and excessive superstition." It is not unusual for church apologists to reach into later centuries for supportive Apocrypha when defending their positions; but here we have an historical support of Christian practices after the Deposit of Faith. Moreover, we find this House-Church is led by women Deacons before the late arrival of "priests."

AFTER THE PATRISTICS

"Two points are important to make about the development of leadership roles in the church in the period from the fifth to the 13th centuries. First the definition of ordination changed radically during the 12th century. Second, women were considered capable of ordination until the 13th century...During the first millennium...Not only bishops, priests, deacons and subdeacons [and lesser offices]...were all considered equally ordained...An ordo (order) was a group in the church that had a particular job or vocation,"[5]

—NCR.

"The meaning of ordination and how women were gradually excluded"

In the second NCR report we are informed that during the first millennium, as explained by Cardinal Yves Congar, the French Dominican theologian: "Ordination did not give a person, for instance, the irrevocable and *portable* power of consecrating the bread and wine, or of leading the liturgy, but rather a *particular* community would charge a person to play a leadership role within that community and he or she would lead the liturgy because of the leadership role they played within the community. So any leader within the community would be expected to lead the liturgy [Consecration]." This specifically comports with the practice of the Didache. Why did this change?

"Only in the 12th and 13th centuries did theologians and canonists devise...another definition of ordination [as it remains today], ordination granted the recipient not a position within a community, but *power* that a person can exercise in *any* community. The central power that ordination granted was the power to *consecrate* the bread and wine at the altar," strictly limited to priests, deacons and subdeacons. "All other earlier orders were no longer considered orders at all." Here we find that all advances made by women since the Patristic era and the third century Didascalia Apostolorum vanished in one fell-swoop. Women were excluded from all the orders, including that of priest, deacon and subdeacons. "In fact, it was taught and believed, and still is, that women never performed any of the roles now limited to those three orders."

THE 10TH – 13TH CENTURIES AND INVESTITURE

During the seven hundred years between Emperor Constantine's legalization of Christianity in 325 and 1049, priests often struggled against later Popes after Siricius' failed Infallible Celibacy Decretal, and sporadic efforts to force celibacy upon priests by selling wives and children of clerics into slavery. During this period much power and wealth fell into the hands of bishops who ruled their far-flung bishoprics as feudal lords since the Dark Ages when Vatican authority nearly vanished across much of Europe. Many bishops appropriated these fiefdoms for themselves and willed it to their heirs, thus depriving the Church of vast property and wealth.

Later, as Imperial power declined and Vatican power and wealth grew it became not a church but a sovereign nation, a theological and political state capable of exercising dominance over vast European populations, ultimately allowing future Popes to rival sovereign rulers of Europe, many of whom greeted him by kissing his slipper. During that time of new-found access to wealth, powerful clerics in far flung reaches of the Empire began treating their Bishoprics as private fiefdoms, their personal business, even buying and selling the office. These bishops became temporal monarchs who were rarely ordained prior to purchasing their office. Ultimately the Vatican state was losing control over its governmental infrastructure that threatened its very existence as a political nation- state. The major papal problem that for centuries had denied total papal control over the church was *Investiture*, that is, the pope's historical inability to control all clerical appointments. Since the Dark Ages, the appointment of bishops was in practice performed by members of the ruling nobility of each country, providing a substantial amount of wealth and land associated with the office of a bishop or abbot. The "Investiture Controversy" was the most significant conflict between Church and state in medieval Europe. In this time of change in the 11th and 12th centuries, a series of Popes challenged the authority of European monarchies over control of appointments, *investitures*, for church officials such as bishops and abbots. Since Constantine, European rulers maintained some control over the appointment bishops who then owed their first allegiance and taxes to their secular ruler, not to popes.

Overcoming this papal problem would ultimately elevate papal authority to its zenith under Pope Gregory VII, who first challenged the practice of investiture by secular rulers in an effort to transfer all such authority to the popes and cardinals. Gregory VII was a vain man who saw his authority as unchallengeable. Gregory declared no one but God could judge a Pope and had statues of himself placed in churches throughout Europe. Asserting Popes were saints on earth by virtue of their succession to Peter's throne, Gregory was determined to become the most powerful *Monarch* in Europe. Ultimately a settlement was reached in 1122 eliminating investiture. In 1074 Gregory had stated: "The church cannot escape from the laity unless priests first escape the clutches of their wives." He succeeded in paving the way for complete control over all clerics, including the threat of female clerics ordained by cardinals. Cardinal Yves Conger in 1995 said: "Gregory VII ended up making the Church itself into a legal institution – ruled by pseudo-infallible Canon Law and Canon law-yers." In the end these two centuries brought about changes for women in the church, parallel in many ways to the changes that occurred in the second and third century.

As reported in NCR research regarding the defrocking of all women, "All this changed over roughly a hundred year period between the end of the 11th century and the beginning of the 13th...women were gradually excluded from ordination. First, many roles in the church ceased to be considered as ordained... Powerful women in religious orders went from being ordained to laity. Second, canon lawyers and then theologians began to debate whether women could be ordained to the priesthood or diaconate. Several canonists argued women had previously been ordained deacons but were no longer. By the end of the 12th century arguments were put forward that women had never been 'really' ordained despite references in canon law to the con-trary. Finally, by the beginning of the 13th century, canonists and theologians argued that women had never been and could never be ordained since they were physically, mentally and spiritually inferior to men." Thus closing the circle back to the Patristic St. Ambrose c. 397 AD who said, "Remember, God took the rib out of Adam's body, not a part of his soul, to make her. She was not made in the image of God, like man...The Ministerial office must be kept pure and unspoiled and must not be defiled by coitus."[6] These centuries would bring about many changes for women in the church.

Thinking back, we recall how Pope Innocent II successfully instituted celibacy in the 12th century, finally bringing all male clerics into chaste submission; but during this epoch of change the previous advances by church women would also be addressed by the popes. The "women problem" was addressed in two can-ons of Innocent's Lateran Council. Fearing women might emulate male clerics we find in canon eight:

"We decree that the selfsame thing is to apply also to women religious if, God forbid, they attempt to marry."

And, apparently even nuns were becoming too independent from church authority to tolerate, as noted in canon twenty six:

"We decree that the pernicious and detestable custom which has spread among some women who, although they live neither according to the rule of blessed Benedict nor Basil nor Augustine, yet wish to be thought of by everyone as nuns, is to be abolished. For when, living according to the rule in monasteries, they ought to be in church or in the refectory or dormitory in common, they build for themselves their own retreats and private dwelling-places where, under the guise of hospitality, indiscriminately and without any shame they receive guests and secular persons contrary to the sacred canons and good morals. Because everyone who does evil hates the light, these women think that, hidden in the tabernacle of the just, they can conceal themselves from the eyes of the Judge who sees everything; so we prohibit in every way this unrighteous, hateful and disgraceful conduct and forbid it to continue under pain of anathema."

As noted by NCR scholars, the 13th century would continue to be a century of change. In 1298 AD Pope Boniface VIII issued a *Decretal* limiting, and subverting, all independent ministry and teaching of nuns, many of whom were becoming important personages within the church. "*Periculoso* (named for its Latin incipit, meaning *dangerous*) was a papal decretal of Pope Boniface VIII issued in 1298, that required the claustration of Catholic nuns." [7] Boniface's Decretal states:

"Wishing to provide for the dangerous and abominable situation of certain nuns, who, casting off the reins of respectability and impudently abandoning nunnish modesty and the natural bashfulness of their sex [...] we do firmly decree [...] that nuns collectively and individually, both at present and in future, of whatsoever community or order, in whatever part of the world they may be, ought henceforth to remain perpetually cloistered in their monasteries [...] so that[the nuns] be able to serve God more freely, wholly separated from the public and worldly gaze and, occasions for lasciviousness having been removed, may most diligently safeguard their hearts and bodies in complete chastity." Today

this Vatican assault on nuns was reinstituted by Pope Benedictine XVI.

Boniface[8] considered himself a universal monarch, "Boniface VIII put forward some of the strongest claims to temporal, as well as spiritual, power of any Pope and constantly involved himself with foreign affairs. In his Bull of 1302, *Unam Sanctam*, Boniface VIII proclaimed that it 'is absolutely necessary for salvation that every human creature be subject to the Roman pontiff.'" Considered by independent historians to be more narcissistic that a theologian; Boniface challenged King Philip IV of France, informing Philip "God has set popes over kings and kingdoms."

It was at this time when Boniface in his desire to marginalize church women, changed the female name of Apostle "Junia" to Junias, a male name that did not exist. Professor of Catholic Thought at Temple University, Dr. Leonard Swidler states, "To the best of my knowledge, no commentator on the Text until Aegidus of Rome (1245-1316) took the name to be masculine." Most surprisingly, regarding this change we find the Patristic "John Chrysostrom, in the 4th century, (337-497) wrote, 'Oh! How great the devotion of this woman that she should be even is counted worthy of the appellation of apostle!'"[9]

Following Boniface's death a "judicial investigation against the memory of Boniface" was held and collected testimonies that alleged many heretical opinions of Boniface VIII. This included the offence of sodomy"

As we examine the church today we must ask: what has changed regarding Catholic *clerics* and women? An informative article on the history of women clerics is presented by *Women Can Be Priests*.[10]

CHAPTER EIGHTEEN

A SUMMARY OF ASCETIC PAPAL DOCTRINES

"Cardinal John Henry Newman is quite blunt about this. Writing just after the definition of papal infallibility in November 1870 he says of the Pope of the time, Pius IX (1846-1878):

'We have come to a climax of tyranny. It is not good for a Pope to live twenty years. It is an anomaly and bears no good fruit; he becomes a god and has no one to contradict him, does not know facts and does cruel things without meaning it'. This comment has a remarkably contemporary ring to it!" [1]

—Theologian Fr. Paul Collins

The most inviolable and vigorously defended concept in Catholic theology is its declaration of Infallibility when explaining and defining Dogmatic truths contained in the Deposit of Faith and Morals. The Church teaches this authority was given to St. Peter individually in the book of Matthew 16:19 "I will give you the keys of the kingdom of heaven, and whatever you bind on earth shall be bound in heaven, and whatever you loose on earth shall be loosed in heaven," and that this authority has been transmitted down to the present through Papal Succession. Therefore, infallible pronouncements, so declared, issued by the Pope individually must be considered by Catholic believers as if coming directly from God, and thus unchallengeable. No passage in all of Scripture has been more abused and misused by the Vatican than this solitary passage. Such a belief would be disproved if one infallible declaration should later override an earlier infallible declaration, certainly including the Doctrines of Christ. Should this Dogma of Papal infallibility be revealed as incorrect, the foundations of

Papal authority would crumble. In such a case the teaching of Popes would be no more valid than that of, say, Billy Graham.

Aware that a significant number of modern historians/theologians no longer accept this papal teaching, but not wishing to challenge New Testament scripture, this belief is now being challenged with a new understanding of Christ's' promise. Does infallible papal teaching continue today, or could it have ended with St. Peter's death? This question is resolved should it be accepted that pseudo-infallible papal doctrines alter or nullify Infallible Doctrines of Christ.

A Byzantine Legal System

"Unless a man is able to say to himself, as in the Presence of God, that he must not, and dare not, act upon the Papal injunction, he is bound to obey it [conscience], and would commit a great sin in disobeying it [conscience]"
—Venerable Cardinal John Henry Newman, 1890.

With Pope Gregory VII, as described by Cardinal-Historian Yves Congar in 1995, "Gregory ended up making the Church itself into a legal institution." Beginning with Pope Siricius' infallible declaration nullifying the Sacrament of Matrimony granted by Christ, until the Vatican Council I's infallible declaration of papal infallibility, a legal system based upon infallible papal declarations became unchallengeable for any who would question papal authority, under threat of excommunication. Today, only the pope and his Curia are authorized to interpret words and terms supporting papal infallibility.

As Canon Lawyers in the 12th century interpreted Church history in order to disenfranchise women from their historical positions, we find Siricius' celibacy definition defended in the same manner. "Orsy, a leading canonist well-known for his theological expertise, acknowledged however that the question of which church doctrines are taught infallibly is 'extremely complex'...No doctrine is understood as defined infallibly unless it is *manifestly evident*," as cited by Canon 749.3 in the Code of Canon Law. In the face of Siricius' transparent insertion into the Deposit of

Faith, asserting "the apostles taught" ascetic celibacy, it is super-fluous for anyone to maintain Siricius' ascetic doctrine of celi-bacy was not *"manifestly evident."* Only in later centuries do we find Siricius' apocryphal celibacy demand, described as a Holy Tradition, described as a discipline initiated by the Apostles. Still today, however, Apostolic celibacy is supported by the Catholic College of Theology, San Carlo al Corso in Rome, *"The obligation of priestly celibacy was already in force since the 4th century. That being the case, the legislators in the 4th century also sustained that this ecclesiastical law was based on an Apostolic tradition."*[2]

Following Vatican Council I and the definition of papal infal-libility it became apparent mandatory celibacy could no longer be defended as a doctrine, "Some new Doctrine." Concerned with this newly defined infallibility giving unchallengeable papal power to define doctrines as he chose, the Cardinals wisely inserted into the Dogmatic Constitution of the Church a "limitation," deny-ing future popes the ability to insert "Some new Doctrine" into the Deposit of Faith. Since that time celibacy has been defended as either a tradition or a Church discipline that may be revoked. Unfortunately for Siricius, however, is that his Directa Decretal from "The Chair of Peter" is *Manifestly Evident,*, denying the sac-rament of Matrimony for priests; his authority did not originate in the Deposit of Faith, it originated with the Apostolic Constitution of 37 0 AD.

CONTRACEPTION

Siricius' appropriation of "papal infallibility" in order to main-tain control over the priesthood was the first such recorded event, but pseudo-infallible encyclicals employed as a tool of theological control over both priests and laity remain with us in the 21st cen-tury. Pope Paul VI s' encyclical in 1968, *Human Vitae,* condemning birth control as a mortal sin is also an attempt to insert "Some new doctrine" into the Deposit of Faith. The ascetic Gnostic phi-losophy that gave us mandatory celibacy brought with it the misogynistic belief that female temptation is traceable directly to the Fall of Eve, and is the first cause of sexual sin. From this belief came the third century teaching of Patristic Fathers that, while procreation is necessary for other than priests, it must be controlled; sexual intercourse between husband and wife was to be strictly confined to acts specifically intended to produce children. Modern Catholics do not realize that aside from reproductive acts, conjugal love was considered a sin after the wife was impregnated.

In the 1960s Bishop Carol Wojtyla, later Pope John Paul II, stated, "If it be declared that contraception is not sin in itself, then we should have to concede frankly that the Holy Spirit had been on the side of the Protestant Churches in 1930. It should likewise have to be admitted that for half a century the Spirit failed to protect Pius XI, Pius XII, and a large part of the Hierarchy from serious error. This would mean that leaders of the Church, acting with extreme imprudence, had condemned thousands of innocent human acts, forbidding under pain of eternal damnation, a practice which would now be sanctioned." With this official insistence that to make this change regarding contraception would destroy the fundamental principle of infallibility we find the Vatican defending "Some New Doctrine." An ascetic doctrine.

Against Women – The Sin of Female Ordination

Ascetic-Christian fears that female temptations threatened the celibate priesthood remains with us today. The Church will relentlessly pursue, investigate, and defrock a priest involved with a woman, but will covertly protect a sexual molester of children. Today a volatile issue has developed concerning the ordination of women to the priesthood.

Historically, doctrinal papal changes consisted of merely adding to or taking from the Deposit of Faith as circumstances of the time deemed necessary, the primary example being Siricius' use of third century Apocrypha to impose celibacy. When the Anglican Church approved the ordination of women Pope John Paul II challenged their understanding with an infallible Encyclical, *Ordinatio Sacerdotalis,* in 1994. The pope replied: *"The Church holds that it is not permissible to ordain women to the priesthood for very fundamental reasons. These reasons include: The example recorded in sacred scripture of Christ choosing His apostles only from Men."*

The pope's reliance on scripture in support from the Deposit of Faith is intriguing; it reveals that women Disciples and Apostles listed in authoritative scripture can be ignored when necessary. In the Book of Romans 16:7 we find St. Paul describing women Apostles, "Greet Andronicus and *Junia* my relatives who have been in prison with me. They are outstanding among the apostles, and they were in Christ before me." It was scriptural authority such as this that would have supported the ordination of women should popes have desired; but, while John Paul II found it appropriate to omit scriptural authority for women apostles, it is deemed appropriate to rely on third century Apocrypha to impose non-Christian celibacy on the priesthood. Equally disturbing for moral theologians in 2001 was the pope's inclusion of female ordination as a heinous sin to be categorized as child abuse. Understanding today, that before the concept of Sacerdotal Priest after 350 A D, women were important Christian leaders, and performed many leadership roles, often with their husbands. We do not know if Junia was married to Andronicus. Once more we find "Some New Doctrine." An ascetic doctrine.

CHAPTER NINTEEN

CONSEQUENCES OF ASCETIC CELIBACY

"[It] is curious for its apparent lack of scriptural foundation. At best there is the injunction from the pastoral epistles 'man of one wife', which would prohibit only widower clerics from remarrying, but in actual fact this was generally interpreted by patristic authorities as being a prohibition against ordaining remarried laymen."[1]
—*Priestly Celibacy in Patristics and in the History of the Church.* Roman Cholij

That illicit priestly sex entered the Church with ascetic celibacy cannot be denied. Before the New Testament was written, a book of instruction for Christian-Jews, *The Didache* was viewed as a Catechism from c.45 AD until well into the second century when unaffiliated traveling "prophets" preached the Gospel as they understood it. These "prophets" were often celibate, viewed with suspicion and permitted to stay only three days. While we have no record of abuse in the first century, we do find in the Didache, *"You shall not seduce boys. You shall not commit fornication."* As early as St. Ignatius of Antioch, after the Deposit of Faith was closed, ascetic celibates who believed their celibacy elevated them above their bishop were condemned. It is also noteworthy that the first attempt by Spanish bishops at Elvira, Spain, requiring priestly celibacy c.306 AD issued a Canon, "Those who sexually abuse boys are not to receive communion, even at death," indicating that even by that time problems existed.

From these early dates until today, papal demands that men who do not possess the gift of chastity as described by Christ, "let those accept who will," but who cannot live a chaste life were well described by a 71 year old nun who first exposed sexual abuse in the Santa Rosa, California, Diocese, "Sexual misconduct of clerics has been an abscess on the Body of Christ."[2] It was only with the priestly abuse scandal revealed in 2002 that elicited the good nun's comment. Unknown by faithful Catholics this "sexual misconduct" goes back to the beginning of ascetic celibacy.

A History of Clergy Sexual Abuse in the Catholic Church

Since the 2002 scandal many Church scholars have revisited the origin of mandatory celibacy and the pain it has visited on the Church and the uninformed Laity. Paramount among these scholars is Cannon Lawyer, Rev. Tomas Doyle, J.C.D., C.A.D.C., formally an aide to the Vatican representative in Washington. Perhaps the most penetrating and informative research on this subject is contained in Fr. Doyle's[3] recent article, *A Very Short History of Clergy Sexual Abuse in the Catholic Church*.[4] This is a distressing report but should be read by Catholics. Here we present excerpts from his research describing Vatican attempts to cover-up priestly sex abuse over the centuries.

"Although clergy sexual abuse has been well documented from the earliest years of the Catholic Church the present era is unique. Victims of clergy abuse had first turned to the Church authorities for help, expecting that the Church's legal system, known as Canon Law, would provide processes whereby victims would be justly treated and perpetrators properly dealt with and prevented from a continued ministry. Instead, Church officials routinely responded to victims by intimidating them in hopes of obtaining their silence...Thus, for the first time in Church history the victims of the clergy turned to the secular legal system for relief.

"The Catholic Church was officially recognized by Emperor Constantine in the early 4th century. With this recognition the religious leaders, soon to be known as the "clergy" gradually evolved into a separate, privileged class, the most exalted members of which were the bishops. Although celibacy did not become a universally mandated state for clerics of the western Church until the 12th century... various church leaders began to advocate it by the 4th century. The earliest recorded church legislation is from the council of Elvira (Spain, 306 AD). Half of the canons passed dealt with sexual behavior of one kind or another and included penalties assessed for clerics who committed adultery or fornication. Though it did not make specific mention of homosexual activities by the clergy, this early Council reflected the church's official attitude toward same-sex relationships: men who had sex with young boys were deprived of communion even on their death-bed... The Council of Elvira was not the only source of early legislative attempts to curb the sexual misdeeds of the clergy. Other gatherings of bishops throughout the Christian world, which encompassed what are now Western Europe, Northern Africa, the Middle East and the British Isles, passed laws attempting to stamp out clerical concubinage, clerical fornication and homosexual activity.

"Early church legislation was passed by individual bishops for their own territory but the more important legislation with lasting historical impact, was that passed by groups of bishops who gathered at periodic meetings known as *councils* or *synods* which were generally named after the place where they occurred. Given the poor state of communications at the time it is remarkable that the various councils and synods produced disciplinary legislation *similar* in tone. Sexual violations by the clergy were not confined to any specific geographic area. Laws were passed throughout the Christian world.

"These laws, whether the product of individual bishops or groups, did not need the approval of the papacy. Although the pope had been respected as the first among bishops from the earliest years of Christianity, the centralization of power was not evident until the middle ages (12th-13th centuries). By the 9th century collections of the growing mass of legislation began to appear. These were unofficial and generally poorly organized attempts at putting at least some of the known legislation. The first truly systematic collection was produced by the monk Gratian in 1140. Known as the *Concordance of Discordant Canons* it consisted of a wide spectrum of texts arranged in a dialectic method with Gratian's own opinions added. Though never officially approved, Gratian's decree became the most important resource for the history of Canon Law. Following the medieval period the major legislative sources were the popes themselves and the general or ecumenical councils, the most recent of which was Vatican II (1962-65).

"The practice of individual confession of sins to a priest started in the Irish monasteries in the latter sixth century. With individual confession came the *Penitential Books*, another valuable source for church history. These were unofficial manuals drawn up by various monks to assist in their private counseling with penitents in confession... The *Penitentials* provide a vivid glimpse into the darker side of Christian life at the time... Several of these refer to sexual crimes committed by clerics against young boys and girls. The *Penitential of Bede* (England, 8th century) advises that clerics who commit sodomy with young boys be given increasingly severe penances. The regularity with which mention is made of clergy sex crimes shows that the problem was not isolated, The *Penitential Books* were in use from the mid-6th century to the mid-12th century. [We will find the 12th century produced more volatility than merely the disenfranchisement of women religious in that century.]

"The most dramatic and explicit condemnation of forbidden clergy sexual activity was the *Book of Gomorrah* of St. Peter Damian, completed in 1051.[?] A Benedictine monk Peter Damian was also a dedicated Church reformer in a society wherein clerical decadence was not only widespread and publicly known, but generally accepted as the norm.[?] His work, the circumstances that prompted it and the reaction of the reigning pope (Leo IX) are a prophetic reflection of the contemporary situation. He begins by singling out superiors who, prompted by excessive and misplaced piety, fail to exclude sodomites. He asserts that those given to "unclean acts" not be ordained or, if they are already ordained, be dismissed from Holy Orders. He holds special contempt for those who defile men or boys who come to them for confession. Likewise he condemns clerics who administer the sacrament of penance (confession) to their victims. His final chapter is an appeal to the reigning pope (Leo IX) to take action... Although Peter Damian had paid significant attention to the impact of the offending clerics on their victims, the Pope made no mention of this but focused only on the sinfulness of the clerics and their need to repent.[?]

"The repeated violations of clerical celibacy were amply documented in the canonical collections of the medieval period. The most authoritative source is the *Decree of Gratian* already mentioned. Though mandatory celibacy had been decreed by the 2nd Lateran Council in 1139, this law was received with neither universal acceptance nor obedience. Medieval scholars attest that clerical concubinage was commonplace. Adultery, casual sex with unmarried women and homosexual relationships were rampant. Gratian devoted entire sections to disciplinary legislation which attempted to curb all of these vices. He demanded that the punishment for sexual transgressions be more severe for clerics than for lay men.

"From the 4th century to the end of the medieval period it is clear that violations of clerical celibacy were commonplace, expected by the laity and highly resistant to official disciplinary attempts to curb and eliminate them. Referring to concubinage for example, one noted scholar said: *From the repeated strictures against clerical incontinence by provincial synods of the twelfth and thirteenth centuries, one may surmise that celibacy remained a remote and only defectively realized ideal in the Latin West. In England, particularly in the north, concubinage continued to be customary; it was frequent in France, Spain and Norway.* Clerical sodomy continued to be a known problem though it did not attract as much legislative attention as clerical concubinage and this quite possibly because of the ongoing attempts to eliminate clergy marriages.

"The documentation from the medieval period indicates that although homosexual liaisons were not uncommon among the secular or diocesan clergy, most celibacy violations involved heterosexual forms of abuse. Illicit sexual activity by the monks was another matter. Although concubinage and even illicit marriages occurred among the monks, the fact that they took vows of chastity precluding marriage and lived a common life theoretically isolated from women meant that their sexual outlets would be considerably restricted. The monks became known for the frequency of homosexual activity especially with young boys. Many monasteries passed local regulations in attempts to curb the rampant abuses. In his Rule, Benedict commanded that no two monks were to sleep in the same bed. Night lights were to be kept burning and the monks were to sleep clothed.

"Following Peter Damian in the *Book of Gomorrah*, at least two general or ecumenical councils took direct aim at church leaders who supported errant clerics by their failure to take decisive action.⏹ The 4th Lateran Council (1215) and the Council of Basle (1449) both recognized the fact that curbing the vices depended on cooperative superiors. The canon from the Lateran Council is succinct: *Prelates, who dare support such in their iniquities, especially in view of money or other temporal advantages, shall be subject to a like punishment.* Church authorities considered celibacy violations to be more than a purely religious matter. They caused some degree of scandal and therefore were a matter of public interest. To enhance the opprobrium the church often tried accused clerics in the ecclesiastical tribunals and then turned them over to secular authorities for additional prosecution and punishment. Penalties were harsh and sometimes included execution.⏹

"The Protestant Reformation of the 16th century was sustained by much more than the controversy over the sale of indulgences. Luther and the other major reformers such as Zwingli and Calvin, all rejected mandatory celibacy.⏹ The rejection was motivated in great part by what the reformers saw as widespread evidence that clerics of all ranks commonly violated the obligations with women, men and young boys. In reference to life in the monasteries on the eve of the 16th century Protestant Reformation, Abbott says that the monks' 'lapses' with women, handsome boys and each other...became so commonplace that they could not be considered lapses but ways of life for entire communities. ⏹ Up to this time the Church's leaders continued to advocate the long-standing remedies of legislation, spiritual penalties, physical penalties and warnings, none of which worked. Living in the midst of a clerical world of non-celibate behavior, the reformers believed that this supposedly celibate world caused moral corruption: *The sexual habits of the Roman Catholic clergy, according to reformers, were a sewer of iniquity, a scandal to the laity, and a threat of damnation to the clergy themselves.*⏹

"No prior reform movement in the Catholic Church had an impact equal the 16th century Protestant Reformation. In spite of attempts to propagate revisionist versions of the Reformation, the Church's primary reaction, the ecumenical Council of Trent (1545-1563), was itself proof of the deeply entrenched and wide-ranging corruption in the Church. Secular princes had urged a reforming council but the popes resisted until 1545 when Pope Paul II summoned one to be held in the Italian city of Trento. The reaffirmation of clerical celibacy did not conclude without strong opposition from a significant number of bishops who argued that mandatory celibacy was simply not working and accomplished no more than denying priests' "wives" and children a share in their estates.⯑_ A canon was proposed which would have permitted marriage for clergy but this was rejected and mandatory celibacy re-enforced. The canon upholding celibacy was followed by one which extolled it as superior to marriage:

If anyone says that the married state excels the state of virginity or celibacy, and that it is better and happier to be united in matrimony than to remain in virginity or celibacy, let him be anathema.
—Council of Trent

"In spite of the reforming legislation and the establishment of mandatory training, education and formation for priests, the bishops at Trent were no more successful at curbing celibacy violations than their predecessors. Illicit sex with women, men and young boys continued but for a time were much less obvious. By 1566, in the first year of his pontificate, Pope Pius V (1566-72) recognized a need to publicly attack clerical sodomy. Two years later the same pope apparently found it necessary to fire another salvo at clerical sodomy. The constitution *Horrendum* specifically named clerics who committed "the sin against nature which incurred God's wrath" (*"quae contra naturam est, propter quam ira Dei venit in filios diffidentiae."*) *and* stipulated that they be punished with deprivation of income, suspension from all offices and dignities and in some cases, degradation.⯑"

"Summarizing the medieval period, it is clear that the bishops were not as preoccupied with secrecy as they are today. Clergy

211

sexual abuse of all kinds was apparently well known by the public, the clergy and secular law enforcement authorities. There was a constant stream of disciplinary legislation from the church but none of it was successful in changing clergy behavior. Finally, and most important, at certain periods church authorities recognized that the problem was not only dysfunctional clerics, but irresponsible leadership.

Solicitation in the Confessional

"In spring, 2003 the American media drew attention to an obscure Vatican document issued in 1962 which prescribed special procedures for processing cases of an especially vile form of clergy sexual abuse: solicitation of sex in the confessional. The Pope and various regional bishops issued a series of disciplinary laws against solicitation, beginning in 1561 and extending to 2001. Papal laws were promulgated in 1561, 1622, 1741, 1917, 1962, 1983 and 2001. The most complete records have been found in the Spanish and Mexican tribunals and reveal a shockingly high volume of complaints from women and men, accusing priests of solicitation and sexual abuse in a variety of forms. The most complete study of cases from the Spanish tribunals revealed that between 1723 and 1820 3775 cases were completed and sentences handed down. The author concluded that this number represents a small portion of the actual cases in that it reflects only those completed and not the total number started and later abandoned.▯" "After the promulgation of the Code in 1917, the Vatican issued special legislation on procedures to be followed in solicitation cases in 1922. This document, like the 1962 document, was sent to the world's bishops but otherwise retained in total secrecy. In 1962 Pope John XXIII approved the publication of renewed special procedural norms for processing solicitation cases. Like the 1922 document but unlike all previous papal legislation on this subject, this document was buried in the deepest secrecy. Although it was promulgated in the ordinary manner and then printed and distributed by the Vatican press, it was never publicized in the official Vatican legal bulletin, the *Acta Apostolicae_Sedis*.▯ The document was sent to all bishops in the world. The dispositive section of the document is preceded by an order whereby the document is to be kept in the secret archives and not published nor commented upon by anyone... It introduced several significant elements including an exceptional degree of confidentiality imposed on the document itself and the persons involved in processing cases.

"It introduced several significant elements including an exceptional degree of confidentiality imposed on the document itself and the persons involved in processing cases. Compared to previous papal documentation confronting clergy sexual abuse this document contains several significant changes which reveal the church's policy on clergy sexual crimes.

"This legislation introduced the following innovations in church policy:

a. **Jurisdiction**: Local ordinaries (bishops and heads of religious orders) have the right to process cases included in this document. However, they retain the option of sending such cases to the Vatican's Congregation of the Holy Office for prosecution.

b. **Secrecy-officials**: Tribunal and other church personnel who are involved in processing cases are obliged to maintain total and perpetual secrecy and are bound by the church's highest degree of confidentiality, known as the Secret of the Holy Office. Those who violate this secrecy are automatically excommunicated and the absolution or lifting of this excommunication is reserved to the pope himself.

c. **Secrecy-parties and witnesses**: Even the accuser and witnesses are obliged to take the oath of secrecy. The penalty of automatic excommunication is not attached to the violation of the oath. However, church official conducting the prosecution can, in individual cases, "threaten accusers" and witnesses with automatic excommunication for breaking the secret.

d. **Anonymous denunciations**: Anonymous accusations are not automatically ruled out though they are generally to be rejected.

e. **Other sex crimes**: Title V of the document specifically included homosexual acts between clerics and members of their own sex, bestiality and sexual acts of any kind with children. The document uses the Latin word "impuberibus" which means "before the age of reason." This is defined in canon 88 as one who is seven or under. The Code also contains a canon prohibiting sex with minors which is defined in canon law as one sixteen or under. A careful reading of the relevant paragraphs of the 1962 document (par. 71-73) leads to some confusion as to whom the crimes apply to. It is clear that sex with children is included and sex with males of any age, as well as sex with animals. The only category of possible victims that is unclear is sex with young girls. Thus, the three classes of clergy sexual abuse were cloaked in the highest degree of secrecy.

"Little was known about the 1962 document until reference to it was included in the recent Vatican legislation on sex crimes, the 2001 Letter sent to all bishops from the Congregation for the Doctrine of the Faith on more grave crimes reserved for consideration to that same Vatican office. The 1962 document is significant because it reflects the church's urgent desire to maintain the highest degree of secrecy and strictest degree of security about the worst sexual crimes perpetrated by clerics. The document does not include any background information about why it was issued nor is there any reasoning available for the imposition of extreme secrecy and the inclusion of the crimes in Title V. One can only presume that cases or concerns had been brought to the attention of the Vatican authorities which prompted the decree.

"Since the archives of the Holy Office, now known as the Congregation for the Doctrine of the Faith, are closed to outside scrutiny it is impossible to determine the number of cases referred to it between 1962 and the present. The other factor impeding a study of cases is the prohibition of local dioceses from ever revealing the very existence of cases much less the relevant facts.

THE CONTEMPORARY ERA

"It cannot be disputed that the bishops as individuals and as a group were aware of the probability of sexual abuse of children and adolescents by clerics by late 1984 and certainly early 1985 in light of the national publicity given to the celebrated case of Fr. Gilbert Gauthe in Lafayette, Louisiana. The claims that they were unaware of clergy sexual abuse or the serious nature of such abuse prior to this time are empty and contrived in light of information that has been uncovered in the various civil and criminal

214

trials since 1985, documents issued by church authorities and various studies conducted under church auspices over the past 50 years.

CONCLUSIONS

"In spite of claims to the contrary, the canonical history of the Catholic Church clearly reflects a consistent pattern of awareness that celibate clergy regularly violated their obligations in a variety of ways. The fact of clergy abuse with members of the same sex, with young people and with women is fully documented. At certain periods of church history clergy sexual abuse was publicly known and publicly acknowledged by church leaders. From the late 19th century into the early 21st century the church's leadership has adopted a position of secrecy and silence. They have denied the predictability of clergy sexual abuse in one form or another and have claimed that this is a phenomenon new to the post-Vatican II era. The recently published reports of the Bishops' National Review Board and John Jay College Survey have confirmed the fact of known clergy sexual abuse since the 1950's and the church leadership's consistent mishandling of individual cases.

"The bishops have, at various times, claimed that they were unaware of the serious nature of clergy sexual abuse and unaware of the impact on victims. This claim is easily offset by the historical evidence. Through the centuries the church has repeatedly condemned clergy sexual abuse, particularly same-sex abuse. The very texts of many of the laws and official statements show that this form of sexual activity was considered harmful to the victims, to society and to the Catholic community. Church leaders may not have been aware of the scientific nature of the different sexual disorders nor the clinical descriptions of the emotional and psychological impact on victims, but they cannot claim ignorance of the fact that such behavior was destructive in effect and criminal in nature."

FAITHFUL CATHOLIC LAITY AND SCANDAL

When the priestly abuse scandal in America first made headlines in 2002 it was only normal for faithful Catholics to reject such distressing revelations as anti-Catholic bias. Historically Catholic faithful have become accustomed to news reports that can be viewed as demeaning to their faith. Most Catholics respect and admire their parish priest, even while understanding that all humans, including priests who dedicate their life to the Church, may fall into sin. Unfortunately, as time passed it became apparent the scandal was not confined to America and the domestic press. Tragically, during the following years it is now apparent this scandal is an internationalcrisis. Across the globe reliable news reports now reveal this scandal has affected all Catholics.[5] What has become most distressing is that this scandal threatens the faith of many Catholics, and the Church. Becoming informed and active, Catholics must realize it is not the Church, the Body of Christ, which has failed, it is the Hierarchy.

Much information is now available based on empirical research by dedicated and lifelong Catholic scholars concerning the history of this scandal. No source is more authoritative than Richard Sipe. Benedictine Monk and Priest (retired) Fr. Richard Sipe is a psychotherapist who over his priestly career of 30 years taught at several seminaries, and during this time clinically treated thousands of priests and their victims, all referred to him by Church authorities for therapy and counseling for their sexual assaults. When complete clinical statistics were not available Fr. Sipe and his colleagues, Canon Lawyer Fr. Thomas Doyle and Catholic Priest and Benedictine Monk Patrick J. Wall dedicated their careers to this field of study and ministry. Today the following are statistical estimates of priestly formation in America. For a current assessment by Sipe and his colleagues consult his web literature.[6][7]

2% of priests have the true *gift* of celibacy and perfect continence.

8% have willed themselves into formation of character necessary to live celibately.

40% struggle and fail to consistently maintain continence.

50% are sexually active at all time, either heterosexually or homosexually.

30 – 50% of priests are homosexually oriented, including our bishops.

A major cause of cover-up for abusive priests by their bishops results from the fact that all bishops were first priests, and are included in the statistics above. Therefore an un-communicated conspiracy of silence exists, don't ask – don't tell, world-wide.

Regarding the homosexual orientation it must be noted this orientation is not a sin in and of itself; medical science reveals it is not consciously chosen. Only when one engages in illicit sex is it considered a sin, in the same manner as heterosexual fornication.

CHAPTER TWENTY

THE FAILURE OF VATICAN COUNCIL II

"The Second Vatican Council addressed relations between the Roman Catholic Church and the modern world. The council, through the Holy See, formally opened under the pontificate of Pope John XXIII on 11 October 1962 and closed under Pope Paul VI on 8 December, 1965. Currently, the questioned validity of the Second Vatican Council continues to be a contending point for religious communities. In particular, some Traditionalist Catholics, who claim that the modernizing reforms which resulted both directly or indirectly from the council consequently brought detrimental effects and indifference to the customs, beliefs, and pious practices of the Church before 1962."[1]

—Second Vatican Council

Excitement permeated the Catholic Church world when newly elected Pope John XXXIII surprisingly called Vatican Council II, the first Ecumenical Council since Pope Pius IX called Vatican Council I in 1870 to formally declare papal infallibility when defining faith and morals as handed down by Christ and the Apostles. The announcement came as a surprise to the conservative Vatican Curia, many of whom had reason to be concerned with the prospect of unforeseen changes, changes that might in some way dilute their historical authority. However, this negative view was not shared by the Laity and clerics who were thrilled when Pope John announced he merely wished to "Throw open the Window of change" in the Church and revisit Church doctrines that in some segments of the laity were being ignored. But as the council progressed, negative attitudes among segments of the Church who previously ignored onerous doctrines such as birth control, the position of women in the Church and the inability of clerics to accept the Sacrament of Matrimony began to manifest themselves. Happily, faithful Catholics became supportive of the council's progress and looked forward to security in their faith with a new understanding of our ancient doctrines.

Informed Catholics across the globe saw a great potential for meaningful change when the council ended after two years, having introduced potential changes that needed only to be fully explained and implemented. However, as time passed a differing view of these potential changes by conservative Church authorities began to appear, changes that today represent the ancient medieval church and many of the laities desired changes were subordinated by church authorities. Apparently, little would change.

"THE CATHOLIC CHURCH'S LOST REVOLUTION: 50 YEARS AGO AT VATICAN II, A PROFOUND TRANSFORMATION OF CATHOLICISM BEGAN — ONLY TO BE CUT SHORT"

"James Carroll, writer and former Catholic priest, put the Church's recent scandals into context, offering an interpretation that is both critical and optimistic. This emphasis on clerical power and the power of the papacy is not an old tradition, but a relatively new innovation."[2]

—Boston Globe

Award-winning author and former Catholic priest James Carroll is often invited to discuss what the permanent "Jewishness" of Jesus meant during His lifetime, and how a recovered appreciation of the importance of His Jewish nature overturns subsequent Christian assumptions, both of doctrine and prejudice. Here we will present selective comments from Carroll's understanding of Vatican Council II, both the enthusiastic support it first received, and the ultimate disappointment in its failure. A devout Catholic, he discusses in a historical and scholarly manner his understanding of this failure.

Beginning with the year before the council was assembled he explains the confident joy he and his seminary colleagues experienced as they prepared to become servants of God, as future priests. "Already we were drawn by the aesthetic glories of high medieval culture, the churches global order, Catholic timelessness, moral rigor – all symbolized by the Latin Mass. If ours was a damming God, ruthlessly consigning enemies (whether Godless Communists or Protestants next door) the eternally boiling lake of fire, we knew that, as Catholics, we were among God's elect. One day as priests, we would be God's elite...Defining our removal from the world was the rejection of newspapers, magazines, 'secular' literature and television. Instead, we were immersed in the study of Latin, scripture, and spiritual classics."[A typical priestly formation]

As time passed the exuberant view of his church and the hopes of the council began to diminish. "The second Vatican Council, which convened 50 years ago has been described as the most momentous event in the 20th century. Meeting in four sessions, over three years, the world's Catholic bishops sought to reimagine the role the church – the spiritual home of more than one sixth of humanity...Yet Vatican II so dramatically failed to fulfill its promise that it registers very little in common memory today, even among Catholics whose faith it was meant to transform...Far more importantly Vatican II, from its half-forgotten place in the past, still points to an urgently needed Catholic Renewal."

"We seminarians fathomed the depth of change by measuring it in ourselves. Having seen, for example, where the 'Christ-killers' charges against the Jews had led, the Vatican II fathers firmly rejected it. But in scripture class we still read Gospels that demonized Jews. So, taking our cue from the Vatican II fathers, we radically changed how we read the sacred texts, abandoning literalism once and for all. Not only a core teaching was upended, but so was a dominant method of biblical interpretation."

"Vatican II dared us to change, and we did. Somber piety gave way to rancorous joy. Instead of mindless subservience, we took initiatives, reinventing the liturgy, throwing ourselves into anti-poverty work, and recognizing Jesus on the bread line...By the end of our six-year training program, it seemed, we would have a happy new mission. Once ordained, we would bring the miracle of Vatican II to the church and to the world.

"Alas, the age of miracles passed. It was naïve of us to imagine that so profound a transformation could happen so easily. The very bishops who had launched the revolution were the first to feel threatened by what it required. Less than three years after the Council concluded, a 1968 papal encyclical tried to arrest change by condemning 'artificial' birth control – in defiance of a consensus then emerging within the church. With that, clerical conservatism staked its program on bringing back a puritanical sexual morality. No equal rights for women. No surrender of clerical power over the inner lives of Catholics. The long pontificate of John Paul II institutionalized this counter revolution. Today, Benedict XVI caps it.

"Yet basic changes of Vatican II could not be thwarted. Primacy of conscience was taken to heart. From the birth-control encyclical forward, the Catholic people began claiming their own right of religious liberty, at times rejecting the authority of the popes and bishops – and still going to communion. Still, many priests and nuns who had embraced Vatican II ideals sooner or later found it impossible to uphold the old authoritarianism. Our situation as servants of a reneging hierarchy became unsustainable.

"By now, the tragic meaning of that betrayal has become evident. Imagine if the other great reform movements of the 1960's had been rolled back. The civil-rights campaign, feminism... Membership in the church, especially in Europe and America, has hemorrhaged. The moral authority of the Catholic hierarchy has been gutted. Priests, at best, evoke pity. Nuns upholding Vatican II values are targeted by inquisitors. The magnificent Roman Catholic church, a millennial font of reasoned faith and ascetic genius, is on the road to becoming yet another fundamentalist cult."

Today this author has not discovered a more penetrating and cogent explanation of Vatican failure, and the Church's efforts to secure church doctrines that were entrenched during its medieval formation of the 11th-13th century, a time when ascetic papal doctrines, founded solely on the first ascetic papal doctrine of Siricius denying the Sacrament of Matrimony, and relying only upon the apocryphal beliefs that penetrated the Christian movement during its second and third centuries. That being said, and speaking as a layman, it is with some timidity that I acknowledge my different understandings of ascetic intrusions into our church. Only by revisiting my early indoctrination of the church's "ascetic genius" have I become bold enough to comment on the seminary formation of modern clerics and theologians who were, as was I, deprived during their formative years as seminarians from the history of changes within the church, changes that are today termed *Holy Tradition* but have no place in Church history. Speaking personally, much discord arose among women relatives when I supported *Ordinatio Sacerdotalis* issued in 1994 by Pope John Paul II. This limited understanding of early Church history is not the fault of clerics, theologians and canon lawyers who are deprived of this information during seminary. This first became apparent for this author when requesting critiques of my first book from knowledgeable Catholic theologians. A nationally prominent church theologian graciously informed me he would rather not comment on my book because he was "not well versed on early church history." Catholic priests no more look for faults in church teaching than Protestants would dare to question *Sola Scriptura*.

The reality of Vatican Council II's failure to institute meaningful changes allowing female ordination, the denial of contraception as a sin, or permitting priests to marry would have challenged three infallible papal doctrines, the consequences of which would be to decimate the concept of papal infallibility. For this reason the subject of priestly marriage was not formally introduced.

The Failure of Vatican Council II

"During a conversation at the beginning of Vatican II Yves Congar OP told his fellow conciliar peritus (theological expert) Hans Kung, If you want to understand the Roman Catholic Church today, look at the eleventh Century. Indeed, it was one of the greatest theologians of the twentieth century and perhaps the greatest ecclesiologists of all time, Yves Congar, who argued that the great turning point in ecclesiology is the eleventh century. The turning point is, of course, embodied in the person of Gregory VII. As Congar pointed out, by seeking to rely on legal precedents for the exercise of what should be only a spiritual

authority, Gregory ended up by making the Church itself into a legal institution with papal power as the basis for everything."
—The Reinvention of the Fisherman. David Timbs. [Melbourne]

Many books and commentaries have been written in an attempt to explain Vatican Council II's failure to institute changes desired by brilliant and sensitive scholars. Slowly in recent years some of those who were disappointed have come to understand why meaningful change failed to flourish, and the reason why. To have implemented changes in the doctrines of most concern – Women's Ordination, birth control and mandatory celibacy – would have nullified Infallible Papal Doctrines, and thus reveal the concept of Papal Infallibility to be untrue. No better explanation of this problem has been put forward than that of Cardinal Yves Conger above when he explains: "Gregory *ended up by making the Church itself into a legal institution* with *papal power as the basis for everything."* Today the Vatican is a legal/theological institution reined over by an infallible Monarch, and defended by an infallible Byzantine legal system designed only to defend papal infallibility. Should the council have challenged these Papal Doctrines in any way, it would have been seen as an attempt to disprove papal authority and power, attempts which must be decimated at all cost, even to the detriment of the laity. No better support for Cardinal Conger's explanation of legal papal power will be found than the penetrating comment of James Carroll above when he writes: "Less than three years after the council concluded, a 1968 papal encyclical [*Humanae Vitae*] tried to arrest changes by condemning 'artificial' birth control – in defiance of a consensus then emerging within the church." With this comment Carroll explains it all – the concept of a church "consensus" nullifying infallible papal doctrines will never be permitted.

This truth was clearly demonstrated when in the process of issuing the Infallible Papal Doctrine, *Humanae Vitae,* this unbending position on the meaninglessness of a church "consensus" is again anathematized. When the "consensus" of a papal commission on birth control advised that the prohibition on birth control should be repealed (60-4) it was rebuffed by Vatican advisors, led by Polish Cardinal Karol Wojtyla.

"If it be declared that contraception is not sin in itself, then **we should have to concede frankly that the Holy Spirit had been on the side of the Protestant Churches** in 1930 [when Casti Connubi was promulgated] *It should likewise have to be admitted that for half a century the Spirit failed to protect Pius XI, Pius XII*, and a large part of the Catholic hierarchy from a very serious error. This would mean that leaders of **the Church,** acting with extreme imprudence**, had condemned thousands of innocent human acts, forbidding under pain of eternal damnation**, a practice which would now be sanctioned. The fact **can neither be denied nor ignored** that these same acts would now **be declared licit on the grounds of principles cited by the Protestants,** which popes and bishops have condemned or at least not approved." This dissenting report was authored by Cardinal Karol Wojtyla of Poland, later Pope John Paul II.

Here, in a most legal manner the definition of Papal Infallibility is protected. Only when those who seek meaningful change come to grips with the fact that absolutely no papal doctrine will voluntarily be acknowledged as heterodox, will "meaningful change" occur.

What are Catholics to Believe?

The Byzantine legal system identified by Cardinal Yves Conger above: "Gregory *ended up by making the Church itself into a legal institution* with *papal power as the basis for everything."* is composed in a manner permitting the Curia to *define* and defend Papal teachings; these definitions are presented with *malleable words and terms* allowing Papal teachings to be defended under all circumstances. The comments below are from an excellent book by Richard Gaillardetz, *By what Authority,* in which he explains for the laity the bewilderment of Church "teaching." For those interested in this subject, it is helpful to examine Gaillardetz's book.

DOGMA: "These teachings communicate God's saving message as revealed to us in Scripture and tradition. [Infallible-Deposit of Faith] At the same time, it is a *human expression* that in its formation can always *be improved."* [Malleable] "Catholic Christians have justifiably given church teaching the presumption of truth."

DEFINITIVE DOCTRINE: "It includes teachings that are *not* divinely *revealed* but are *necessary* for safeguarding and expounding divine revelation. [Malleable] Because it is *assumed* these teachings are necessary for preserving divine revelation, these teachings, like dogmas, are taught with the charisma of infallibility and, as such, are also irreversible." [Malleable Infallibility]

AUTHORATIVE DOCTRINE: Authorative doctrine is drawn from the *wisdom* of the church as it *reflects* on *scripture.* and *tradition*...yet even as these teaching are proposed authoritatively, the Church's teaching office is not ready to commit itself irrevocably to them." [Deposit of Faith –Malleable]

"But what about more specific teachings like the Church's prohibition of birth control...Few theologians believe that teachings of this sort have been taught infallibly, but the more difficult question concerns whether they *could* be taught infallibly." [Malleable]

The Vatican Curia, however, has its own response to this malleability challenge. "...the only appropriate response of the believer to dogma is what Vatican II called an 'assent of faith.' Unfortunately however, Roman Catholicism has traditionally held that, due to the central role that dogma plays in communicating God's saving Word, membership in the Church of Jesus Christ would be called into question by the obstinate and public denial of dogma. This kind of formal rejection is called *heresy*."

With this last statement in mind it may be assumed by some this Catholic author's rejection of certain Papal Doctrines threatens the allegation of heresy. If so, it will be helpful for the reader to juxtapose this writer's position on Papal Doctrines with St. Thomas Aquinas' definition of "Heretic": *One who having accepts the Faith of Christ corrupts its Doctrines.*" This threat is also to be considered by those who reject any of the Papal Doctrines described i

CHAPTER TWENT-ONE

THERE IS NO INFALLIBLE MONARCH

As previously stated, the primary focus of this book is to explain why there is no infallible papal monarch. Admittedly, this is a distressing concept for faithful Catholics to accept. Having personally experienced the distress faced by Catholics when life-long beliefs are challenged as untrue; it is with empathy I ask the reader not to consider this book to be an affront to the Catholic Church. Rather, this book is intended only to expose a failing medieval power structure that had no place in first century Christianity, a Hierarchy that is today decimating the Catholic Church. The truth or error of this book must be accepted or rejected by Catholics as they reach their personal conclusions based on the historical events described above. As Catholics, we must come to acknowledge this failed leadership while continuing to rely on our faith. This author believes the illicit nature of this hierarchy will ultimately bring about its own downfall.

With the modern availability of ancient literature, new understandings of Christian history is now attainable to average Christians, should they seek it. Beliefs unknown to clerics unless they personally invest years of personal research into first and second century Christianity that is omitted during seminary formation is readily attainable. For instance, little known by Catholics today, first century Christian history informs us Jesus' brother, St. James the Just, was elected by the Apostles as their leader following the Crucifixion of Jesus c. 30 and assassinated in 62 AD. St. James, who wrote the New Testament *Book of James,* remained in Jerusalem as the sole leader of Christianity, whom St. Peter followed, while Jesus' Apostles traveled the Empire and beyond, orally spreading the Gospel before the New Testament was written. Following his death no historical record exists, from any source, that anyone replaced St. James as Christian leader, not even the Bishops of Rome. Only in the fourth century, c. 385 AD, do we find Bishop Siricius of Rome assuming the title of "Pope" when he issued his infallible Decretal "from the chair of Peter" nullifying the Sacrament of Matrimony for married clerics, contrary to the teaching imparted by Christ who said, "It is not everyone who can accept what I have said...let them accept who can."

Since 1870, the Bishop of Rome is defined by the Church as the only human divinely endowed by God to infallibly explain Christ's revelations concerning Christian faith and morals. Therefore, to reject such papal teaching is to reject the representative of God on earth: *The Pope possesses full and supreme power of jurisdiction over the whole Church, not merely in matters of faith and morals, but in Church discipline and the government of the Church."* (De fide) This belief has been rejected since earliest Christianity, as did St. Cyprian, the Bishop of Carthage. In 255, St. Cyprian rejected the concept that monarchial authority was possessed by the Bishop of Rome. At that time Cyprian and the pope were in heated conflict over Church teaching when he issued his famous insult to Pope Stephen I: "There is no Bishop of Bishops." Subsequently, St. Cyprian was supported by Christian bishops across the Empire. Over the centuries Papal authority ascended to a Monarchial status after the medieval period, and determined to increase Vatican wealth and control over married bishops and priests of his time, Pope Gregory VII declared in 1074: "The Church cannot escape the laity unless priests first escape their wives," thus leading to the re-imposition of Clerical celibacy and denying the Sacrament of Matrimony first imposed by Siricius. A millennium after the imposition of a Monarchial Papacy we write today of the same visceral scandals that surrounded medieval bishops and priests, scandals that inspired St. Peter Damian, 1049 AD, to write *The Book of Gomorrah (Liber Gomorrhianus),* addressed to Pope Leo IX seeking change.

Without belaboring the history of Papal Infallibility described in this book we realize that papal infallibility has, unknown by the

Catholic laity, been rejected throughout history, as described by the epigraphs in Chapter Fourteen. Currently the Catholic Church is facing its most serious challenge since the Reformation, stemming from the Papal Doctrines of which we write. Until Catholicism acknowledges the papacy is merely the Bishop of Rome, elected as were all bishops in the beginning by diocesan citizens, as St. Cyprian insisted, the Church will continue to diminish. Belief in an Infallible Monarch has been rejected since the earliest Centuries of Christianity. St. Ignatius of Antioch c. 110, who was a student of Apostle St. John expressed high esteem for Bishops of Rome where Peter and Paul had jointly served as Apostolic leaders. Still, Ignatius preached that all bishops were autonomous: "Let no man do anything connected with the Church without the bishop." This letter was written to the Church of Smyrna as Ignatius was being transported to Rome for slaughter in the Coliseum. In Ignatius' day bishops were supreme in their diocese.

Securing Papal Power

With Constantine, Christianity became the dominate religion in a pagan world and the papal office became the dominate Roman power, subservient only to the Emperor. After Pope Damasus, 385 AD, assassination and war were often employed in the struggle for papal supremacy. Damasus' election over his papal opponent, Ursinus, became deadly. Both claimants were elected simultaneously by opposing factions; power was up for grabs. Within one month, 137 supporters of Ursinus' were killed in the basilica where they had fled for protection. Damasus was elected.

In later centuries it would primarily require wealth to secure the papacy. The papacy of Pope Benedict IX, 1032 AD, was purchased and sold three times. St. Damian wrote of Benedict in his *Book of Gomorrah*, "A demon from hell disguised as a priest... feasting on immorality." Benedict's papacy was first purchased at age 12 by his father Alberic III. Two popes, Pope John XIX and Pope Benedict VIII were Benedict's uncles, brothers of his father Alberic. Benedict was forced from Rome in 1036 AD, and again in 1044 AD. Returning to Rome the second time, he arrived with forces to expel Pope Silvester III. He then sold his throne to his godfather, Pope Gregory VI, for 1,450 lbs. of gold. This was not an uncommon change of power. In 1492, Pope Alexander VI, the father of Caesarea Borjia who assassinated his brother Giovanni Borjia, and his notorious daughter Lucretia Borjia, with whom he was reported to have had an incestuous relationship, purchased the papacy with seven mule loads of gold in order to secure the votes of the French Cardinals. Modern Catholics should not consider such changes of power to be unusual.

ANTI-POPES AND CARDINALS

Over centuries, political infighting for power became intense between Cardinals and popes. In 1159, only ten years after the Second Lateran Council, Pope Hadrian IV died and schism appeared. Immediately after Pope Hadrian's death, power and authority once more hung in the balance; contending groups of Cardinals elected different Popes. Pope Alexander III was contested by four anti-Popes between 1159 and 1180.

The first contender opposing Alexander III was *anti-Pope Victor IV*, 1159-1164 AD; although residing in Germany Victor wished to maintain political authority in Rome. In this conflict Anti-Pope Victor was supported by Roman citizens, to no avail. In reprisal for Emperor Fredrick's support of the challenger, Victor, Pope Alexander claimed papal authority and excommunicated the Emperor. Anti-Pope Victor in turn also claimed the papacy and excommunicated Pope Alexander who was forced to flee Rome. Both Popes maintained support of the Cardinals who elected them until Victor's death five years later.

Upon the death of Victor, *anti-Pope Paschal III*, 1164–1168, was elected by the same group of Cardinals who supported Victor. Paschal was able to prevent Pope Alexander III, whose residence was then in France, from re-entering Rome. Paschal served four years.

The next opposition for Alexander came from *Anti-Pope Callistus (Callixtus) III,* 1168-1178. Callistus was a follower of anti-Pope Victor IV, who had elevated him to Cardinal. However, as the political winds shifted Emperor Fredrick, who initially supported Callistus, reversed his position and supported Alexander

III. Following Emperor Fredrick's reversal ten years later, Callistus submitted to Alexander III, for which he was rewarded.

In 1179-1180 *Anti-Pope Innocent III* became Alexander's final opponent. Innocent was elected by, again, Cardinals who continued to oppose Alexander III. However, Alexander III was able to bribe Innocent III's supporters into giving him up – whereupon he was imprisoned. After more than two decades of political conflict and the disposal of this fourth anti-Pope, it was time to convene another Lateran Council and try to pick up the pieces.

Finally, during the Third Lateran Council in 1179, Pope Alexander III was successful in reaching a political agreement with his Cardinal adversaries in an attempt to nullify their power: Canon 1 of the Lateran Council stated: *"To prevent future schisms only Cardinals are permitted to elect the Popes. Anyone declaring himself Pope will be excommunicated."* With his papal power to install Cardinals, who would likely support his papal authority, a truce was instituted, but would ultimately fail.

CARDINAL-NEPHEWS

Pope Paul II, 1464, was considered among the worst of the Renaissance popes. Paul was apparently an acknowledged homosexual who spent vast sums of church money on Mardi Gras-like parades and banquets. He spent much time adorning himself with priceless jewelry and associating with his numerous male companions. He was also into voyeurism and bondage, and perhaps sadism, often watching naked men being racked and tortured in the papal dungeons. It was said that on July 26, 1471 Paul died while engaged in a sex act.

However, Pope Paul II offers us another insight into the Renaissance papacy – nepotism. Paul II was initially trained as a merchant, but upon the elevation by his uncle to the papacy he changed careers with an *appointment* to the clergy. His uncle, Pope Eugene IV, had himself become Cardinal by appointment of his father Pope Gregory XII, 1406-1415, as a *Cardinal-nephew*. Every Renaissance Pope appointed relatives, often their own illegitimate sons, termed Cardinal-nephews, to the College of Cardinals. Cardinals, continually in power struggles with Popes attempted to increase their individual powers by limiting the number of

Cardinals; papal conflict was common. A Pope without a Cardinal-nephew was rare. The word "nepotism" originated with this practice. Fourteen notable Popes began as Cardinal-nephews: John XIX, Benedict IX, Anastasius IV, Gregory IX, Alexander IV, Adrian V, Gregory XI, Boniface IX, Eugene IV, Paul II, Alexander VI, Pius III, Julius II and Clement VIII..

The struggle for Vatican power between Cardinals and the pope continue as this book is being written.

OPPOSITION

With the early introduction of Cardinals into the Catholic hierarchy, a new level of ranking had entered the Church, elevating Cardinals, all of whom are *not* bishops, above the authority of first century bishops. With such an agreement first century bishops were disenfranchised with the loss of all ability to have a voice in papal elections. The Cardinals and the papacy forever changed the Church power structure. Today the Vatican power structure has eliminated the office of Bishop as it existed in the Didache, in the Deposit of Faith.

Catholic rejection of papal infallibility became prominent prior to the modern declaration of infallibility of1870. Prior to this belief in papal infallibility was not a defined requirement of Catholic faith, but was anticipated with fear by many bishops. In an attempt to placate Irish Catholic Bishops, the Vatican permitted them to reject papal infallibility by publicly stating: "it is not an article of the Catholic Faith, neither am I thereby required to believe or profess that the Pope is infallible" These Irish bishops later repeated their position in an address to both the Catholic clergy and laity in Ireland, stating: "The Catholics of Ireland not only do not believe, but declare upon oath ... that it is not an article of the Catholic faith, neither are they required to believe, that the Pope is infallible, and that they do not hold themselves 'bound to obey any order that is in its own nature immoral." Today, should any cleric question the concept of an Infallible Monarch he would be immediately defrocked. Surprisingly, a joyful moment of hope arrived when one pope came close to the cliff of denying papal infallibility. The most beloved Pope in modern time, Pope John XXIII, who was the first pope to seek meaningful change in the Church addressed a conclave of priests, saying: "I am only infallible if I speak infallibly but I shall never do that, so I am not infallible." Unfortunately Pope John died before concluding the Second Vatican Council.

The Catholic Church is not the Vatican; the *Church* is the Body of Christ firmly ensconced in dioceses around the globe. Until the Church returns to its origin, when Monarchs did not exist and the Didache taught in the Deposit of Faith: *"Elect for yourself, therefore, bishops and deacons worthy of the Lord, humble men and not lovers of money; for they also serve you in the ministry of the prophets and teachers,"* the Church will continue to fail. Today bishops are often serfs who merely serve at the pleasure of the Pope; any who question papal authority or fail to cover-up un-Christian immorality of other Churchmen are immediately defrocked. Only by returning to the equal authority of all bishops, all of whom are elected by their parishioners as taught and practiced by all Christians in the beginning, and permit bishops to vote in some manner for a pope, who serves with their consent, will the Church again come together.

A Failed Papacy

As Pope Benedict voluntarily leaves the papacy, ominous reports of his complicity in covering up priestly sex abuse of children has been alleged against him in his positions as Cardinal, Prefect of the Congregation for the Doctrine of the Faith, and finally as pope. Additionally, he leaves under significant criticism from former colleague Fr. Hans Kung for failure to introduce changes that would end the churches' unjust "authoritarian rule."

Fr. Hans Küng[1] is a Swiss Catholic priest, theologian, and author, "A Catholic priest in good standing." Following the publication of his book, *Infallibility? An Inquiry,* questioning the veracity of Vatican Council I's definition of papal infallibility, Pope John Paul II rescinded Kung's authority to teach Catholic theology. Forced to leave the Catholic faculty, he remains at the University of Tübingen as a professor of ecumenical theology. Although Kung is not officially allowed to teach Catholic theology, neither his bishop nor the Holy See have revoked his priestly faculties. Ironically, it was Fr. Kung who provided his colleague Joseph Ratzinger the first step up the Hierarchical ladder. At Kung's instigation the Catholic faculty at Tübingen appointed Ratzinger as professor of dogmatic theology, ultimately leading to his 1962 appointment as *peritus* during Vatican Council II, serving as an expert theological advisor to its members until its conclusion in 1965. For some time Fr. Kung has challenged the papacy for failure to correct ancient doctrines that have no place in Christianity:[2] Such as allowing divorced and remarried Catholics to receive Communion in some circumstances; taking steps to "correct" the 1968 encyclical "Humanae Vitae" denying the use of birth control in some cases; abolish the rule of priestly celibacy in the Latin-rite church; institute a new way of electing bishops with the involvement of local Catholics. Father Kung said it would be helpful to call a third Vatican council to deal with these and other issues. Today Fr. Kung is actively suggesting a universal priestly challenge to the church's "Authoritarian rule."[3] Today, with the arrival of Pope Francis papal detractors pose the pejorative question: "Is Pope Benedict XVI still infallible?"

Sadly, this author does not believe meaningful change will occur under the new pontiff, Pope Francis, a Jesuit. Founded and approved by Pope Paul III in 1540, Jesuits are sometimes referred to colloquially as "God's Soldiers." Among the Jesuit's first defined missions is to "serve and defend" the Pope. The Jesuits were the principle founders of the Counter-Reformation, a movement to reform the Catholic Church from within and to counter the Protestant Reformers, whose teachings were spreading throughout Catholic Europe. Perhaps their greatest contribution to the power and temporal authority of the papacy was the Jesuit leadership role in support of Pope Leo IX's declaration of papal infallibility during the 1870 Vatican Council I, which is acknowledged by scholars to be an effort to overcome the disastrous results of the failed Papal State in the 1870s, and the Protestant Reformation which elevated Protestantism to the largest Christian belief system worldwide.

As Catholics seeking change continue in their efforts to recapture the failed hope of Vatican Council II we must recall the article's comments in the beginning of this book.

"Rather than wring our hands over what the church has become under back-to- back popes who have acted in an arrogant and authoritarian manner, we should celebrate what Vatican II has already done for us. It has given us a new view of ourselves. It's made us more free, more human and more at the service of a world that Jesus loved. It has given us a new view of the church. It's our church, not the pope's church, or the bishops' church, or a priest's church. It has given us a new view of our place in it. We can think, we can speak, and we can act as followers of Jesus in a world that needs us."

KEEP THE FAITH, CHANGE THE CHURCH

At eighty years of age this lifelong Catholic author is associated with no Catholic activist group, but supports all who seek change. Shortly after the troubling news reports of priestly abuse in 2002 many concerned Catholics sought to understand why. With that in mind the first Catholic group to form with the mission of understanding why, and to work within the Church for change, was organized, VOTF Voice of the Faithful.[4] Their slogan was appropriate, "Keep the Faith, change the Church," a movement this writer embraced. Other groups are active: Bishops Accountability[5]; Survivors of Those Abused by Priests[6]; National Survivor Advocates Coalition[7]; Women Can be Priests[8]; Future Church[9]; Association for the Rights of Catholics in the Church[10]; *National Catholic Reporter* (The Independent News Source)[11]; Catholic web Catholica (news and discussion forum). Based in Australia Catholica is the most read international website for Catholics of all views.[12] For Catholics who wish to be active and/or informed, these and others should be viewed.

And from this Catholic writer: For faithful Catholics who remain confused on the truth of our Christian history I ask you to consider this: Today Catholic Canon Law 1037 prevents St. Peter from becoming a Catholic Priest. For those confused Catholics I appeal to you, "make a visit" to the Eucharist, examine your conscience. Think about it.

In closing, I quote two Christian apologists. First, Catholic apologist Karl Keating from his book *Catholicism and Fundamentalism;* although he speaks here of biblical fundamentalism his comment is appropriate for Catholics searching for truth: *"Only once the doctrines are understood in themselves should you turn to their* justifications, but showing what doctrines mean is the principal task you have. Until you do that you cannot move forward."

Lastly, priest Martin Luther from his book, *Works*; when he speaks of why he nailed his 96 Theses to the church door: *"I had intended to say and to assent to nothing except what is contained primarily in Holy Scripture and then the church fathers...and in Canon Law and papal decrees."*

This is the state of the church today.

"Yahweh God said, 'It is not good that man should live alone. I will make for him a Helpmate." Genesis 2:18_

APPENDIX

Approximately three months before my book, *Why St. Peter Could Not Become a Catholic Priest Today,* was completed, the publication of a new book revealing theological changes within the early Catholic Church was published. Differing from my book which is based on historical events that introduced foreign beliefs, this new book examines early theological changes that remain with the Church today. This new book, *Why Priests?: A Failed Tradition,* is authored by Emeritus Professor of history at Northwestern University, Gary Wills,[1] a Roman Catholic scholar of impeccable credential who prays the Rosary every day.

Part One of Professor Wills' book, *Priest Power: The Eucharist,* and its first two chapters, *A Priestless Movement* and *Holy Men,* will intrigue faithful Catholics. With this beginning Wills then explains misleading Scriptural interpretations that continue to effect the Catholic Church.

Approaching early Christianity from different perspectives, this author believes most Theological changes revealed by Professor Wills are conformed by little known historical events this author attempts to expound.

The New York Times Sunday Book Review

Apostolic Transgression

'Why Priests?' by Garry Wills

By RANDALL BALMER

Published: February 15, 2013

Garry Wills wants us to know that he really bears no animus toward priests. Truly. Some of his best friends, not to mention his mentors, are priests. His quarrel is not with priests but with the notion of the priesthood, which, he argues, finds no precedent in the early church and precious little warrant in the New Testament.

WHY PRIESTS?
A Failed Tradition

By Garry Wills

Jesus never claimed for himself the mantle of priesthood, nor did he, a Jew, hail from the priestly tribe of Levi. The sole reference to Jesus as priest in the New Testament, Wills says, occurs in the Epistle to the Hebrews, an enigmatic letter of unknown provenance. The writer of the letter introduces the notion of Jesus as priest not in the line of Aaron (Levite) but in the tradition of Melchizedek, the obscure Canaanite king of Salem who makes a cameo appearance in Genesis and is mentioned again briefly in Psalm 110.

Using his linguistic skills and his impressive command of both secondary literature and patristic sources, Wills raises doubts aplenty about "the Melchizedek myth," and the priestly claims for Jesus in the "idiosyncratic" Epistle to the Hebrews. He notes

237

as well the linguistic anomalies of the Genesis passage and even questions the inclusion of Hebrews in the canon of Scripture.

The Epistle to the Hebrews also posits a novel interpretation of the Crucifixion, Wills argues, that of substitutionary atonement: the death of Jesus was necessary to placate the anger of a wrathful God against a sinful humanity. In this scheme, God demanded the blood sacrifice of his own son. Wills challenges this notion on several grounds, including its regressive "substitution of human sacrifice for animal sacrifice." In fact, he points out, the Greek word for "sacrifice" occurs 15 times in Hebrews, more than in the rest of the New Testament combined.

Jesus, moreover, understood himself as a prophet, not a priest. "Jesus was acting in the prophetic tradition when he cleansed the Temple, driving out the money changers," Wills writes. "Though he attended the Temple, as any Jewish layman would, he performed no priestly acts there; presided over nothing; did not enter the Holy of Holies; made no animal sacrifice," according to Wills. "He excoriates priests, and priests in return contrive his death."

So, to quote the book's title, "why priests?" The standard Roman Catholic teaching is that all priestly authority derives from Peter, to whom Jesus bestowed "the keys of the kingdom"; the authority of every priest, according to Catholic doctrine, can be traced through a line of "apostolic succession" back to Peter, the first bishop of Rome. The teachings of Jesus, however, were radically egalitarian: "The last shall be first, and the first last." Neither Jesus nor his followers claimed to be priests, Wills maintains, and "there is no historical evidence for Peter being bishop anywhere — least of all at Rome, where the office of bishop did not exist in the first century C.E."

Having attributed the abiding conundrum of the priesthood to "the Melchizedek myth" propagated in the Epistle to the Hebrews, Wills writes that this new priestly class began over the centuries to arrogate to itself powers and prerogatives unimagined by Jesus and his disciples. Although Jesus had instructed his followers not to "address any man on earth as father," priests demanded that very honorific.

Central to the priestly claims to authority, Wills says, was the importance of the sacraments, especially celebration of the

Eucharist, which could be performed, the church declared, only by priests. "The most striking thing about priests, in the later history of Christianity," the author writes, "is their supposed ability to change bread and wine into the body and blood of Jesus Christ."

This exclusivity, according to Wills, derives from Thomas Aquinas rather than Jesus. The Thomistic view of the Eucharist understands the Mass as re-enacting the sacrifice of Christ, from which all other graces devolve to the believer. The church, following Aquinas, vested the power of transubstantiation — the bread and wine of holy communion actually becomes the body and blood of Christ — in the priesthood. With that magical power, the priesthood increasingly set itself apart from the laity.

Wills argues that an alternative understanding of Jesus and the Eucharist, one more consonant with the New Testament (Hebrews excepted) and informed by Augustine, sees Jesus as coming to harmonize humanity with himself. The Eucharistic meal remains a meal (as it was in the first century), not a sacrifice, one that celebrates the union between Christ and his followers. "One does nothing but disrupt this harmony by interjecting superfluous intermediaries between Jesus and his body of believers," Wills writes. "When these 'representatives' of Jesus to us, and of us to Jesus, take the feudal forms of hierarchy and monarchy, of priests and papacy, they affront the camaraderie of Jesus with his brothers."

If some elements of Wills' thesis sound familiar, they are. In the not-so-distant past, another formidable thinker and critic — someone who also favored Augustine over Aquinas — mounted a similar case. In his 1520 "Address to the Christian Nobility of the German Nation," Martin Luther argued against "Roman presumption" and punctured the pretensions of the clergy: "Priests, bishops or popes . . . are neither different from other Christians nor superior to them."

Similarly, in "The Babylonian Captivity of the Church," published the same year, Luther wrote that "priests are not lords, but servants," and "the sacrament does not belong to the priests, but to all men."

If the priesthood is superfluous, if priests are indeed an accretion of church history, where does that leave Wills himself, a cradle Catholic who spent more than five years in a Jesuit seminary preparing to become a priest? His final chapter is a model of elegant simplicity, a contrast (intended or not) to the flummery often associated with his own church. He opens by repeating that he feels "no personal animosity toward priests," nor does he expect the priesthood to disappear. "I just want to assure my fellow Catholics that, as priests shrink in numbers," he writes, "congregations do not have to feel they have lost all connection with the sacred just because the role of priests in their lives is contracting."

If the early followers of Jesus had no need for priests...What does Wills believe, if not in "popes and priests and sacraments"? With legions of other Christians, he affirms the Nicene Creed; the mystical body of Christ, "which is the real meaning of the Eucharist"; and the afterlife. Wills also expresses appreciation for the Blessed Virgin and for the saints: "I do not want to get along without the head of Augustine or the heart of Francis of Assisi to help me."

"There is one God, and Jesus is one of his prophets," Wills concludes, "and I am one of his millions of followers." For those millions, scattered across time and space, that's an affirmation worthy of celebration.

Randall Balmer, an Episcopal priest, is chairman of the religion department at Dartmouth College.

Footnotes can be found at:
www.illicitcelibacy.com/SPfootnotes

Made in the USA
San Bernardino, CA
01 September 2014